The Programmer's Job Handbook

About the Author...

Gene Wang is Executive Vice President of Applications and Development Tools at Symantec Corporation. Formerly Vice President and General Manager of Programming Languages at Borland, he was responsible for the success of Borland C++. Under his guidance at Symantec, Wang's groups have released the award-winning Symantec C++.

The Programmer's Job Handbook

Gene Wang

***Osborne**/McGraw-Hill*

Berkeley New York St. Louis San Francisco
Auckland Bogotá Hamburg London Madrid
Mexico City Milan Montreal New Delhi Panama City
Paris São Paulo Singapore Sydney
Tokyo Toronto

Osborne **McGraw-Hill**
2600 Tenth Street
Berkeley, California 94710
U.S.A.

For information on translations or book distributors outside the U.S.A., or to arrange bulk purchase discounts for sales promotions, premiums, or fundraisers, please contact Osborne **McGraw-Hill** at the above address.

The Programmer's Job Handbook

1234567890 DOC 99876

ISBN 0-07-882137-1

PUBLISHER ***Lawrence Levitsky***
AQUISITIONS EDITOR ***Scott Rogers***
PROJECT EDITOR ***Emily Rader***
COPY EDITOR ***Judy Ziajka***
PROOFREADER ***Linda Medoff***
COMPUTER DESIGNER ***Peter F. Hancik***
ILLUSTRATOR ***Randall Marsden Design***
QUALITY CONTROL SPECIALIST ***Joe Scuderi***

To my wonderful wife, Leslie,
and my precious daughter Gina

Contents

Acknowledgments

During the time that I spent writing this book, I was continually gratified by the support I received from friends in the industry, all of who wanted to contribute something to help programmers succeed in their careers. I sincerely wish to thank the many friends and colleagues who helped by contributing their wisdom. At Symantec, I talked to dozens of people, including Gordon Eubanks, Walter Bright, Bill Coleman, Mansour Safai, Steve Singh, Enrique Salem, Gary Barbato, Peter Norton, and Pat Vermont. Brad Silverberg and Jim McCarthy of Microsoft were tremendously supportive and helpful, as was Jerry Barber of Adobe, Dan Putterman of Maximum Information, Jeffrey Tarter of *Softletter 100*, Paul Gillin of *Computerworld*, Bruce Brereton of Novell, Anders Hejlsberg of Borland International, Githesh Ramamurthy of CCS, and Yulun Wang of Computer Motion. Bill Donovan and Susan Yun added a lot of insight from their recruitment experience successfully placing programmers in high-paying jobs. My mother, Jo Szeto, helped out by continually reminding me that she was an English major. And I'd like to thank Scott Adams, the creator of *Dilbert*, for letting me use some of his *Dilbert* comics in this book, for sharing his insights on choosing the right company, and for enriching my life every day with his humor. I especially wish to thank Janel Garvin for helping out with this project, and my editor at Osborne/McGraw-Hill, Scott Rogers. Thanks also to Emily Rader and Daniela Dell'Orco.

Introduction

Programming is a great career. Technology is changing the shape of our civilization from one year to the next, creating great new job opportunities with high financial rewards and a multitude of software specialty areas to master. Computer software and the programmers who create it are literally at the heart of the information age and all the new opportunities that it brings. Truly, programming is one of the most exciting professions to pursue as we head into the twenty-first century. But you have to carefully plan and manage your career path to aim it on a high-growth trajectory. If you master the fine art of programming, you will have a highly desired skill set and a bright job future to look forward to. This book is meant to help programmers, technical managers, software analysts, quality assurance engineers, and all others associated with software development, to find that right path to the future.

Together, we will explore the programmer's job market of tomorrow by examining in depth the job market as it exists today. We'll take a look at what programming skills are in demand and how much different companies are paying by industry and geographical region. I boldly predict seven software technologies that I think will be hot in the future and hope that I'm right **;-)**. In addition, from interviews with many of the top software industry experts, I provide a list of seven skills of successful programmers. Hopefully, by reading this book, you will be able to optimize your personal career path in life and improve your job selection process to find and get the best jobs.

This book is not a technical book. It is not designed to show you any specific tricks and techniques for writing good code or designing software architectures. There are plenty of excellent books around on those topics, and there are also classes and conference sessions available to help you get the technical expertise you need to succeed. This book is designed to develop your skills in managing your career path in order to put you in line for the jobs that will be the most rewarding and fulfilling as you progress through your career.

Are you aware that programmers in the United States on average make more than twice as much as the average American? Did you know that programmers with a knowledge of C++ command better salaries and get jobs a lot easier than programmers with other language specialties? Did you know that Microsoft Foundation Classes (MFC) is the framework that you need experience with in order to get most of the programming jobs for creating desktop software? Did you know that surfing the Net is one of the fastest, easiest, and cheapest ways to find the perfect job?

How This Book Is Organized

In Chapter 1, I talk about what makes a successful programmer. Next, in Chapter 2, on the programmer's job market, I arm you with the statistical information you need to shape your career in the direction you want it to go.

Once you're oriented to the programming job market overall, Chapter 3 provides some nitty-gritty, down-to-earth advice on actually getting the job you want. Unfortunately, it's not enough to be a great programmer. To get a great job you have to also know how to write a résumé, how to conduct yourself in an interview, and where to look to find the positions that are available. This chapter gives you plenty of inside tips on getting the job you really want. It talks about how to prepare for an interview, how to create a dynamite résumé, when to use recruiters, and even how to know when it's time to leave your old job and move on. It also includes a checklist of items to review before you go into an interview, to help you when you're at a new employer's office trying to convince them you're right for the job. This chapter provides you with tools to assess yourself and your career in order to determine how you're doing at providing yourself with the career you want and deserve.

Chapter 4 outlines seven skills of successful programmers and introduces the idea of career management, as opposed to simply getting a job. It discusses how to manage your career both when looking for a different job and when executing the job you have now. The advice here comes from years of experience—my experience and the experience of software development vice presidents and directors from such companies as Microsoft, Apple, Adobe, and Symantec.

Chapter 5 covers the subject of choosing your programming tools. Great programmers need the best tools. I have dedicated much of my professional career to building great development tools, starting in 1983 with an AI programming tool called Golden Common LISP, then building Borland's C++, and now Symantec's award-winning Symantec C++. This chapter lists some of the tools available and I give you some pretty good insider advice on selecting tools that are powerful, versatile, and that save you time and effort.

Chapter 6 explores seven hot technologies for programming careers. From the Internet and networking, to Windows 95 and multimedia, to client-server development and distributed computing, some of the fastest growing technology trends lead to the biggest job opportunities.

Chapter 7 discusses component programming, which to me is one of the most exciting technologies since the introduction many years ago of object-oriented programming. I believe this is one of the most important technologies for programmers to know to get ahead in the future. Component programming will form the cornerstone of rapid application development in the next 10 to 15 years.

In Chapter 8, I talk about optimizing the software lifecycle. The challenge of delivering high-quality software on time has never been higher. Here I discuss a process for software project management used successfully at Symantec.

Finally, in Chapter 9, I highlight some key factors in picking the right organization to work for and list the top 100 software companies today.

Writing this book has been a real learning experience for me. I hope that reading the assembled information will be rewarding for you and put you on the right path to a brilliant career.

1 The Successful Programmer

High technology is one of today's fastest growing fields. The need for software is accelerating as the information age moves into the twenty-first century. In virtually every industry, in every country around the world, organizations need programmers. This creates great job opportunities for programmers who are successful. The natural question is how do you become a successful programmer? As you might expect, there is more than one answer.

Albert Einstein said, "Try not to become a man of success, but rather, try to become a man of value." Being good at programming is a prerequisite to job success. One way to amplify success is to gain unique expertise in technical areas that many companies are focusing on. For example, if you become an expert in Windows 95 programming, client-server applications, usability testing, embedded systems development, or object-oriented programming, your career opportunities will improve considerably. This book discusses hot technology areas for programmers in more depth in Chapter 6, "Hot Technologies for Programming Careers," and Chapter 7, "Component Programming." Suffice it to say here that developing your skills in the following areas will increase your value as a programmer:

- Windows 95 programming
- Object-oriented programming

- Multimedia
- Internet
- Networking
- Wireless communications and mobile computing
- Client-server development

Measures of Success

There are many different ways to measure success. Money is a common metric. The highly successful programmer gets paid more than his or her peers. The average programmer who has been in the profession for a few years makes just over $54,000 a year. Senior programmers can make more than $80,000, and many lead programmers or architects writing significant programs can earn well into the six-figure range. A survey by *Fortune* magazine (June 26, 1995), summarized in Table 1-1, compares the entry level and average salary of programmers with the salaries of several other professional occupations.

In addition to salary, a person often receives bonuses and other recognition for work well done. Benefits such as retirement plans, stock options, extensive health-care coverage, and generous vacation time are also common in the programming field.

As you will see in Chapter 2, "The Programmer's Job Market," salary levels vary a great deal depending on where you work and what industry you choose. Being in the right place at the right time is a key ingredient of success. Although there are programming jobs in virtually every industry, some industries pay better than others. For example, on average you'll be better rewarded financially in banking or real estate than in government or education. Also, of course, while

	Entry Level	**Average Salary**
Software engineer	$33,702	$54,470
Accountant	$24,750	$36,500
University professor	$39,050	$49,490
Government economist	$21,486	$46,852
IRS tax auditor	$19,500	$38,500

Table 1-1 *Average Salaries for Programmers and Selected Other Professionals*

senior technical positions in the computer industry pay handsome salaries, entry-level positions typically pay less than the average.

Not only does salary vary according to industry, but also according to geographical location. The majority of programming jobs are located near large cities, since most programming activities are conducted at a company's head office and these tend to be located in large cities. In addition, the rate of pay varies according to which area of the country you live in. On average, the pay in the U.S. is highest in Northern California, with New York not far behind. On the low end of the pay scale is the Pacific Northwest. Of course, the cost of living is less in Seattle than it is in Silicon Valley or New York City, so in some ways the difference evens out.

Dilbert reprinted by permission of United Feature Syndicate, Inc.

Of course, money is not the only measurement of success in life, and it's certainly not the only type of reward that comes from programming. Good programmers receive great satisfaction from the work itself, from meeting the challenge of solving a problem, from creating an elegant application, from constructing an algorithm that works smoothly and efficiently. They also frequently are allowed flexible work hours, with the ability to work at home if they want and with calm and quiet surroundings in a private office in the workplace.

An important measure of success as a programmer is involvement in successful software projects—software that gains popularity, or that achieves some significant advance for the program's end users. We can all think back on some applications that have literally changed the world. Remember Visicalc, the first spreadsheet program? Conceived by Dan Bricklin, Visicalc launched an industry and was largely responsible for the success of the Apple II. And then there was WordStar. Introduced in 1978, this was the first program to offer advanced word processing features to personal computer users. These software applications made enormous differences in the way people work, in the amount of work people can get done in a day, and even in the way people think; yet both of these programs have been superceded by new and better products. Of course, most applications don't have the same visible impact on people's lives as the invention of the spreadsheet, but there are many opportunities to make highly significant contributions to the evolution of science and industry through software engineering.

The Path to Successful Results

How can you ensure that the projects you work on will provide you with the opportunity to fulfill yourself and make a difference? You can do so by managing your career. This doesn't mean taking the first job you can get or even taking the job that starts out with the highest pay. Managing your career involves many activities, including finding the right job, finding the right specialization where you'll have an opportunity to grow, picking the right tools to use, selecting the right languages and platforms to

> **"Thanks to the growing popularity of computers as management tools, software programmers who know a language named C++, popular for building databases and other business applications, are ardently sought. So are LAN/WAN specialists..."**
> **—*Fortune* magazine**

learn, doing the best you can within the job that you have, and knowing when it is time to make a change and move on to another job.

You need to pick the right projects to work on. To do this, you need to know which software technologies offer growth opportunities and which do not. This book will help you find out where the opportunities are. You will learn about emerging technologies that have excellent potential. I've tried not to be negative about any particular software specialization, but you'll see that some types of jobs may not be the best choices for interesting and challenging growth opportunities in the future. If you want your career to evolve in ways that will continue to give you pleasure and keep you interested well into the next century, then pick an area that I discuss in Chapter 6 instead of a job maintaining COBOL applications for an outmoded mainframe-oriented system. Of course, this is not to say there's no need for mainframe COBOL programmers. Many lines of old COBOL code still exist and will continue to exist for years, and this code needs to be maintained. However, this is not an area I'd recommend to someone starting out who wants to be in a growth area with lots of potential.

"Thanks to the growing popularity of computers as management tools, software programmers who know a language named C++, popular for building databases and other business applications, are ardently sought. So are LAN/WAN specialists who are good at linking a company's computers." This quote from *Fortune* magazine illustrates the importance of making the right choices in programming in order to cultivate skills that will be in hot demand both today and in the future. Intelligent planning is essential in managing your career for good growth and opportunity.

Once you're established in a good organization with strong prospects for the future, then manage the way you work and turn in the best job performance you possibly can. To do that, you need to follow some processes and procedures that will help you create great software on time and on budget.

The Software Lifecycle: A Blueprint for Successful Results

All software, whether commercial software or internal corporate applications, embedded systems or low-level communications drivers, has exactly the same purpose: to fill a user's needs. In Chapter 8, "Optimizing the Software Lifecycle," you'll learn how to increase the odds that your software project will be successful in meeting those needs on time and on budget. The lifecycle has eight distinct phases, and if each one is properly executed, great software will result.

During the concept phase, you define the user needs. After you feel you really know what they are, then a software project enters the proposal phase. In this phase, you create the project proposal and project the human, monetary, and time resources you will need. After the project proposal is approved, you define the architecture, functional specifications, and engineering and test plans for the software. Next, you build the software (so easy to say, so hard to do). In the test phase, you manage the project through alpha and beta testing to improve software quality. Next, you create the "green master" version of the software and look for any final show-stopping bugs. The pay-off phase is shipping the software. Finally, you go into maintenance mode, responding to user feedback and gearing up for the next release.

Each of these phases needs to be managed carefully within the software creation process. You'll do much better in your career if you learn how to maximize your personal contribution within each of these phases. Remember: Managing your career is something you do every day at work. It is not just getting or switching jobs.

Getting along well with your team is a critical talent to master. Only people who work well with other people get along well in professional careers, and this rule is just as true for programmers as it is in any other profession. In programming, learning a few other axioms will also help. For instance, don't put bugs in your software. This sounds like a statement so obvious as to be foolish, doesn't it? But you'd be surprised how many programmers excuse sloppy initial coding practices with the notion that the bugs can be found and fixed later in the test cycle. Being thorough and meticulous and following through to the end is a trait that will get you successfully through many software projects and will earn you the respect of your co-workers as well as your boss.

Once you develop the traits and practices to get you from concept to maintenance of your software projects, you'll find that you'll start to have a history of successful projects that you can add to your résumé and use to get a better job. Keep a portfolio. In it, include details of your software, maybe a copy of each application, a list of any awards that the projects you've been involved with have won, and any commendations you receive from your boss or your users. A project portfolio is a valuable tool for getting even better projects in the future at the company you work for or at a company for which you'd rather work.

Another measure of success is a bit more subtle than the ones discussed so far, but it's every bit as powerful and significant. That measure is the amount of influence you have on others. Many programmers are considered to be computer experts outside of the programming community because that is precisely what they are. You'll find that nontechnical friends and colleagues will look to you for advice on almost any computer-related subject. Bear with them and be patient with questions that may seem stupid to you. That's automatically part of the territory of being a programmer.

What is not automatic, and what you'll find much more meaningful, is other programmers' looking to you for advice. Great programmers are the ones that other programmers seek out for help. They are often nudged into a position of leadership even though they may by nature be shy or retiring. Have no fear; when others ask you for advice on the best way to integrate one piece of an application into another, when they use techniques you have created, or when they ask you for help with an algorithm, your heart will swell up like a melon, and you'll feel an overwhelming satisfaction. This is truly one of the great rewards of programming.

Successful Programmers

One of the world's most successful people started as a programmer. Bill Gates wrote a BASIC system for the Altair 8800 in 1974. Today, his company, Microsoft, defines much of the PC software landscape with the Microsoft Windows operating system and the Microsoft Office and Home products. Bill is the richest person in the United States. His personal wealth is counted in the billions of dollars. His influence extends throughout our entire civilization.

Other successful programmers may not be as well known, but they are certainly in the top percentiles in terms of wealth and personal success. Consider Walter Bright, for instance. Walter wrote the Symantec C++ compiler. He started out much like anyone else—simply a programmer who liked working on compilers. Now he's a multimillionaire who lives in a mansion beside a lake, drives a Ferrari, has a speedboat docked outside his house, and works at home. He telecommutes with the rest of the team and occasionally flies down from Seattle to Cupertino to visit. Most people would think Walter has an ideal life, and I'm sure Walter would agree.

Anders Hejlsberg is another example of a programmer-turned-superstar. Anders wrote the original Turbo Pascal compiler that Borland made famous in the 1980s. Anders' latest work is a rapid application development tool called Delphi. Today Anders has more money than I even like to think about, and he has his choice of projects to lead. I asked Anders why he thought programming was a good career choice. Anders explained that "every two years, the speed of the processor doubles, the capacity of memory quadruples, but our brains remain the same size. So obviously it is going to take more programmers to fill the capacity!"

Throughout this book I quote many great programmers and technical managers to present their perspectives on what makes a programmer great.

Managing Your Career

I cannot stress enough that you need to plan your career to reach your full potential. Just floating along doing what comes up and taking (and keeping) just any job is the way that most people operate. That's why most people are not actually that successful. To be successful, you need to have a plan and to execute it. Can you imagine spending all the time and energy needed to learn to sail, investing in a boat and supplies and tools, declaring to friends and family that you're going to dedicate your life to a sailing journey, and then just sailing out of port into the open ocean without a clue as to where you're going or which direction you should travel to get there? If you want to get somewhere, then first you have to figure out where you want to go, and second what to do to get there. Successful people aren't aimless, and that includes successful programmers.

So don't be content to just drift along, making the best of what life gives you. If you want to be a success, you have to figure out what that means to you and how to get to the place you want your career to be, and then you have to keep yourself on track as you go along.

I recommend that you create five- and ten-year plans. An example of a ten-year plan appears later in this chapter, and it should help you with your own plans. To create a five- or ten-year plan, you need to assess your goals honestly and realistically. What technologies interest you? Where, geographically, would you like to work? Are you interested in foreign travel or in working in another country? Do you want to go into management, or would you rather be an individual contributor? Figure 1-1 is a flow chart showing the two distinct ways that programming careers typically evolve. You can go into management if working with and guiding people appeals to you. Otherwise, you can stay on the technical track and still attain as much financial success and job satisfaction.

When you feel you really know where you want to be, then determine what intermediate steps you need to take to reach your goal and set some measurable milestones along the way that you can use to see if you are still on course. Assess your skills and research your goals. If you want to be a software architect at a

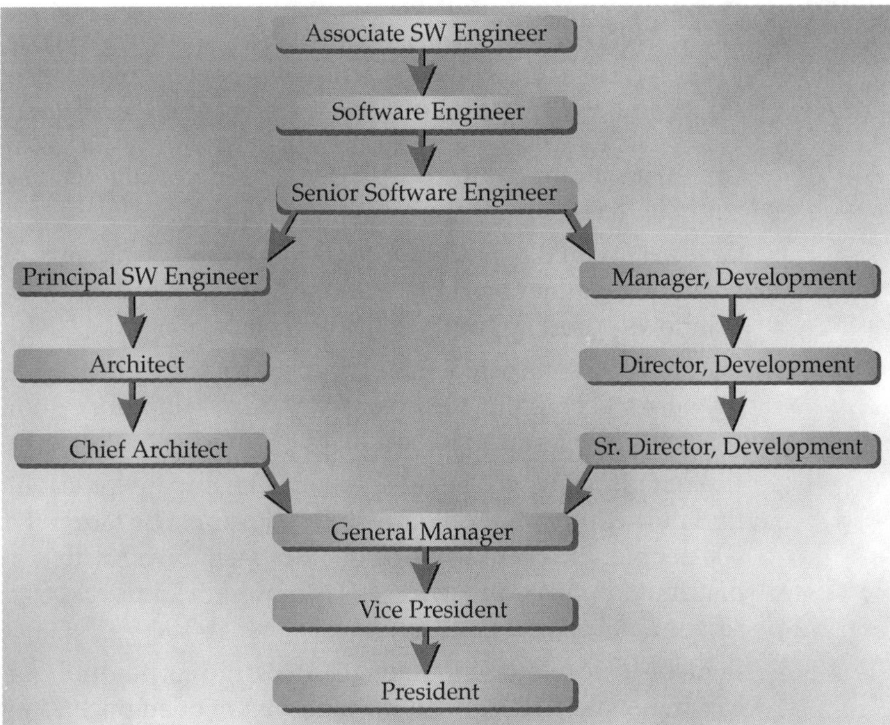

Figure 1-1 *Management track career versus technical track career*

leading commercial software firm in five years, talk to someone who is in that position and ask that person how he or she got there. Read the want ads and note the qualifications required of people in the position you seek to attain. Look in Chapter 2 and read some real job descriptions. This type of research will reveal what you need to reach your goal.

With this information in hand, take an honest look in the mirror and assess your skills. Maybe you'll find you're lacking in some area. Maybe you don't know object-oriented programming. Maybe you're clueless about distributed processing, but your goal is to become a chief information officer in a large corporation using client-server applications. It doesn't matter what skill you lack; if you figure out what it is well ahead of time, then you've got plenty of time to gain proficiency and round out your background so you can eventually reach your goal.

When you create your five- or ten-year plan, make it realistic, attainable, and detailed enough to be meaningful. "I'm going to be a vice president of engineering in ten years" isn't enough of a plan all by itself. Be more specific so you can measure your progress against your milestones.

Ten-Year Career Plan

Here is an example of a ten-year career plan. It is a hypothetical plan for someone who wants to become a vice president of engineering at a large corporation.

1996	Complete summer internship at Symantec working on C++ compiler testing.
1997	Graduate with B.S. in Computer Science. Get job as entry-level programmer working with the C/C++ language on a Windows-based application. Target salary: $36,000.
1999	Should have completed at least two major software projects at my current company. Complete M.S. degree in Information Science. Target salary: $45,000 with promotion to Project Lead.
2000	Promoted to Project Manager at current company or leave to find new company. Company I work for must be larger than 500 people. Projects I work on should be involved with distributed processing, wide-area communication, and client-server database programs. Target salary: $60,000.
2001	I will be a Development Manager at a large corporation earning over $80,000. I will manage a team of engineers, and all the projects I am in charge of will be done on time and on budget. I will join a professional organization and be actively developing a network of colleagues.
2003	I will be Director of Engineering at a large corporation managing more than 100 people creating distributed applications for long-distance wireless communication and for database processing. Target salary: $120,000.
2006	I will be Vice President of Engineering for a large corporation. Salary: over $150,000.

Look over this ten-year plan. One thought that may occur to you is that it will be difficult for someone to make such rapid advancement at the same company. To make large leaps in salary or responsibility, you sometimes need to leave your current company and find a more promising opportunity elsewhere.

When to Make a Change

When every morning you get up and find you don't want to go to work, it may be time for a job change. When you feel like you're just not contributing when you are at work or that you just aren't connecting with and getting along with your supervisor, maybe it's time to move on. When you've spent the last several years doing the same programming tasks and they lack challenge, perhaps it's time to find a new challenge. When the organization you work for is downsizing or planning layoffs, make sure you keep abreast of what's going on. These are all signs that you should think about looking for a job somewhere else.

I spoke at length with Bill Donovan. He's a highly successful recruiter specializing in placing top programmers, and he is more familiar with helping programmers move from one job to another than anyone I know. Bill's viewpoint is that there usually comes a time when you have to leave your current job and company and look for something better if you are going to actively manage your career.

While most Human Resources people wish it was not the case, the truth is that job hopping is a vital part of most successful people's careers. It is only when you leave one job and go to another, for example, that you can totally remake your job along the lines of what you want to do. It is really the only way to get a range of experience on your résumé. It is frequently the easiest way to get a big boost in your salary and sometimes the fastest way to get a promotion.

Traditional wisdom says that those people who stay with a single company for many years are more desirable as job candidates than those who don't. This used to be true, but now it is no longer the case. If you stay at a company three or four years, that's often enough to fulfill your potential there. Although it still is undesirable to have ten jobs at ten companies in as many years, there is no stigma attached to people who change companies at reasonable intervals. What's a reasonable interval? "It varies from one person to another," says Bill. If you have a good reason for moving on, then there is no reason not to do so. Just be sure to state clearly what that reason is.

Attaining Success

The road to success in programming is well marked and relatively easy to follow. Choose a technical specialization that is of interest to you and that will be hot in the future. Manage your career as you go to earn the respect of your colleagues and your bosses. Figure out where you want to be and how to get there. Don't be afraid to venture out of the comfortable confines of the job you have in order to advance. Put it all together in a plan and then do it!

2 The Job Market for Software Developers

You've chosen a field that is likely to provide you with strong employment prospects, a good salary, comfortable working conditions, and interesting projects for the rest of your career. Programming is a great field to be in as we progress through the information age.

The average programmer in the United States today makes over $54,000, which is more than twice as much as the average American makes in a year, and the potential for future job growth and opportunities is much better than average compared to most other professions. Programmers work within teams of other programmers that vary in size from three to ten people. They work in pleasant, quiet environments—and because of the nature of the work, it is becoming more common for many to work in home offices. Programmers work for large corporations, for small entrepreneurial shops, or for themselves as contractors. The demand for programmers in the U.S. varies from one geographical area to another, with the highest demand being in California and the New York areas; but almost all major cities have many jobs for programmers.

Dilbert reprinted by permission of United Feature Syndicate, Inc.

The Overall Job Market

According to all sources, the total number of programmers worldwide is increasing. However, the degree to which that increase occurs and the projections for its future expansion vary considerably according to which sources are consulted and which segments are viewed. Overall, the U.S. Department of Labor estimates that the job of programmer/analyst is one of the fastest growing occupations in the United States (see Figure 2-1). In a recent report, the estimates for total current and projected size rise from more than 1.2 million in 1990 to almost 1.6 million in 1996.

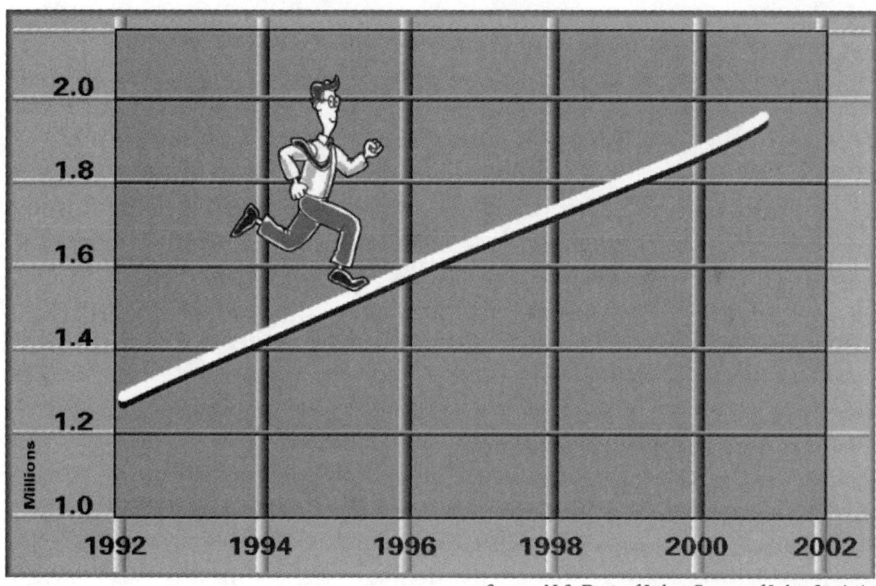

Source: U.S. Dept. of Labor, Bureau of Labor Statistics

Figure 2-1 *Predicted growth in developer market*

As new technologies arise, the demand for programmers can be expected to rise along with them. Client-server systems, mobile and remote computing, embedded systems, multimedia, and interactive communications are all technologies that are changing the way businesses operate—and all these changes are fueled by programming.

Software development as a field has matured greatly in the last 30 years; and when a profession matures and expands as much as programming has, it invariably becomes subject to specialization. Today programmers are not only categorized by which languages, operating systems, and hardware architectures they know, but also by what industry they work in and what advanced techniques they know and use.

Industry Segments

According to Forrester Research, 57 percent of employed programmers work in corporate development settings of all sizes, with 18 percent of the total employed in large Fortune 1000 corporations. Another 21 percent are employed by independent software vendors (ISVs), 10 percent are employed by value-added retailers (VARs) or as consultants, and 12 percent are employed doing embedded systems work. In addition to those professionally employed, there are a significant number of "hackers," or home hobbyists and students, who develop small applications for themselves or others. (See Figure 2-2.)

The largest segment of programmers is corporate developers. This segment is growing at a higher rate than the others, and its growth is mainly in database and client-server solutions. Another rapidly growing segment is programmers who work with embedded systems. With computer chips, and thus programs, being embedded into cars, telephones, office equipment, and almost every system one can think of, the demand for embedded systems programming is poised to boom.

International Opportunities

The international market for programmers is also an area of strong growth and can provide excellent opportunities for programmers who want to travel to other countries. Most of the western European countries already have strong development communities, with many firms producing software. Software sales in Germany, France, Italy, the United Kingdom, and the Scandinavian

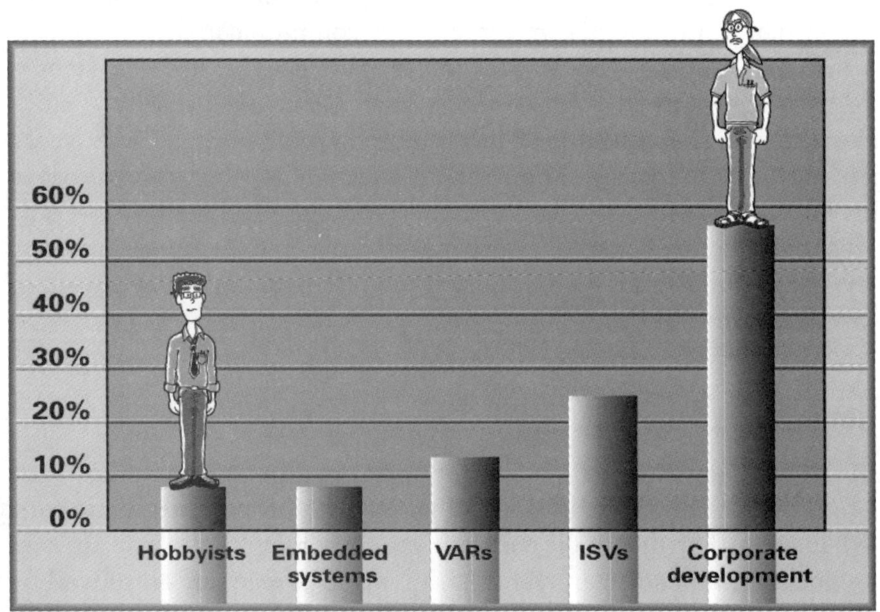

Figure 2-2 *Programming industry segments*

countries are increasing at about the same rate as they are in the United States. Software production and sales in Eastern Europe, Asia, India, Australia, and some Latin American countries are also growing. The software industry in India, in particular, shows excellent growth and offers many opportunities for programmers starting out.

One way to gauge how fast the programming community in any area is growing is to examine the sales of software development tools. Although international sales revenues in 1993 still were behind those in the United States, international revenues from Windows development tools from 1991 to 1993 increased by 300 percent; by contrast, U.S. revenues only slightly more than doubled during the same period (see Table 2-1).

More than a third of the international growth was fueled by Japan alone. Symantec has experienced the same trend with its localized language products for the Macintosh and Windows. The market for programming in Japan is really taking off.

The opportunities for programmers in a particular country are not entirely dependent upon the demand for software within that country. We live in a global economy, and people from literally all over the world compete for the same goods and services. Recently, developers living in other parts of the world have made some inroads into the U.S. and European software development job markets. When a firm asks others outside the company to perform jobs, it is called outsourcing. Global outsourcing means engaging for services across country boundaries. Global outsourcing of programming jobs is becoming more and more common.

According to Datamation, the global outsourcing market is growing quickly and is projected to surpass $240 billion by the mid-1990s.

The number of firms and countries participating in the global software development market is rapidly increasing. The main reasons for this growth are

	Windows Domestic	**Windows International**
1991	$40.3	$19.2
1992	$68.8	$30.4

Table 2-1 *Software Tool Sales in Millions*

- Relatively low entry costs in terms of capital expenditure
- Worldwide availability of low-cost PCs
- Proliferation of affordable high-speed telecommunications networks
- The movement toward free market economies and free trade
- The high salaries and overhead costs in the U.S. and other industrialized countries

Another factor is that programming languages are universal—the same C++ syntax is understood around the world.

Of the countries active in providing outsourcing development services to the U.S. market, India is a leader. Indian software exports grew from $24 million in 1985 to $350 million in 1993. Much of Indian software development is performed via high-speed satellite links for U.S. firms on mainframes located in the United States. More than 250,000 information systems specialists graduate annually from more than 100 technical institutions in India, and U.S. firms using Indian software engineering include Citibank, Digital Equipment Corporation, Texas Instruments, and Hewlett Packard.

Clearly, there are many opportunities for programmers in all parts of the world. The obstacles to living overseas and working as a programmer vary with the country; but English usually is taught in schools and widely spoken, so American programmers are highly valued in most communities even when they don't speak the native language.

If you decide that you'd like to explore working in another country, you need to consider all the relevant factors. The implications of working in another country are complex and outside the scope of this book. Suffice it to say that you will need to consider a cost of living that will likely be far different than in the United States, a different set of tax calculations, different benefits, relocation expenses, work restrictions, home visits, and visas, among many other factors. Most libraries have books on working overseas, and you should be able to get a good general idea of the issues involved from reading these. If you want to work in a particular country, you can also call that country's consulate in New York or San Francisco and ask for information.

No matter where you want to go in your career or even in the world, the fact that you chose programming as your occupation gives you the freedom to make very fine distinctions in choosing a path to follow. You can pursue leading-edge technologies and try to make a breakthrough in some specific area, or you can become a star in a well-established industry. You can work for a bank in Manila, a hospital in Chicago, a government agency, or in almost any industry in any geographical area that interests you. It's up to you.

Types of Programming Jobs

Many different types of jobs are available to you as a programmer. You can choose among a wide variety of systems and applications. Jobs range from writing shrink-wrapped software like programmers do at Symantec, to developing database programs within a large corporation, to writing test programs for benchmark applications, to creating embedded systems that run inside an automobile. With such a wide variety of job opportunities, you should be able to find the right challenge to match your particular talents and inclinations.

Corporate Programming

The most common type of programming job is also the one that is easiest to get: the job of in-house corporate programmer. Although most people tend to think of the shrink-wrapped software industry when they think of programmers, the vast majority of programmers work in industries other than the computer industry. That's because almost all businesses today rely heavily on computer technology driven by custom software. Banking, health care, retail, real estate, insurance—there is literally no major industry that doesn't use custom software.

In-house corporate programmers often work in MIS departments creating software that spans an entire enterprise. Applications that corporations usually have programmers create include accounting systems, payroll, network systems, communications, and virtually anything that either the whole enterprise or small groups within the enterprise require.

Today, corporate programmers typically are concerned with the downsizing or "right-sizing" efforts prevalent within large companies—that is, with companies' efforts to stop relying on mainframe computers and workstations as the major source of corporate computing and information and instead to use local area networks (LANs), wide area networks (WANs), and various remote connectivity technologies to manage enterprise-wide tasks. Client-server systems, or applications distributed across a network and using multiple-networked CPUs for processing, are becoming a required implementation at most larger companies. Industry experts report that in the next few years more than 70 percent of corporations deploying new applications will use some form of client-server implementation, and 60 percent of all corporations will rework existing applications to take advantage of the client-server paradigm. Thus, the corporate programmer is well advised to have at least some knowledge of how to distribute applications across a network environment.

Business modeling is also an important consideration for many corporate programmers, and a knowledge of business rules and decision processes often is important. Also, fourth-generation languages (4GLs) are becoming more customized to the large corporate environment and are playing an ever-increasing role. Forrester Research predicts a dramatic upswing in the number of 4GLs sold between 1992 and 1996 (see Figure 2-3). Forrester predicts that the growth of 4GLs such as Powersoft's PowerBuilder, Symantec's Enterprise Developer, and Microsoft's Visual Basic will top the billion dollar mark in 1995. Much of that growth will come from the corporate development environment.

COBOL is the long-established standard in business software, though many people are now migrating to the more powerful and sophisticated object-oriented languages. Nevertheless, there are millions of lines of COBOL code out there that need to be maintained, and many firms are still generating new business applications in COBOL. Mainframe languages such as PL/1 are in a similar category. The job market for programmers with a proficiency in main-

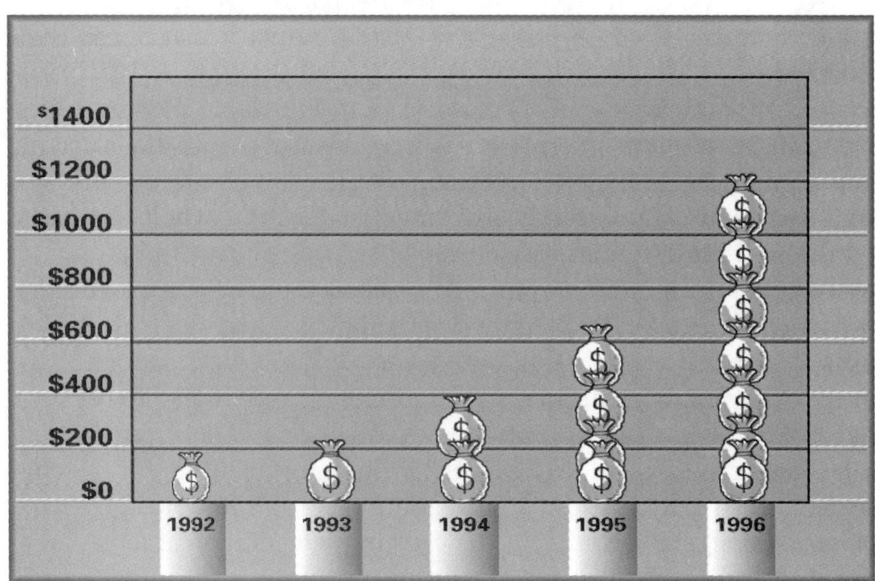

Source: Forrester Research, 1994

Figure 2-3 *Growth of 4GLs in the United States*

frame languages is shrinking, but there are still jobs available, and most of them are in the corporate environment. If you wish to work with COBOL in a large corporate environment and you're not within five years of retirement, then you may be able to find a job, but you'd be well advised to learn new skills at the same time—skills that will take you into the future.

Since most programming for large corporations is done at or near the company headquarters, these jobs tend to be clustered near larger cities.

Shrink-Wrapped Software Development

A great programming job is creating shrink-wrapped software. More than 5,000 software companies in the United States create and sell software products for the end-user. Within these companies, software developers typically are among the most respected people. They are the creators of the products that are the purpose of the company. These jobs are driven by product schedules—and during the final push to get a particular product out the door, programmers often work extra-long hours. Although the short development cycles can be stressful, the rewards can be great, both financially and psychologically, arising from a sense of successful completion of an effort within a team. Companies often give bonuses and great celebrations upon the shipment of a shrink-wrapped software product to compensate for the long hours programmers and others have invested. Programmers also have the opportunity to make friends and contacts that will last a lifetime as the pressure of getting the product out the door firmly cements relationships among the members of the development team. Furthermore, having experience in successfully shipping shrink-wrapped software is very valuable for future career growth.

The market for shrink-wrapped end-user software products is growing at a very respectable rate. IDC reports that overall growth of the worldwide end-user software market in 1994 was 11.2 percent and had a total revenue of $77.2 billion, and in 1995 IDC predicts a growth rate of more than 12 percent.

Applications created for end users span the distance from simple educational games for tots, to recipe indexes for home use, to multimedia film designers, to class libraries for professional developers. One of the most fascinating features of the shrink-wrapped software industry is the diversity of products sold and projects that you can be involved in. Regardless of your interests, the chances are good that you can find a company that is creating and selling programs in that area—and if you can't find one, then maybe you should create one. After all, it is the shrink-wrapped software industry that has given rise to more new software endeavors than any other segment.

The shareware concept gives developers a chance to try out new software ideas and see how they fly before finding capital to create a software company. If you create a program that you think may be useful and therefore popular, you can publish it on various bulletin boards where other people can download it and try it free of charge. If users like the program, you request that they send some money to the developer—you. Some great programs, such as Doom and Mosaic, got their start as shareware. Producing shareware isn't a way to get rich, but it is a way to get your own unique application into the hands of end users. If they like it, you'll hear about it, and perhaps so will investors with the capital to start a small company.

The predominant language now used in the commercial shrink-wrapped software industry is C, with C++ gaining momentum. Developers like the flexibility the C language gives, and the C++ extension provides additional functionality as well as object-oriented capabilities. In addition, Apple, Microsoft, and most other major vendors of system software use C++ as their standard. Thus, if you want to be involved in this industry segment, become a C++ expert, and you will be popular.

Geographically, the places in the United States where commercial software vendors are located is fairly limited. Most large software vendors are in the Silicon Valley area just south of San Francisco, in the Boston area, and in Atlanta, Dallas, Houston, Seattle, and Los Angeles. Of course, ISVs can be located anywhere, and many smaller ones are popping up in more remote locations such as outlying areas of Colorado, Arizona, and the Midwest. In Europe, developers cluster around the larger cities in Germany, France, and the United Kingdom. Bangalore is the development capital in India.

Pure Research and Development

An attractive job for someone with a creative tendency is working within a research group. Typically, these jobs are in larger corporations, universities, or government agencies. As a person involved in pure research, you will not have any actual product as a goal. Instead, you have the opportunity to make breakthroughs in software technology that others throughout various segments of the industry can use far into the future. In a research department, you have the thrill of "going boldly where no one has gone before." This field requires a lot of creativity and vision and pays off with career possibilities unequaled in any other segment. If you should be the one to make a true breakthrough in software technology, like Bjarne Stroustrup did, for instance, your name will be known throughout the world, and you will be a much-sought programmer.

Because research departments typically exist through the auspices of government grants or the long-range vision of a very large corporation, research jobs are not as easy to find as many other types of programming jobs. Many people who do go into pure research get their foot in the door while still in college. If you are currently studying at a university and think you may be interested in continuing your career in pure research, then ask your professors for information on any ongoing research at your school or elsewhere.

Contracting

Contracting is an increasingly popular type of work for programmers. In today's economy, many companies that require custom programming services on a semi-regular basis can't afford to keep a large full-time in-house staff. These firms often employ contractors to write applications and train staff personnel to maintain them. Sometimes the contractor has a maintenance agreement with the company, with the programmer returning every so often or answering questions and fixing bugs as needed. Usually, however, once the application is finished, so is the contract job. Then it's off to a completely new job. Contract programmers work for corporation system integrators (SIs), value-added retailers (VARs), or on their own. The benefits of this type of life are new challenges, new environments, and new people to deal with fairly frequently as one job ends and another begins. In addition, programmers who want to travel can move all over the globe, wherever there are jobs. The pay is usually better up front for solo contractors than for staffers, but contractors who work for themselves miss such benefits as health insurance, retirement plans, and life insurance.

Independent contractors are usually hired to complete a portion of a project and integrate it into the overall team effort. In this scenario, they typically work at home, coordinating their work through the project leader, and are relatively isolated from the company and team. Contractors also may be hired to come in and work as part of the team, in which case they operate almost exactly like employees. Nevertheless, even contractors of this type do not receive the normal employee benefits.

Another type of development contracting opportunity is employment by a VAR, SI, or other development contracting firm. These firms keep staffs of programmers available to perform jobs for companies that need software developed only periodically and so don't keep a resident programming staff.

Contractors who work for VARs or SIs may actually be employees of the VAR or SI and receive all the normal benefits that come to a full-time employee of any company. On the other hand, contractors who work for a contracting firm that specializes in short, temporary jobs may not have any benefits and may be on call whenever they are not actually working.

According to the *U.S. Industrial Outlook*, 4,100 firms in 1994 (other than sole proprietorships) provided computer professional services as their primary activity. This number will continue to increase. Of these, systems integration was the principal offering at 1,800 companies. Four hundred new firms of this variety opened during that same year.

In addition to companies whose primary activity is providing computing services, other companies, such as manufacturers and distributors of computer equipment and some telecommunications companies such as AT&T, have begun to offer contract services. These companies employ large teams of developers whose services are then hired out.

In the June 1994 *Journal of System Management*, the Yankee group estimated that the U.S. market for information systems outsourcing was growing at a rate of 15 percent annually and would reach $50 billion in the next year or two; but even though the number of development contracting firms may be growing at that rate, custom programming services—whether provided by house staff or contractors—actually is growing more slowly than in previous years. More contractors are being hired to create reusable objects and to modify existing software. This shift is largely attributed to more user-friendly prepackaged software, GUIs, 4GLs, and CASE tools, which have created an increased demand for training services, component software, and software modifications (rather than for completely new applications developed from scratch).

The following types of activities are most commonly outsourced:

- Applications development
- User training
- Data center management
- Systems analysis

The following phases of the software development cycle are most likely to be outsourced:

- Detailed design
- Coding

- Testing

Acceptance testing is almost never outsourced because in-house testing is needed to verify contracted work upon completion of a project. The same is true for the initial requirements analysis, which is almost always performed by in-house staff to define the work required. The preliminary design is also usually developed in house.

Contractors who are well established can live and work practically anywhere. Often people perform programming jobs in their homes hundreds of miles from where the company whose project they're working on is located. They may even work outside the country. Almost every language is in demand by some segment at some time, so language skills aren't a limitation.

The biggest hurdle to jump to become a successful independent contractor is gaining a name for yourself. If you're just starting out, the wisest course is probably to get some jobs under your belt at a large company or at a VAR or SI and then break out on your own once you've become known in the development community.

Embedded Systems Programming

One of the fastest growing segments of the programming industry is embedded systems, small applications encoded onto computer chips and used for a wide variety of purposes. Embedded systems are everywhere. If you have a new car, it undoubtedly has a computer that runs off chips with embedded applications. Remote communications, cellular telephones, industrial machinery—the list goes on and on—all use embedded systems.

Applications written for embedded systems are low level and have no user interface. Thus, the programmer can skip many of the cumbersome details of creating GUIs and concentrate on the task at hand. This clean, functional approach is appealing to those who like to create programs with few frills.

Industry experts say that embedded systems applications currently account for 15 percent of all applications built with CASE/AD tools and 11 percent of those built with traditional 3GLs. With the number of everyday uses of embedded systems increasing every year, this percentage is going to increase quickly.

The number of programmers needed to create embedded systems by the year 2010 is projected to be 10 million people, and the jobs are going to be everywhere. In this field, the reigning 3GL is C, and the number of lines of C code used in embedded systems doubles every year. Embedded systems offer a terrific opportunity for anyone wanting to work in an expanding field with excellent prospects for continued growth.

Client-Server Programming

Creating client-server distributed network applications is another programming occupation in much demand with high potential for continued growth. Most analysts and research firms agree that the overwhelming majority of large companies with mainframe legacy systems are either considering or actively pursuing the downsizing of their current configurations—that is, they are moving their applications from the older systems to wide-area networks. These companies used to rely on mainframes and workstations, but increasingly they depend on local-area networks (LANs) and wide-area networks (WANs). Thus, client-server applications and remote connectivity have become necessities at many large companies.

Consider the way downsizing occurs. Usually a company implements a network and has "big iron" that it wants to continue to use in some way (usually as a network server). To achieve this goal, companies integrate SNA into the network environment and implement TCP/IP connectivity. There tends to be an increasing importance of network technology as businesses' old mainframe configurations evolve into new network-centric configurations.

New applications written for almost any large corporations will need, at minimum, to be network aware and able to take advantage of network services. However, more likely they will need to be true distributed applications that can use multiple CPUs on a network to accomplish their tasks. Creating such applications requires a knowledge of network technology, protocols, and since most networks are heterogeneous, cross-platform considerations.

Other network programming jobs are at the network operating system level or at lower levels, such as writing programs that control network cards, gateways, Internet routers, and communication with large WANs. Some network software vendors are creating new opportunities with new tools for creating remote procedure calls (RPCs) in a heterogeneous environment, implementing network security across a variety of WAN technologies, or performing any of a number of operations at any of the seven ISO network levels.

Jobs in client-server programming offer much diversity and give the programmer a broader perspective on the whole enterprise computing paradigm than do many other types of jobs.

Database Programming

A field that has been popular since the early PC days is database programming. Jobs in this area have in the past been an excellent way to break into the programming field. They still are, but the work has become more sophisticated. From programming in older languages such as dBASE, programmers now work with PC databases such as Access and Paradox and client-server relational database products such as those from Oracle and Sybase and SQL Server. The demand for database programmers remains high and will continue to grow.

Databases are now expected to be relational and distributed, with an application server host and client software running on a workstation.

Database programmers need a solid knowledge of one of the popular 3GLs (such as C or C++) as well as of database-specific languages such as SQL. Database programming jobs can be found almost everywhere.

Akin to database programming is the development of enterprise-wide business applications using fourth-generation languages (4GLs), such as Symantec's Enterprise Developer. 4GLs allow programmers another layer of abstraction between the objectives of the project and the code. That is, 4GLs eliminate or automate much of the coding usually needed in an application. They allow the programmer to quickly create applications using business rules and logic and connections to standard databases. The advantage of using 4GLs is the rapidity with which programmers can create applications or prototypes for applications.

Other Fields

The fields discussed on the preceding pages are just a sampling of the areas open to programmers. There are literally hundreds of different types of jobs for programmers, and you will be able to find one that suits your talents, interests, and financial needs. Think about creating new manufacturing systems or retail-point-to-sale software. If you like games, then nothing could be more satisfying than creating new games that use the latest technologies available in sound, multimedia, and virtual reality. And speaking of virtual reality, if you like the excitement of being on the cutting edge, VR provides vast new horizons to explore. VR is a fascinating field with a very big future.

Industries for Programmers

The following industries and products all depend on programmers in some capacity:

- Accounting
- Airlines
- Automotive manufacturing
- Banking
- Central processors
- Computer peripherals
- Education
- Entertainment
- Games
- Government
- Health care
- Hospitality
- Industrial systems
- Insurance
- Investment management
- Management
- Medicine
- Multimedia
- Nonprofit organizations
- Nursing
- Pharmaceuticals
- Publishing
- Real estate
- Remote communications
- Remote computing
- Retail
- Securities
- Space industry
- Sports
- Telephones
- Television
- Transportation
- Virtual reality

And there are many more. As software increasingly pervades our lives, the number of programming jobs will continue to grow. If you want a career that will provide you with enormous variety, excellent opportunity, and a great future, you have made a wise choice with programming.

Jobs by Language and Platform

Yet other considerations in planning your programming career are the platform and language in which you want to specialize. Although it is true that most programmers have a command of more than one computer language and of at least the fundamentals of more than one platform, it is also true that today you need to specialize. The specializations that you select are very important as your choices will shape the future of your career. Most people want to select a language and platform that will be in demand tomorrow as well as today.

Platforms Today and Tomorrow

Platforms range from CICS and MVS in the mainframe world, to UNIX, Windows, OS/2, and Macintosh in the PC world, all the way to the Newton environment for hand-held devices and a wide variety of embedded systems for as many uses as you can imagine. Change is the only constant in the programming field, so some of these platforms are still emerging while others reign dominant and still others are receding.

DOS

In the early 1980s, Microsoft's disk operating system (DOS) became the de facto standard for personal computers. It also became the cornerstone of the mighty Microsoft empire that has dominated the software industry since personal computing became popular.

Figure 2-4 shows sales of development tools for the DOS environment over the years. Sales of development tools are an excellent measure of market size because active developers buy tools regularly. As you can see, the popularity of programming for DOS has faded drastically since the introduction of GUIs in the PC environment.

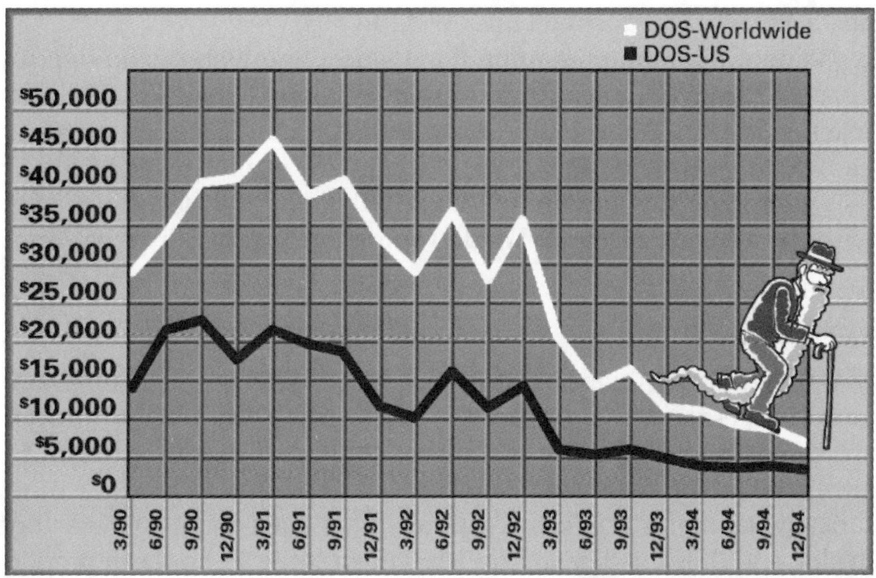

Source: Software Publishers Association

Figure 2-4 *Dollars (in thousands) spent on programming tools for the DOS platform*

There are still programs being written for the DOS environment, and there is still a demand for programmers to write them. However, these implementations are usually found in manufacturing or industrial applications where an attractive user interface is not important and where computers may be too old or slow or small to handle the new GUI interfaces.

If you're looking for a growth segment of the software industry, DOS is not the place to be.

Windows

The one platform definitely poised for more growth and thus more demand for knowledgeable programmers is Microsoft Windows in all its many forms. Windows was announced in 1982, but it wasn't until the early 1990s that version 3.1 brought Windows into the forefront of operating systems. Though purists will argue that Windows 3.1 is not an "operating system," the fact remains that it is treated like one, and it created a huge demand for Windows programming specialists.

The release of Microsoft's Windows 95 was one of the most significant events in the history of the industry, and literally millions of people are switching to it. This new 32-bit operating system takes a quantum leap ahead of everything else on the market in terms of performance, functionality, and ease of use. Windows 95 is boosting Windows sales even past its historic heights. Heads up—whatever you do, don't miss Windows 95.

Today, Windows is omnipresent on the desktop, and it shows no signs of retreating as Microsoft continues to develop new versions with new capabilities. If you center on Windows as your operating system of choice, you are virtually ensured a rich future with lots of work and continuing challenges as Microsoft continues to upgrade the operating system with more advanced versions. Figure 2-5 shows the dollars spent on Windows programming tools in recent years.

Macintosh

The Macintosh systems software has been well loved by a minority of programmers and end users for as many years as it has existed. The Macintosh OS is excellent for multimedia implementations and continually leads the other OSs in intuitive, graphics-oriented applications.

Historically, sales of Macintosh computers have been about 10 percent of total PC sales, and thus the demand for Macintosh software has been proportionately lower than that for other software products. However, Apple's new

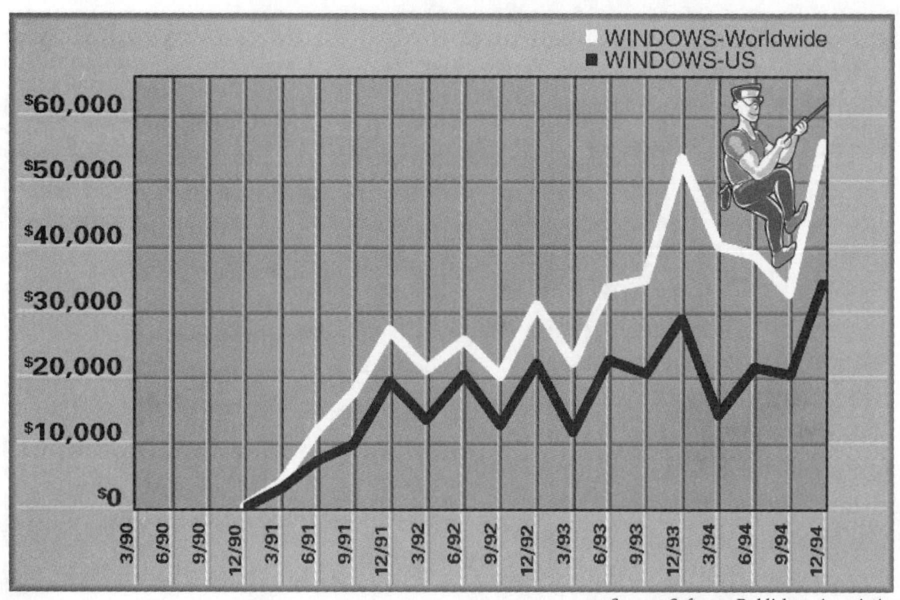

Source: Software Publishers Association

Figure 2-5 *Dollars (in thousands) spent on programming tools for the Windows platform*

Power Mac computer, based on the PowerPC RISC processor from Motorola, is creating considerable new demand for the Macintosh system. Apple sold more than 1 million Power Mac computers in the first year. Apple is moving its entire product line to the RISC chip, and that means a large demand for new applications for the Power Mac. This could provide a great opportunity for you if you're interested in programming for the Macintosh system. With the release of the Copland operating system, Mac programming should experience a renaissance.

OS/2

OS/2 is promoted heavily by IBM, who is working to get this system into the large corporations that have traditionally bought hardware and software from IBM. OS/2 has excellent underlying multiuser technology, great networking hooks, and a rich, object-oriented interface. However, OS/2 made little headway against Windows 3.1, and now that Windows 95 is here, the chances of OS/2 becoming a dominant factor in the industry seem slim.

Programmer's Perspective

"Everybody knows Windows is hot today and will continue to be hot. Windows, Windows 95, and in the longer term, NT, will all be important. I think the processors that will be important are still the x86-based ones. It's still going to be Intel. Power PC is interesting, but I don't see that happening as Intel is so dominant. And as for really interesting technologies, I think because of all the miniaturization, we're going to see more hand-held devices like message pads. I think wireless is going to be tremendously important. Some of the things that General Magic is doing are nice, but they're still missing the connectivity. When the cost of connecting comes down, we're going to see a whole lot of growth in that area. Wireless will become much more affordable and hand-held devices much better connected."

Enrique Salem
General Manager,
Systems Architect Unit,
Symantec

UNIX

UNIX has offered a multiuser environment since its inception. It is the mainstay of workstations that have traditionally been connected to large servers and is a mature OS that's well placed for continued growth. UNIX is not confined to dumb terminals anymore. It's appearing on more and more desktops.

The market for UNIX is very different from the markets for other operating systems and has different characteristics. For instance, it is not possible to estimate whether the market is growing or shrinking based on the size of the market for UNIX tools. Such market reports do not exist. In addition, there are many "flavors" of UNIX; it is not a unified operating system.

The lack of standardization in the UNIX environment makes it hard to pursue a career based on UNIX and still feel secure enough in your choice of UNIX types to sleep well at night. However, UNIX is far and away the most popular operating system used in universities. The fact that many people use UNIX while still in school also makes many programmers comfortable with it.

Network Operating Systems

Microsoft is now building networking functionality into the Windows operating system, and this is going to entirely change the future face of the network operating system landscape. In fact, independently sold network operating systems may eventually disappear altogether, though this won't happen for a long time because of the huge installed base of existing systems.

The major player in the network field right now, with over 60 percent market share, is Novell. Novell's NetWare took off in the late 1980s and hasn't slowed down since. Although proprietary to Novell, the IPX/SPX protocols pervade the industry, and NetWare is the NOS of choice. Other network operating systems include older NetBIOS-based systems such as IBM's PC Net and MS Net and newer multi-threaded systems such as LAN Manager. Writing applications for these networks will bring you into contact with new developments in network and remote communications as they arise. Working in the network operating system field can be exciting and can lead into many areas of job growth.

Mainframe Operating Systems

Mainframe operating systems are becoming less and less attractive as platforms for new programmers to specialize in. That's because these older mainframe "legacy" systems are quickly being phased out of most business enterprises and are being replaced by local-area networks, wide-area networks, and distributed client-server technologies that spread the work load over a network of PCs instead of relying on huge monolithic mainframe servers. This development is very important to the programming field; less than five years ago, legacy systems were used for the vast majority of software implementations in large- and medium-sized businesses. This fundamental change is having tremendous impact on the way applications are built and the expectations that users have for them.

Future Object-Oriented Operating Systems

The technology that is replacing legacy systems is distributed client-server computing. Specializing in this field will ensure that you're in high demand both now and in the foreseeable future.

It's always difficult to accurately predict the future. Will Taligent, the joint IBM-Apple venture into object-oriented operating systems, become a dominant player in the OS wars? Somehow, I don't think so. Will General Magic's Magic Cap pervade every nook and cranny of our lives as it controls the software of remote hand-held devices? Again, this wouldn't be my guess. Will Cairo be the place to be? Perhaps.

Taligent is a dark horse. Its technology incorporates some wonderful ideas, but the creativity behind the operating system functions is not generally what makes or breaks an operating system. Rather, the real requirement for a successful OS is plentiful applications, the drive of a large manufacturer, and sometimes a new niche that needs filling.

For these reasons, I think Cairo will be the next big success. It will supersede NT with Microsoft's blessing and with Microsoft's extraordinary muscle pushing it. Cairo will be the natural successor to all the Windows and NT applications and to the OEM deals that Microsoft makes with hardware vendors.

"The current version of NT is Daytona, and that will transition probably in early 1997 to Cairo or some derivative of Cairo," predicts Symantec's Enrique. "The direction and future of NT is Cairo, so that really makes sense. Taligent is a neat concept, but there's not enough market share and there's not a compelling reason for people to switch, so I don't think it's going to be a huge success.

"Other technologies that people need to consider are OLE and OpenDoc. Instead of building a whole application, programmers can use these components that are parts of other applications, and so really understanding OLE and OpenDoc is going to be key. A limitation of these technologies today is that neither has really been successful. Microsoft is really pushing OLE, which is making it pick up steam, but still the requirements of OLE are obstacles. It needs a really fast processor, plenty of RAM, and some pretty heavy hardware to bring up two applications and have them run in sync and not bog down the user. But every year the price-performance ratio for processors is getting better, and we have to believe that's going to continue and that technologies that are currently hardware intensive will become more accessible to larger audiences. OLE is one of the technologies that will really gain."

I agree with Enrique's sentiments, as do many other people in the industry.

Of course, my predictions could be wrong, but I don't foresee any major change in who supplies the operating system for the majority of PCs.

Speaking the Language of Jobs

It used to be simple: If you wanted a job programming for business applications you learned COBOL. If you were a scientist and wanted to use the computer to work on scientific problems, the language of choice was FORTRAN. Well, things have changed. Now languages are not necessarily confined to specific implementations. You can be a C or C++ programmer and work on any platform creating almost any type of application. FORTRAN and COBOL, while still with us and still used in their traditional arenas, are fading. Pascal, which was a popular hobbyist's tool, is also losing ground to the much more popular C language and its object-oriented extension, C++.

Figure 2-6 shows estimates of the growth potential and current number of lines of code in use today for each of the most popular languages. As you can see, the object-oriented 3GL C++ language and various 4GLs are expected to show the most growth over the next several years. Component programming, with its object-oriented roots, is expected to dominate the future of 3GLs, and C++ is the obvious object-oriented favorite. The other object-oriented languages in the figure have much less potential. SmallTalk was never very widely accepted, and there's no indication that it will gain more proponents. Object-oriented Pascal has gained quite a few users at the hacker/home-hobbyist level,

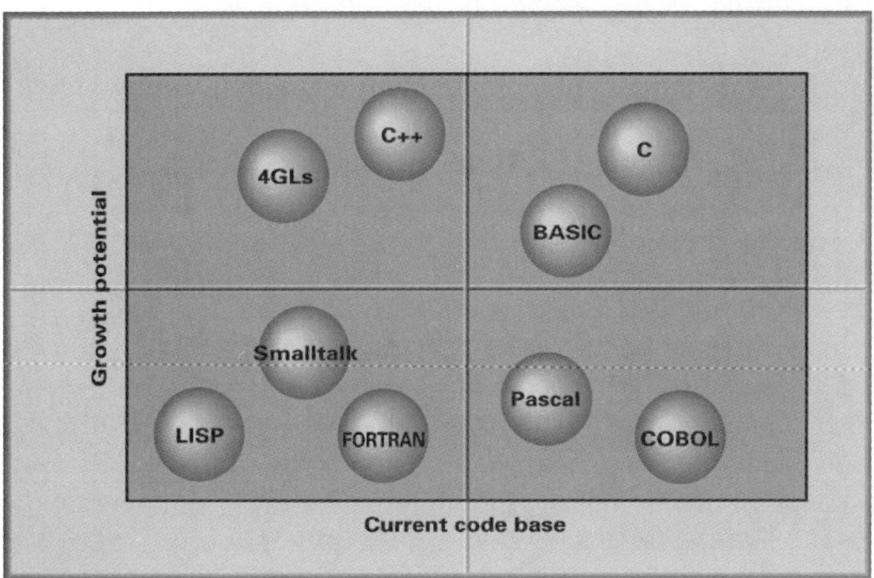

Figure 2-6 *The most popular computer languages in use today*

but it is almost never used in corporate or commercial settings and so is not a good bet for future programming jobs.

COBOL presents a different type of opportunity. The growth potential of COBOL is limited as the language is being abandoned at many sites in favor of C or, more commonly, object-oriented C++. However, so many lines of COBOL code exist that there is real opportunity for programmers who know *both* COBOL and a more modern language such as C++. IDC states that in 1993, PC COBOL revenue still represented 34 percent of the total market for language tools, and this figure relates directly to jobs.

Another way to examine the popularity of languages is to compare shipments of each language. Figure 2-7 shows total worldwide revenue and units shipped for each of the major languages. As you can see, C/C++ dominates both in revenue and, even more important, in shipments. Traditionally, C/C++ tools have a lower price point than do other languages. This lower price makes them more readily available to a wide range of programmers. Couple that with the remarkable flexibility of the C language and the object-oriented capabilities of C++, and it's clear that this is the language you need to know.

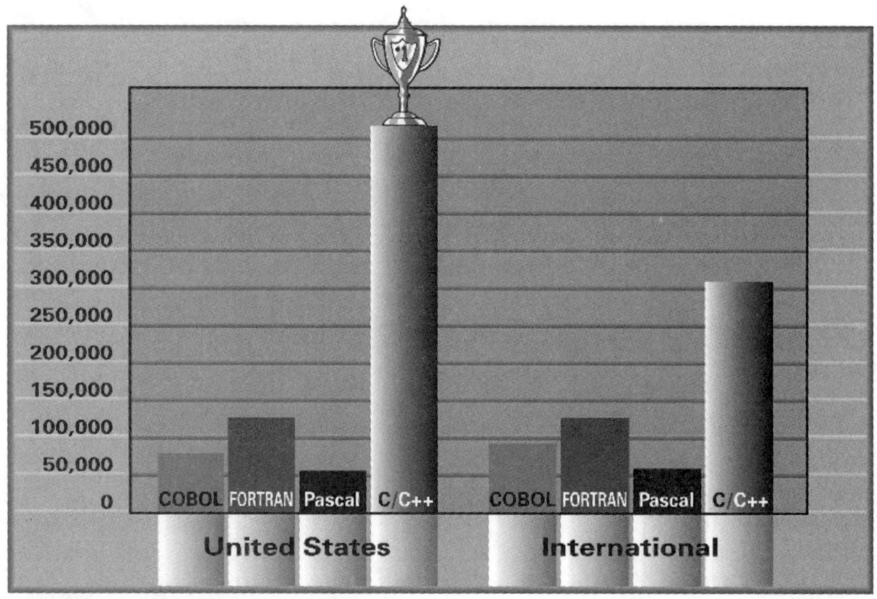

Figure 2-7 *The desktop 3GL market*

Source: IDC, 1994

Job Titles and Categories

The most common job title or category for a programmer is quite simply "programmer." That's not to say that all programmers have that title. They may be known as software engineers, developers, development engineers—and by many other titles. The semantics may vary, but basically the job is programming: designing programs, writing code, building components and applications, debugging, and maintaining code.

There are, however, other areas in which programmers are in high demand. Just scan the following list. Positions with any of these job titles can involve programming.

- Build engineer
- Computer science educator
- Customer service representative
- Documentation manager
- Graphic designer
- Internationalization engineer
- Program architect
- Quality assurance engineer
- Sales engineer
- Software engineer
- Systems analyst
- Systems engineer
- Systems integrator
- Technical support representative
- Technical writer
- Usability engineer
- Value-added retailer

Quality assurance (QA) departments often have a great need for test engineers well trained in programming. Test engineers write test programs that automate much of the software testing routine. They also are involved in testing complex parts of an application and may be responsible for actually creating utilities, installers, or other pieces of an application. Test engineers form a cornerstone of any programming effort and are absolutely essential to shrink-wrapped software, embedded systems, and virtually any type of commercial software creation cycle.

Documentation engineers are another type of professional whose job is closely related to programming. As programs and their operation become more complex, a high degree of expertise is required to create the documents that explain how the software works and how to troubleshoot problems when the software doesn't work as planned. Although not many programmers aim to end up as documentation engineers, this occupation is an excellent place to start, and you can use it to get your foot in the door at a company for which you particularly want to work.

Systems analysts and systems integrators usually are well versed in both hardware and software, and they often have an interest in cross-platform design and implementation. They may work as independent contractors, in-house staff, or more commonly, as employees of value-added retailers (VARs) or independent system integration (SI) firms.

The general programming job categories and each software development team also have jobs with specialized titles and duties. Most projects have a project leader or manager. These people are generally responsible for one or more components of a software program and so usually have some informal management duties in addition to their programming tasks. Engineering managers usually do nothing but manage a project. Most engineering managers don't write any code at all and usually have only a supervisory role in the design and architecture of an application. Their job is the management of people, time, costs, and project execution.

As you move up the organizational ladder, the top jobs are usually engineering vice president or chief information officer. People in these high-level jobs often don't have any actual involvement in ongoing projects. VPs and CIOs focus on strategic planning and forecasting trends rather than on coding or debugging. These jobs also involve a high degree of interaction with other functional areas of the company. The pay at this level is always excellent, as are other perks such as stock grants or options, vacations, and bonuses.

The job descriptions listed in the remainder of this section will help you get a clearer idea of what various jobs entail. These are actual job descriptions recently posted for positions in the Silicon Valley area.

Internationalization Engineer

Consultant with expertise in DOS to work on internationalization (Japanese and/or Chinese), setting up text files for these languages, translating the languages into the appropriate fonts, and displaying the languages on the screen. Must understand the process of getting text built by using translation program(s). Experience with medical instrumentation a plus.

Quality Assurance Engineer

Consultant to work with system developers to drive quality in test design, development, and execution. Ensure quality of testing procedures and results. Responsibilities will include test-case design (working with application developers and end users to design the necessary test cases to confirm functional requirements and system integration), test-case development (develop test cases designed above), test-case execution (working with application developers, establishing testing time-tables), execution of test scenarios, and documentation of the results/issues. Required ability to define testing methodology as well as execute unit, integration, and system testing, with emphasis on system testing.

Software Engineer—UNIX

Consultant to help with the development effort for a diagnostic instrument control system using C++. Must have minimum two years of C++ in the UNIX environment and experience with standard UNIX development tools (MAKE, RCS, VI or EMACS, shell scripts, debug facilities). Expertise with real-time systems helpful.

Software Engineer—Database

Senior relational and object-oriented database developer very experienced in design and development of both relational and object-oriented databases. Particularly familiar with Oracle and Sybase. Very experienced in developing client-server systems with SUN servers and both SUN and Mac clients. Must be very good at working with junior people and willing to take the time necessary to further his/her skills development. C++ programming, knowledge of one or more document management systems, knowledge of electronic publishing systems and various data formats, and knowledge of related meta-data design are all significant pluses.

Software Engineer

Senior Symantec C++ developer experienced in front-ending various tools with Symantec C++. Strong knowledge of DDE, OLE, and the building of VBX extensions required. Extensive knowledge of MS Windows graphical user interface standards required. Experience with Acrobat and World Wide Web preferred.

Software Engineer—Internet

World Wide Web developer experienced in setting up World Wide Web–readable HTTP servers. Strong knowledge of multiple Web search engine implementations required (particularly WAIS, Verity, and PLS). Experience in implementing multiple-source Web sites (HTML, PDF) required. Experience with implementing Verity/Acrobat/Web integration preferred.

Technical Support Engineer—Networks

Consultant to provide hands-on level 2 technical support to the Windows NT and Pathworks environments. Responsibilities include the distribution, installation, operation, maintenance, and troubleshooting of multiple PC network operating systems, as well as capacity/performance management of servers and the Santa Clara network. The successful candidate will also participate in large, cross-site projects affecting the PC NOS environment.

Technical Writer

Consultant with 4+ years of experience writing software engineering documentation. Experience writing user manuals and service manuals for the medical or scientific instrumentation a definite plus. Must have 2+ years experience using MS Word for Windows. Must be able to work effectively with engineering, marketing, and project management personnel.

Software Quality Assurance Engineer

This person will act in a QA role for the Norton product line, with special emphasis on the CPS products. Will work on Win 95 programs in the year ahead. Will report to a senior QA person. The person should have good experience in both testing and writing QA script. Requirements: BS in computer-related field. Experience testing and writing QA scripts. Localization and international S/W experience. Good QA experience. Good team player.

Release Lab Engineer

The person should have in-depth knowledge of how to run release lab support for localization. The person will deal with the various development teams in the U.S. to facilitate close working relationships. Requirements: Strong network and build environment skills.

Quality Assurance Engineer—Japanese

This person should be experienced in the Japanese aspect of software QA. The person should be able to develop and test-run QA scripts to test our software in a Japanese environment. Japanese language skills are a major requirement of the job. Requirements: BS in computer-related field. Experience in both writing and running Japanese QA scripts. Experience in living in Japan. Knowledge of Japanese culture.

Software Engineer—Localization

To act in a software role within the development team. The person will work on software localization for Windows 95. Should have good experience in debugging language code and releasing clean masters. Requirements: BS in computer-related field. Software experience: DOS and Windows experience. Language skills will be a bonus.

Technical Support Analyst—International, Central Europe

The person filling this position will provide technical answers and solutions in two or more languages to customers calling, faxing, or writing in with problems using Symantec software. The person will maintain an up-to-date case and customer reference in the case-logging database. Requirements: Secondary education (Dutch HAVO or equivalent), with several foreign languages. Solid knowledge of and experience with operating systems (DOS and Windows). Solid knowledge of IBM (-compatible) and/or Mac hardware. Preferably, experience in using Symantec and Central Point products. Fluency in English and at least one other foreign language (French, Dutch, German). Strong problem-solving and communication skills.

Quality Assurance Supervisor

This successful candidate will own entire testing effort for shipping a product in the Advanced Utilities group of Peter Norton. Manage all aspects of testing including QA and test-plan writing and verification, test-tool evaluation and development, test-plan execution, defect tracking, defect fix verification, and regression testing. Manage QA engineer and QA analyst teams of up to 20 persons, including writing reviews and developing team members. Requirements: BS in Computer Science, Computer Engineering, or Electrical Engineering (with computer emphasis). MBA a plus.

Development Manager

Qualified candidate will have experience in designing, developing, and managing DOS/Win products and will develop or supervise development of functional specifications, development schedules, and user interface specifications and will supervise development of code to functional specifications. Experience requirements include five to seven years experience in hands-on design of software. Necessary skills include proficiency in C and 680x0 family assembly language and demonstrated proficiency in software and UI design. Knowledge of object-oriented software design and networks helpful. Proven technical leadership influence within organization. Requirements: BS or equivalent in Computer Science or related field. Knowledge of C language and 680x0 family assembly language; experience with C++, OOP, or networks a plus. Leading software development teams.

Software Engineer—UI Specialist

The successful candidate will specify, create, and manage the development of all application artwork, work with developers to create visually accurate prototypes; manage the creation of and coordinate the maintenance of functional specifications, and ensure that all interfaces are consistent and share innovations. Requirements: BS or MS in Industrial Design or Graphic Arts desired. Requires Windows programming experience with proficiency in UI innovations on popular commercial applications, Visual Basic for developing prototypes, painting tools, resource editors, Word for Windows, and Aldus Super Paint. Good negotiation and communication skills.

Quality Assurance NLM Engineer

With minimal supervision and some management direction, this person will suggest, implement, and evaluate approaches to testing strategies in a Novell NetWare environment. The applicant must be able to define, create, document, verify, and execute test cases for an NLM product; participate in reviews, inspections, and walk-throughs of development, quality assurance, and technical publications documents/code with appropriate member of our QA staff. Write test automation and testing tools as required in both C and Windows programming languages. Requirements: BS in Computer Science or equivalent work experience, CNE certified. Thorough knowledge of innerworkings of PCs, Novell NetWare (3.x and higher), NLM DOS, and Windows is a must. Knowledge of C and Windows programming would be helpful. General knowledge of PC software/hardware setup/configuration would be helpful. Must have some quality assurance experience. Writing, executing, and evaluating test plans and cases for an NLM product. Developing QA tools and programs in both C and Windows programming languages as required. Self-starter who is able to work in a high-pressure, time-sensitive atmosphere with little direction and minimal supervision. The applicant must be a team player.

Development Manager—Network Communications

Qualified candidate will have experience in designing, developing, and managing DOS/Win products and will develop or supervise development of functional specifications, development schedules, user interface specifications, development schedules, and user interface specifications and will supervise development of code to functional specifications. Experience requirements include five to seven years experience in hands-on design of software. Necessary skills include proficiency in C and 80x86 family assembly language and demonstrated proficiency in software and UI design. Knowledge of object-oriented software design and networks helpful. Proven technical leadership influence within organization. Requirements: BS or equivalent in Computer Science or related field. Knowledge of C language and 80x86 family assembly language; experience with C++, OOP, or networks a plus. Leading software development teams.

Senior Quality Assurance Analyst

This person will own significant parts of the testing responsibilities for products in the Networking Product Group of Peter Norton. Responsibilities include ensuring these products meet the highest quality standards by executing and developing a wide variety of comprehensive tests and utilizing internal and commercial test tools to meet this goal. This person will utilize knowledge of platforms that the products run on to ensure that all possible test cases are identified and execute tests on DOS, Windows 3.x, Windows for Workgroups 3.11, and/or Macintosh platforms. Ensuring defects are correctly fixed is also included in the responsibilities for this position. Requirements: Associate of Science or similar education from a technical college. Expert power user of DOS, Windows, and/or Macintosh. Knowledge of all aspects of installment, maintenance, and upgrading of these platforms, Knowledge of settings, applications, and utilities on the platform. Two years of increasing challenges and demonstrated results in commercials S/W QA environment (relevant experience considered in lieu of this).

Senior Development Director

Qualified candidate will have experience in managing multiple DOS/Win/Mac development teams and will supervise development of functional specifications, development schedules, and user interface specifications. Experience requirements include seven to ten years experience in hands-on design of software and five to seven years management experience. Necessary skills include proficiency in C and 80x86 family assembly language and demonstrated proficiency in software and UI design. Requirements: BS or equivalent in Computer Science or related field. Knowledge of C and 80x86 or 6800 assembly language. Experience with C++, OOPS, or networks a plus. Experience managing multiple software teams. Proven technical leadership influence within an organization.

Software QA Engineer

This individual will maintain bug tracking system and manage external test sites, matrix functionality testing and specification, UI design and feedback, software debugging using C++ and Soft-Ice. Requirements: BS in Computer Science or equivalent one year of experience. Knowledge of testing methodologies, C and C++, Windows, Windows 95, PCs and PC architecture, Novell NetWare. Previous QA experience with DOS/Windows products or equivalent.

Associate QA Engineer I

The qualified candidate will own significant parts of the testing responsibilities for products in the Advanced Utilities Group of Peter Norton. Ensure these products meet the highest quality standards by writing, executing, and validating a wide range of comprehensive tests. Propose and develop internal test tools where appropriate. Validate test cases by code inspection and utilize source-level analysis tools. Utilize knowledge of operating system (DOS, Win 3.x, Mac) internals to test OS-level utilities and validate that test cases are sufficient. Ensure that defects are correctly fixed. Requirements: BS in Computer Science, Computer Engineering, or Electrical Engineering (with computer emphasis). MBA a plus. Extensive platform knowledge (including some internals) of DOS, Windows, and/or Macintosh. Demonstrated effective communication, planning, organization skills, two years of increasing challenges and demonstrated results in commercial PC S/W QA applications programming or relevant experience considered.

Software Quality Assurance Manager

The successful candidate will oversee several QA teams simultaneously. In addition, this person must be able to write QA test plans. Requirements: BS in Computer Science or equivalent. Five to seven years experience in software QA with management experience. Must be able to program in C or C++. Network product experience is highly desirable. Must be well organized, interact well with people, and be self-motivated.

Principal Software Engineer

Qualified candidate will have experience in designing, developing, and managing DOS/Win products and will develop or supervise development of functional specifications, development schedules, and user interface specifications and will supervise development of code to functional specifications. Requirements: Leading software development teams. Experience requirements include five to seven years experience in hands-on design of software. Necessary skills include proficiency in C and 80x86 family assembly language and demonstrated proficiency in software and UI design. Knowledge of object-oriented software design and networks helpful. BS or equivalent in Computer Science or related field. Knowledge of C language and 80x86 family assembly language; experience with C++, OOPS, or networks a plus.

Senior Technical Writer

This person will be responsible for writing and maintaining product documentation and may act as project lead. Must have proven writing skills and good technical and product knowledge, including familiarity with UI design guidelines for Macintosh platform. Must be able to scope work required and manage schedule and have basic understanding of publication process. Must be well organized, interact well with people, and demonstrate a capacity for initiative and self-motivation. Requirements: Must have technical writing experience with a retail-software product and a degree or equivalent experience in a computer-related or technical-writing field. Must have superior technical knowledge of Macintosh operating system with emphasis on file system architecture.

Senior Manager, Product Marketing

This individual will drive and manage the product launch process for all commercial products. Responsible for ensuring that products are clearly defined and positioned early enough to execute well-coordinated, successful product launches. Requires coordination of product management, product marketing, and central functional marketing entities (advertising, PR, creative services, channel marketing, direct mail) and product management of successful cross-functional launches. Add to various functional plans to ensure that strategies are achieved. Requirements: BS/BA or equivalent, MBA strongly preferred. Seven to ten years work experience (related). Knowledge of product management software a plus; general knowledge of product development process; cross-functional marketing experience.

Senior SQA Analyst

This person will design and implement test plans and test suites to evaluate software; design and document test scenarios; perform validation of client-server areas of products based on back-end engine-specific knowledge; interact with engineering department for design, specification, and implementation of software throughout product life cycle. Requirements: BS in Computer Science or related field, MS preferred. Database design experience, SQL experience, knowledge of object-oriented techniques; QA experience preferred. Superior problem-solving skills, highly motivated, strong communication skills with leadership potential.

Software Architect

The successful candidate will design, implement, enhance, and maintain different development tool components for the next generation of software development tools. Requirements: BS in Computer Science or equivalent. Fluent in C++ and object-oriented design; product design and development experience in Windows 16- and 32-bit environments; OLE2 and MFC experience a plus. Independent problem solver as well as a team player, creative, strong attention to detail, ability to master complex technical issues.

Computer Operator

This individual will operate and monitor critical corporate network and business computer systems on 24-hour/7-day basis. Data Center systems consist of a variety of DOS, Windows, and OS/2 based servers and gateways, HP3000 and HP9000 minicomputers and associated peripherals, and network backbone equipment. This position requires an individual who will ensure that procedures are followed to maximize uptime of network systems supporting cc:Mail and other critical company functions. Requirements: Prefer two-year or four-year degree in Computer Science, MIS, or related field. Specific experience with HP3000/XL commands and operation, OCS job scheduler, NBSPOOL output management. Experience using DOS, Windows; general network system knowledge desirable.

Software Tools Engineer

You will join the Development Tools group developing various components of our visual 4GL client-server product set. This includes development of a database repository and its administrative tool set. Focus is predominantly on user interface and usability issues. Requirements: BS in Computer Science or equivalent, 3+ years related coding experience. Fluency in C++ and Windows. Knowledge of object-oriented design and techniques. Knowledge of OLE2, MFC, Windows 95, Windows NT, relational database concepts, and application development a plus. Ability to work in a collaborative environment, as well as independently. Ability to suggest solutions to problems of limited scope. Ability to follow through coding implementations with minimal supervision. Ability to provide useful input that enhances the usability and usefulness of the product. Ability to prioritize tasks and commit to scheduling deadlines.

Technical Writer Specialist

This working writer and documentation manager will have responsibility within a software operating environment for documentation project planning, resource assignments, operation of projects within budget and schedule constraints, overall document quality and recruiting. Responsible for researching and proposing new documentation techniques and cost-reduction alternatives, investigating new technologies for online documentation and production. At least five years of professional technical writing experience applied to software products. Must have demonstrated management skills, initiative, self-motivation, and independence. Requirements: client-server development tools experience preferred.

Where the Money Is

Although money usually is *not* the most important criterion for job satisfaction among programmers, it is an important factor for almost everyone and should be a consideration when planning your career.

Although almost every industry employs programmers, all industries do not pay the same. In addition, the rate of salary increases also varies. For example, from 1994 to 1995, goverment programmers received the smallest salary increases (3.1%), while retail industry programmers received the best average salary increases (6.2%). Tables 2-2, 2-3, and 2-4 show the results of an annual salary survey conducted by *Computerworld* for 1995.

Average salaries vary quite a lot for all programmer job classifications by industry. They also vary by job function, with Programmer representing the entry-level developer and CIO/VP/Director representing the highest position in most programming fields.

Some of the best-paying programming jobs are in industries that are also in the forefront in the development of new technologies. Media, for example, requires knowledge of special effects techniques, morphing, virtual reality, and lots of other software "magic," and media programmers are paid handsomely for their cutting-edge expertise.

Another factor in compensation is geographical location. As Table 2-5 shows, you can expect to make more money throughout the course of your career in some geographical areas than in others. Jobs in New York and California consistently pay better than jobs in other regions. But don't forget that the cost of living also is higher in these regions.

Industry, Nonmanufacturing

Systems Analyst		Senior Systems Programmer		Systems Programmer		Senior Programmer/ Analyst		Programmer/ Analyst	
Bus. Svc. IS	$49,000	Bus. Svc. IS	$67,000	Bus. Svc. IS	$53,625	Banking	$57,465	Banking	$46,147
Utils.	$48,250	Banking	$57,900	Banking	$49,150	Bus. Svc. IS	$49,800	Utils.	$43,271
Trans.	$46,655	Media	$54,000	Utils.	$45,900	Health	$47,769	Bus. Svc. IS	$39,000
Banking	$46,500	Health	$51,334	Nonprofit	$45,333	Trans.	$47,200	Trans.	$37,544
Media	$44,667	Distrib.	$50,667	Trans.	$45,000	Utils.	$46,577	Distrib.	$37,500
Insurance	$44,518	Trans.	$49,000	Retail	$44,875	Media	$45,214	Insurance	$37,072
Gov't	$43,557	Insurance	$49,804	Media	$42,500	Bus. Svc. Non-IS	$44,776	Health	$36,705
Health	$43,314	Nonprofit	$49,750	Health	$41,925	Gov't	$43,796	Gov't	$36,019
Distrib.	$43,071	Utils.	$49,500	Insurance	$40,900	Insurance	$43,117	Bus. Svc. Non-IS	$35,792
Retail	$42,417	Retail	$48,527	Distrib.	$40,800	Distrib.	$42,429	Media	$34,667
Bus. Svc. Non-IS	$38,214	Bus. Svc. Non-IS	$45,600	Gov't	$39,324	Retail	$42,006	Retail	$34,209
Nonprofit	$38,000	Educ.	$42,964	Educ..	$34,364	Nonprofit	$40,650	Educ.	$32,796
Educ.	$37,833	Gov't.	NA	Bus. Svc. Non-IS	$30,000	Educ.	NA	Nonprofit	$32,409

Source: Computerworld

Table 2-2 *Programmer Salaries, 1994–1995*

Industry, Nonmanufacturing (*continued*)

Database Manager		Database Analyst		Data Security Administrator/ Analyst		Computer Operations Manager		Computer Operations Supervisor	
Media	$79,500	Banking	$55,000	Bus. Svc. IS	$51,500	Bus. Svc. IS	$62,500	Utils.	$50,250
Distrib.	$70,500	Retail	$53,625	Nonprofit	$50,000	Insurance	$58,256	Trans.	$44,500
Utils.	$62,000	Insurance	$51,125	Retail	$48,200	Utils.	$57,267	Bus. Svc. IS	$43,000
Banking	$60,000	Educ.	$50,500	Educ.	$47,750	Trans.	$51,667	Insurance	$39,693
Insurance	$59,763	Utils.	$48,250	Health	$46,600	Banking	$51,317	Media	$39,050
Nonprofit	$58,000	Health	$47,071	Banking	$46,357	Distrib.	$46,864	Health	$38,660
Retail	$56,800	Gov't	$43,765	Insurance	$46,138	Media	$46,667	Banking	$38,417
Gov't	$52,438	Media	$43,500	Gov't	$45,273	Nonprofit	$46,429	Bus. Svc. Non-IS	$38,250
Health	$52,425	Distrib.	$42,800	Bus. Svc. Non-IS	$35,500	Health	$46,406	Nonprofit	$37,900
Bus. Svc. IS	$51,500	Nonprofit	$42,750	Distrib.	NA	Retail	$45,600	Gov't	$37,655
Educ.	$47,944	Trans.	$41,500	Media	NA	Bus. Svc. Non-IS	$44,300	Educ.	$37,636
Bus. Svc. Non-IS	$46,845	Bus. Svc. IS	$40,500	Trans.	NA	Gov't	$43,988	Retail	$37,055
Trans.	$43,000	Bus. Svc. Non-IS	$38,333	Utils.	NA	Educ.	$39,536	Distrib.	$34,250

Industry, Manufacturing

Systems Analyst		Senior Systems Programmer		Systems Programmer		Senior Programmer/ Analyst		Programmer/ Analyst	
Consumer Prod.	$62,667	Chemical	$60,500	Consumer Prod.	$57,500	Consumer Prod.	$54,417	Consumer Elec.	$43,274
Met/Plas./ Rubber	$56,000	Consumer Prod.	$58,667	Chemical	$44,000	Ind. Equip.	$53,600	Consumer Prod.	$42,750
Food/Bev.	$55,250	Ind. Equip.	$56,500	Food/Bev.	$43,000	Consumer Elec.	$55,234	Forest Prod.	$40,083
Chemical	$53,000	Consumer Elec.	$55,660	Forest Prod.	$42,333	Chemical	$49,000	Food/Bev.	$39,180
Consumer Elec.	$51,667	Food/Bev.	$49,800	Apparel/ Textile	$41,667	Food/Bev.	$45,667	Chemical	$38,834
Forest Prod.	$43,333	Forest Prod.	$45,250	Consumer Elec.	$40,000	Forest Prod.	$44,188	Apparel/ Textile	$37,893
Apparel/ Textile	$36,333	Apparel/ Textile	$42,333	Ind. Equip.	$39,867	Apparel/ Textile	$44,000	Met./Plas./ Rubber	$36,726
Ind. Equip.	NA	Met./Plas./ Rubber	$41,429	Met./Plas./ Rubber	$37,767	Met./Plas./ Rubber	$42,700	Ind. Equip.	$34,001

Source: Computerworld

Table 2-2 *Programmer Salaries, 1994–1995* (continued)

Industry, Manufacturing (*continued*)									
Database Manager		**Database Analyst**		**Data Security Administrator/ Analyst**		**Computer Operations Manager**		**Computer Operations Supervisor**	
Food/Bev.	$71,750	Consumer Elec.	$55,000	Food/Bev.	$56,500	Consumer Prod.	$72,000	Chemical	$49,667
Consumer Prod.	$68,375	Ind. Equip.	$55,000	Chemical	$50,000	Food/Bev.	$57,460	Food/Bev.	$44,850
Consumer Elec.	$64,000	Food/Bev.	$54,333	Forest Prod.	$46,500	Ind. Equip.	$54,738	Apparel/ Textile	$39,937
Chemical	$52,000	Consumer Prod.	$52,000	Met./Plas./ Rubber	$45,000	Chemical	$53,750	Met./Plas./ Rubber	$39,625
Apparel/ Textile	$50,000	Chemical	$45,000	Consumer Prod.	$41,000	Consumer Elec.	$51,500	Consumer Elec.	$38,500
Met./Plas./ Rubber	$45,708	Apparel/ Textile	$42,000	Apparel/ Textile	NA	Met./Plas./ Rubber	$51,429	Consumer Prod.	$37,500
Forest Prod.	$43,625	Met./Plas./ Rubber	$41,000	Consumer Elec.	NA	Apparel/ Textile	$47,321	Forest Prod.	$31,000
Ind. Equip.	NA	Forest Prod.	$40,000	Ind. Equip.	NA	Forest Prod.	$46,417	Ind. Equip.	NA

Source: Computerworld

Table 2-2 *Programmer Salaries, 1994–1995* (continued)

The turnover rate also varies according to region, as shown in Table 2-6. However, the turnover rate in this profession is lower than the national average for all professions.

Forms of Compensation

In many programming jobs, your salary is not the only monetary reward you receive. Especially in the commercial software industry, there are often large bonuses associated with completing or shipping a software product. As you can see in Table 2-7, bonuses represent anywhere from 5 percent to almost 12 percent of the total compensation received in various types of software development jobs. Also, the higher your salary, the higher the bonus amount. Thus, as you move up through an organization, you can expect bonuses to become increasingly important to your overall income.

Other common forms of compensation are health insurance, 401K plans, relocation payments, and stock options. Thus, when you consider a job opportunity, be sure to consider all of these factors as well as salary. They can make a big difference in the actual value of your total compensation package.

Industry, Nonmanufacturing							
Lead Computer Operator		Computer Operator		Technical Specialist		Microcomputer, End-User Computing Manager	
Bus. Svc. Non-IS	$33,209	Trans.	$30,875	Utils.	$45,025	Bus. Svc. IS	$69,000
Insurance	$32,979	Utils.	$27,900	Distrib.	$44,400	Media	$61,800
Media	$32,042	Gov't	$26,686	Insurance	$40,313	Insurance	$60,550
Bus. Svc. IS	$32,000	Insurance	$25,609	Media	$36,667	Utils.	$58,500
Gov't	$31,341	Media	$25,278	Bus.Svc. Non-IS	$35,571	Trans.	$54,000
Utils.	$30,806	Educ.	$25,208	Health	$35,520	Distrib.	$49,333
Health	$30,306	Bus. Svc. Non-IS	$24,885	Nonprofit	$35,500	Gov't	$49,199
Banking	$29,367	Nonprofit	$24,643	Educ.	$33,958	Health	$48,736
Educ.	$28,787	Distrib.	$24,559	Retail	$33,950	Banking	$48,031
Trans.	$28,717	Banking	$24,155	Trans.	$33,500	Educ.	$46,233
Retail	$28,529	Bus. Svc. IS	$23,750	Banking	$32,571	Bus. Svc. Non-IS	$43,667
Nonprofit	$28,357	Health	$23,453	Gov't	$31,206	Retail	$36,682
Distrib.	$26,255	Retail	$22,788	Bus. Svc. IS	NA	Nonprofit	$35,100

Technical Support Manager/Help Desk Manager		Help Desk Operator		PC Technical Support Specialist		Business Services Analyst	
Insurance	$53,250	Utils.	$39,167	Utils.	$40,825	Bus. Svc. IS	$49,000
Trans.	$44,500	Bus. Svc. Non-IS	$34,500	Banking	$36,765	Utils.	$43,000
Bus. Svc. Non-IS	$42,668	Trans.	$34,400	Trans.	$30,833	Banking	$41,800
Health	$40,833	Banking	$31,591	Nonprofit	$34,350	Media	$40,600
Gov't	$40,447	Distrib.	$31,250	Gov't	$33,804	Retail	$39,333
Banking	$39,250	Health	$30,088	Distrib.	$33,400	Bus. Svc. Non-IS	$38,200
Media	$38,500	Insurance	$29,138	Insurance	$33,182	Health	$37,625
Retail	$37,100	Bus. Svc. IS	$28,750	Bus. Svc. IS	$32,567	Educ.	$35,643
Nonprofit	$36,714	Nonprofit	$28,071	Bus. Svc. Non-IS	$32,155	Nonprofit	$35,500
Educ.	$34,806	Gov't	$27,393	Health	$31,911	Insurance	$32,667
Distrib.	$32,167	Educ.	$24,364	Retail	$30,778	Gov't	$29,636
Utils.	$24,500	Media	$23,667	Educ.	$30,541	Distrib.	$29,500
Bus. Svc. IS	NA	Retail	$22,857	Media	$27,571	Trans.	NA

Source: Computerworld

Table 2-3 *Technical Operations Salaries, 1994–1995*

Industry, Manufacturing

Lead Computer Operations		Computer Operator		Technical Specialist		Microcomputer, End-User Computing Manager	
Consumer Prod.	$36,000	Consumer Elec.	$28,813	Consumer Prod.	$45,000	Consumer Prod.	$73,500
Food/Bev.	$35,333	Consumer Prod.	$28,056	Consumer Elec.	$41,641	Food/Bev.	$71,650
Consumer Elec.	$33,344	Food/Bev.	$27,056	Food/Bev.	$41,275	Chemical	$71,000
Chemical	$31,333	Forest Prod.	$25,800	Met./Plas./ Rubber	$38,740	Apparel/ Textile	$49,333
Forest Prod.	$30,500	Ind. Equip.	$24,233	Forest Prod.	$37,167	Forest Prod.	$45,750
Met./Plas./ Rubber	$27,164	Met./Plas./ Rubber	$23,669	Ind. Equip.	$24,733	Met./Plas./ Rubber	$45,000
Ind. Equip.	$26,510	Apparel/ Textile	$22,436	Apparel/ Textile	NA	Ind. Equip.	$44,000
Apparel/ Textile	$26,043	Chemical	NA	Chemical	NA	Consumer Elec.	$43,625

Technical Support Manager/Help Desk Manager		Help Desk Operator		PC Technical Support Specialist		Business Services Analyst	
Consumer Prod.	$56,250	Chemical	$33,667	Chemical	$41,000	Food/Bev.	$51,667
Consumer Elec.	$52,000	Met./Plas. Rubber	$31,125	Forest Prod.	$40,000	Consumer Prod.	$50,000
Forest Prod.	$40,000	Forest Prod.	$30,750	Consumer Elec.	$39,750	Consumer Elec.	$44,000
Apparel/ Textile	NA	Consumer Prod.	$29,667	Consumer Prod.	$38,700	Ind. Equip.	$39,000
Chemical	NA	Consumer Elec.	$29,000	Food/Bev.	$36,357	Forest Prod.	$37,500
Food/Bev.	NA	Food/Bev.	$28,375	Apparel/ Textile	$33,083	Chemical	$35,000
Ind. Equip.	NA	Apparel/ Textile	$23,000	Met./Plas./ Rubber	$31,857	Apparel/ Textile	NA
Met./Plas. Rubber	NA	Ind. Equip.	NA	Ind. Equip.	$28,925	Met./Plas./ Rubber	NA

Source: Computerworld

Table 2-3 *Technical Operations Salaries, 1994–1995* (continued)

Industry, Nonmanufacturing

CIO/CP		Director, Systems Development		Director, Networks		Director, IS Operations		Manager of Voice/Data Communications	
Bus Svc. IS	$140,500	Banking	$96,500	Banking	$94,953	Banking	$81,380	Trans.	$80,000
Banking	$118,973	Bus. Svc. IS	$87,400	Bus. Svc. IS	$79,500	Bus. Svc. IS	$70,500	Banking	$78,375
Media	$98,292	Bus. Svc. Non-IS	$75,194	Utils.	$76,833	Media	$68,463	Utils.	$73,500
Insurance	$96,056	Insurance	$74,742	Insurance	$74,325	Retail	$68,236	Bus Svc. IS	$72,000
Retail	$95,778	Media	$72,750	Media	$65,500	Insurance	$67,606	Insurance	$71,638
Bus. Svc. Non-IS	$90,881	Retail	$71,235	Retail	$65,400	Bus. Svc. Non-IS	$64,205	Distrib.	$70,000
Health	$88,853	Trans.	$69,633	Health	$64,750	Utils.	$62,600	Media	$62,500
Utils.	$88,334	Health	$69,311	Bus. Svc. Non-IS	$60,857	Trans.	$61,167	Nonprofit	$60,700
Trans.	$85,591	Utils.	$69,000	Distrib.	$55,000	Gov't	$60,371	Bus. Svc. Non-IS	$58,857
Distrib.	$78,955	Distrib.	$60,818	Gov't	$54,941	Nonprofit	$60,271	Gov't	$54,100
Educ.	$73,764	Gov't	$59,528	Nonprofit	$54,375	Distrib.	$59,293	Retail	$52,325
Nonprofit	$72,329	Nonprofit	$58,950	Educ.	$54,267	Health	$57,617	Health	$51,864
Gov't	$69,440	Educ.	$57,957	Trans.	$53,650	Educ.	$52,239	Educ.	$47,167

Communications Specialist		Network Administrator		LAN Manager		Project Manager, Systems and Programming		Senior Systems Analyst	
Media	$82,667	Utils.	$49,000	Banking	$54,376	Banking	$72,706	Bus. Svc. IS	$60,250
Utils.	$58,000	Bus. Svc. IS	$48,250	Insurance	$50,858	Bus. Svc. IS	$71,250	Banking	$59,913
Banking	$53,914	Banking	$46,035	Bus. Svc. IS	$48,500	Media	$62,125	Media	$56,143
Bus. Svc. IS	$53,250	Nonprofit	$45,938	Health	$46,094	Distrib.	$60,900	Trans.	$53,358
Distrib.	$51,000	Insurance	$44,076	Nonprofit	$45,714	Insurance	$59,117	Insurance	$52,665
Nonprofit	$46,250	Bus. Svc. Non-IS	$42,656	Bus. Svc. Non-IS	$45,545	Utils.	$57,214	Utils.	$52,633
Insurance	$44,957	Gov't	$41,552	Utils.	$44,875	Retail	$57,105	Health	$51,936
Retail	$44,450	Educ.	$41,200	Media	$43,000	Health	$55,459	Bus. Svc. Non-IS	$51,120
Trans.	$44,000	Health	$41,018	Trans.	$41,500	Nonprofit	$53,833	Nonprofit	$50,550
Health	$43,000	Retail	$40,184	Distrib.	$41,375	Bus. Svc. Non-IS	$53,620	Distrib.	$48,833
Gov't	$40,946	Trans.	$39,333	Educ.	$39,739	Trans.	$53,448	Gov't	$48,372
Bus. Svc. Non-IS	$40,083	Media	$39,155	Retail	$39,218	Gov't	$51,990	Retail	$47,864
Educ.	$39,154	Distrib.	$38,500	Gov't	NA	Educ.	$50,176	Educ.	$46,132

Source: Computerworld

Table 2-4 *Technical Manager Salaries, 1994–1995*

Industry, Manufacturing

CIO/CP		Director, Systems Development		Director, Networks		Director, IS Operations		Manager of Voice/Data Communications	
Consumer Prod.	$130,700	Food/Bev.	$96,778	Chemical	$118,500	Food/Bev.	$96,967	Food/Bev.	$72,800
Food/Bev.	$122,455	Consumer Prod.	$95,278	Consumer Prod.	$112,133	Chemical	$82,250	Consumer Elec.	$72,750
Consumer Elec.	$108,173	Met./Plas./ Rubber	$83,111	Food/Bev.	$108,250	Consumer Prod.	$81,375	Met./Plas./ Rubber	$70,500
Forest Prod.	$100,938	Consumer Elec.	$79,906	Apparel/ Textile	$79,000	Consumer Elec.	$62,069	Consumer Prod.	$66,000
Apparel/ Textile	$94,889	Forest Prod.	$69,125	Forest Prod.	$65,000	Met./Plas./ Rubber	$58,221	Chemical	$61,667
Chemical	$91,800	Chemical	$68,879	Ind. Equip.	$62,000	Forest Prod.	$55,343	Apparel/ Textile	$54,667
Ind. Equip.	$79,958	Apparel/ Textile	$63,600	Met./Plas./ Rubber	$55,125	Apparel/ Textile	$53,500	Forest Prod.	$51,250
Met./Plas./ Rubber	$77,642	Ind. Equip.	$63,233	Consumer Elec.	NA	Ind. Equip.	NA	Ind. Equip.	NA

Communications Specialist		Network Administrator		LAN Manager		Project Manager, Systems and Programming		Senior Systems Analyst	
Food/Bev.	$55,350	Food/Bev.	$51,583	Consumer Prod.	$59,300	Consumer Elec.	$71,750	Consumer Elec.	$61,000
Chemical	$51,250	Consumer Elec.	$48,000	Food/Bev.	$56,000	Consumer Prod.	$69,929	Food/Bev.	$59,250
Consumer Elec.	$45,350	Consumer Prod.	$44,200	Chemical	$52,500	Chemical	$68,929	Consumer Prod.	$57,500
Forest Prod.	$44,500	Chemical	$41,667	Met./Plas./ Rubber	$47,786	Food/Bev.	$63,667	Ind. Equip.	$56,820
Met./Plas./ Rubber	$40,857	Met./Plas./ Rubber	$40,556	Consumer Elec.	$46,542	Ind. Equip.	$62,009	Chemical	$54,000
Apparel/ Textile	$40,000	Forest Prod.	$40,167	Forest Prod.	$44,667	Met./Plas./ Rubber	$52,714	Met./Plas./ Rubber	$47,167
Consumer Prod.	$39,333	Ind. Equip.	$37,816	Apparel/ Textile	$44,182	Forest Prod.	$52,667	Forest Prod.	$46,000
Ind. Equip.	NA	Apparel/ Textile	$33,667	Ind. Equip.	$43,729	Apparel/ Textile	$52,583	Apparel/ Textile	$45,000

Source: Computerworld

Table 2-4 *Technical Manager Salaries, 1994–1995* (continued)

	CIO/VP/ Director	Manager	Project Manager	Senior Systems Analyst	Systems Analyst	Senior Programmer/ Analyst	Programmer/ Analyst	Senior Programmer	Programmer
Other	$95,000	$42,500	$36,500	$31,500	$28,000	$28,250	$26,000	$43,000	$22,300
New York	$80,038	$58,562	$57,156	$47,860	$44,944	$47,763	$42,119	$44,833	$34,090
Atlanta	$79,400	$56,204	$47,969	$48,166	$39,184	$42,476	$33,615	$36,750	$30,366
Northern California	$78,596	$58,678	$49,428	$51,083	$50,214	$50,208	$41,676	$53,388	$40,846
Southern California	$78,007	$61,562	$56,333	$54,666	$46,090	$46,696	$37,742	$45,000	$33,642
Boston	$74,490	$57,550	$54,411	$47,625	$37,615	$44,346	$33,597	$40,428	$30,937
Baltimore/D.C.	$74,274	$56,847	$55,261	$46,952	$35,429	$43,742	$37,651	$31,799	$29,172
Chicago	$73,060	$55,984	$52,323	$49,227	$43,107	$41,578	$36,263	$39,500	$30,652
Texas	$72,500	$54,000	$50,470	$46,500	$41,088	$44,240	$37,322	$40,700	$31,520
Detroit	$65,209	$53,782	$51,066	$43,576	$39,500	$42,521	$37,109	$39,500	$30,000
Denver	$64,438	$52,000	$49,533	$44,049	$39,081	$39,593	$33,101	$40,125	$28,882
Florida	$63,550	$50,869	$46,642	$43,027	$41,100	$40,880	$35,100	$30,750	$26,044
Arizona	$63,413	$54,531	$54,833	$48,388	$43,600	$40,743	$32,171	$44,928	$31,041
Minnesota	$62,891	$56,000	$45,500	$45,000	$37,266	$41,480	$33,695	$35,750	$28,470
Pacific Northwest	$56,031	$48,921	$43,370	$44,709	$40,045	$38,987	$34,519	$38,388	$27,681

Source: Computerworld

Table 2-5 *Programmer Salaries, by Region*

How IS Turnover Compared in 1994

IS turnover	8.7%
Total U.S.	12.0%

Average Turnover Rate in 1994 by Region

	Northeast	Midwest	South	West	Average
IS department	9.8%	7.5%	7.9%	10.1%	8.7%
Companywide	10.3%	11.2%	16.5%	13.0%	12.1%

Average Turnover Rate by Company Size

	Less than $100M	$100M–$500M	Over $500M
IS department	7.9%	9.8%	9.5%
Companywide	11.7%	13.1%	12.4%

Table 2-6 *Turnover Rates*

Women in Programming

There was a time when 90 percent of all programmers were male. If you went into any software development group and looked around, all you would see is men. That has certainly changed. Today there are as many women in programming as there are in most professions. Women have made great strides in this occupation, as Table 2-8 shows. Women are still underrepresented in top management positions, but hopefully this will change in the future.

Future Outlook

As noted before, the overall outlook for programming jobs is excellent. This is especially true in high-growth areas such as object-oriented component programming, embedded-systems development, and client-server development. The *EDGE Workgroup Computing Report* produced in 1994 by Uniforum and Pencom reported that open systems client-server developers currently are paid better than mainframe programmers, and that developers with skills in object-oriented programming are in high demand and command an average salary across the board of $64,000 yearly—that's a high average salary with the added benefit of great future prospects.

Other specialties are even more timely. Currently, there is high demand for developers and IS professionals qualified to create Lotus Notes implementa-

CIO/VP	Director, Systems Development	Director, Networks	Director, IS Operations	Manager of Voice/ Data Communications	Communications Specialist	Network Administrator	LAN Manager	Project Manager, Systems and Programming	Senior Systems Analyst
Average: $82,129	Average: $67,276	Average: $65,110	Average: $60,196	Average: $57,139	Average: $44,588	Average: $41,240	Average: $44,175	Average: $55,331	Average: $50,388
Bonus: $9,439	Bonus: $5,706	Bonus: $4,940	Bonus: $5,179	Bonus: $3,139	Bonus: $2,386	Bonus: $1,640	Bonus: $2,627	Bonus: $3,055	Bonus: $1,522
Total: $91,568	Total: $72,982	Total: $70,050	Total: $65,375	Total: $60,278	Total: $46,974	Total: $42,880	Total: $46,802	Total: $58,386	Total: $51,910
Company Size									
Under $100M: $74,112	Under $100M: $61,460	Under $100M: $56,398	Under $100M: $55,658	Under $100M: $53,851	Under $100M: $42,663	Under $100M: $39,580	Under $100M: $42,920	Under $100M: $53,900	Under 100M: $48,069
$100M–$500M: $97,518	$100M–$500M: $71,814	$100M–$500M: $63,345	$100M–$500M: $66,869	$100M–$500M: $56,599	$100M–$500M: $46,342	$100M–$500M: $43,977	$100M–$500M: $45,298	$100M–$500M: $60,347	$100M–$500M: $52,163
Over $500M: $131,639	Over $500M: $93,526	Over $500M: $90,721	Over $500M: $84,682	Over $500M: $69,157	Over $500M: $51,635	Over $500M: $47,401	Over $500M: $50,715	Over $500M: $62,896	Over $500M: $56,765

Systems Analyst	Senior Systems Programmer	Systems Programmer	Senior Programmer/ Analyst	Programmer/ Analyst	Database Manager	Database Analyst	Data Security Admin./ Analyst	Computer Operations Manager	Computer Operations Supervisor
Average: $43,710	Average: $48,635	Average: $41,117	Average: $44,263	Average: $36,274	Average: $53,610	Average: $46,766	Average: $46,170	Average: $47,624	Average: $38,167
Bonus: $1,706	Bonus: $3,096	Bonus: $770	Bonus: $1,718	Bonus: $929	Bonus: $2,059	Bonus: $1,008	Bonus: $1,314	Bonus: $1,921	Bonus: $1,358
Total: $45,416	Total: $51,731	Total: $41,887	Total: $45,981	Total: $37,203	Total: $55,669	Total: $47,774	Total: $47,484	Total: $49,545	Total: $39,525
Company Size									
Under $100M: $40,806	Under $100M: $48,514	Under $100M: $39,898	Under $100M: $43,589	Under $100M: $35,304	Under $100M: $48,365	Under $100M: $41,490	Under $100M: $43,625	Under $100M: $44,662	Under 100M: $37,396
$100M–$500M: $46,174	$100M–$500M: $50,358	$100M–$500M: $42,031	$100M–$500M: $48,278	$100M–$500M: $38,060	$100M–$500M: $56,069	$100M–$500M: $50,520	$100M–$500M: $50,750	$100M–$500M: $47,267	$100M–$500M: $36,509
Over $500M: $50,144	Over $500M: $54,977	Over $500M: $45,500	Over $500M: $48,160	Over $500M: $39,932	Over $500M: $61,062	Over $500M: $49,628	Over $500M: $48,034	Over $500M: $59,517	Over $500M: $44,180

Lead Computer Operator	Computer Operator	Technical Specialist	Microcomputer, End-user Computing Manager	Technical Support Manager/ Help Desk Manager	Help Desk Operator	PC Technical Support Specialist	Business Services Analyst
Average: $$29,361	Average: $24,681	Average: $35,927	Average: $47,543	Average: $40,440	Average: $28,940	Average: $32,239	Average: $36,569
Bonus: $943	Bonus: $702	Bonus: $874	Bonus: $2,282	Bonus: $1,316	Bonus: $546	Bonus: $806	Bonus: $636
Total: $30,304	Total: $25,383	Total: $36,801	Total: $49,825	Total: $41,756	Total: $29,486	Total: $33,045	Total: $37,205

Source: Computerworld

Table 2-7 *Programmer Salaries Including Bonuses*

Lead Computer Operator	Computer Operator	Technical Specialist	Microcomputer, End-user Computing Manager	Technical Support Manager/ Help Desk Manager	Help Desk Operator	PC Technical Support Specialist	Business Services Analyst
Company Size							
Under $100M: $29,215	Under $100M: $24,108	Under $100M: $32,729	Under $100M: $45,228	Under $100M: $35,937	Under $100M: $29,934	Under $100M: $31,683	Under $100M: $35,053
$100M– $500M: $30,376	$100M– $500M: $26,147	$100M– $500M: $38,583	$100M– $500M: $47,228	$100M– $500M $41,342	$100M– $500M: $28,073	$100M– $500M: $32,853	$100M– $500M: $39,500
Over $500M: $32,448	Over $500M: $27,161	Over $500M: $40,665	Over $500M: $59,309	Over $500M: $49,877	Over $500M: $30,561	Over $500M: $36,499	Over $500M: $39,510

Source: Computerworld

Table 2-7 *Programmer Salaries Including Bonuses* (continued)

tions. A New York firm recently hired a Notes administrator for a salary of $60,000, which is 20 percent more than what a NetWare administrator gets in that region. Consultants can earn $1,200 to $1,500 per day for Notes work. Professionals versed in Notes are in demand because the Notes application is currently very popular in large corporations, and thus companies need applications that can interact with that environment. This is not to say that Notes is a specialty you should enter. Notes may not be as popular by the time you read this book as it is at the time of this writing. However, if it isn't Notes, then something else will be "hot." The real message here is to watch new technologies as they emerge. Keep up with trade journals and weekly PC newspapers. When you hear about something new that sounds exciting, explore it, learn about it. Keep current with the various tools and technologies, watch for trends, and follow your interests. In this way, you should always have a wealth of job opportunities and a host of exciting new challenges.

Job Title	Percent of Women in IS
Management	
CIO/VP IS	16.7%
Director, systems development	25.7%
Director, networks	16.7%
Director, IS operations	16.7%
Networks	
Manager, voice and data and communications	26.9%
Communications specialist	22.9%
Network administrator	27.5%
LAN manager	28.7%
Systems Development	
Project manager, systems and programming	36.3%
Senior systems analyst	39.0%
Systems analyst	45.2%
Senior systems programmer	31.2%
Systems programmer	35.0%
Senior programmer/analyst	39.7%
Programmer/analyst	45.7%
Database manager	31.6%
Database analyst	31.0%
Data security administrator/analyst	42.2%
Technical Services and Operations	
Computer operations manager	23.8%
Computer operations supervisor	31.9%
Lead computer operator	40.0%
Computer operator	40.9%
Technical specialist	25.4%
PC End-user Support	
Microcomputer, end-user computing manager	38.9%
Technical support manager/help desk manager	45.0%
Help desk operator	60.4%
PC technical support specialist	30.1%
Business services analyst	58.8%
Total Percent of Women in IS	37.3%
Percent of Women in Total U.S. Workforce	43.7%

Table 2-8 Women in Programming

Getting the Job: The Perfect Résumé and Interview

Okay, so now you know the market segment and geographical location where you want to be. You're familiar with the types of programming jobs available today, and you have some idea of where you want your career to be in ten years. So, how do you actually get the job you want?

How Jobs Become Available

It takes a company considerable time and money to hire any full-time professional. In a typical scenario, a manager first must identify a need for a permanent employee with specific job-related skills and talents. If the position is a new one, then the manager usually has to champion the idea of adding staff to the "higher-ups" within the company, division, or business unit and show how a project or task cannot be completed in a timely manner if the company doesn't hire an additional person. To buttress the request for additional staff, the manager may use forecasts of the projected revenue from a project, time tables for completion of the project, and anticipated profit and loss figures with and without the new hire.

Of course, less paperwork and official justification may be needed in a small company or to hire a replacement for someone who has left. However, in almost every situation there must be financial justification for hiring staff, and that justification usually is the need for the successful and timely completion of some project to achieve the revenue associated with the project.

Programmers are hired because a particular project needs to be worked on and completed.

The expectation is that you'll be able to continue contributing in a similar way to other projects after the current one is finished, and that's why the company is hiring a full-time employee instead of a contractor. But knowing that the hiring manager probably has a particular project in mind gives you a clue to how to win the job.

Identify the project that needs to be done and then market yourself as someone particularly qualified for that project.

This strategy is basic but powerful and is actually quite easy to implement, as you will see.

A hiring manager usually has to jump through several hoops to get a new position approved because hiring someone is so expensive in both time and money. Not only does the company have to pay the new employee's salary, but also social security, workmen's compensation, taxes, and benefits. Most companies figure they pay an additional 34 percent of salary for benefits, including government-mandated payments. Thus, if the salary for a particular job is $40,000, the actual cost to the company is $53,600. In addition, there may be relocation expenses to pay, or for an experienced senior-level position, there might be a hiring bonus. Stock options are sometimes granted as an incentive to keep people at a company, and these options have to be approved by the company's board of directors. If a professional independent recruiter, or "headhunter," is used, the company may have to pay an amount equal to perhaps 20 percent of the new employee's first-year salary as a finder's fee. Want ads in newspapers also can be expensive. A small display ad in a major city newspaper can cost $2,000 to $5,000, and large ads in the Sunday paper cost much more. In addition, the company incurs considerable expense in the first few months after someone is hired as a result of training and low productivity while the new recruit learns the ropes.

Obviously, a company does not hire people without giving the decision a lot of thought. Thus, even if you're the hottest programmer in your class or have great experience in the industry, don't expect a job to be created especially for you. If you are hired, it will be because the company thinks you're the right person to fill a need the company already has.

How Companies Recruit Applicants

Once the decision has been made to open a position and hire someone to fill it, the Human Resources (HR) department takes over and begins to publicize the availability of the job. At the same time, other people within the company find out about the job and may apply for it or tell friends and colleagues about it, associates at other companies find out about the job, and sometimes head-hunters are employed to look for appropriate candidates. Figure 3-1 shows the percentage of people recruited and hired at a prominent software company by recruiting vehicle.

Sometimes you hear that no one ever gets a professional job through the classified ads. This is not so. Look at Figure 3-1. The large display ads that you see on Sundays can cost $10,000 or more to run just once in a large metropolitan newspaper. Companies spend those thousands of dollars advertising professional programming jobs with the expectation that the ads will pay off. Don't neglect the classifieds.

Don't forget to check out-of-town newspapers, too. Probably no newspaper in the world has as many ads for programming jobs as the *San Jose Mercury News,* and you don't have to live in San Jose to get the paper. You can call from anywhere in the country and for a fee the company will send you the paper. You need only order the Sunday edition, as that's when the most jobs are listed. Other large metropolitan newspapers that you may want sent to you include the *Los Angeles Times*, the *Boston Tribune,* and *The New York Times*. By Monday morning, the papers should also be available in your local library.

"Foot-in-the-door" jobs, or those that result from referrals by someone within the company, also account for a large percentage of new hires. However, this route doesn't require you to know the hiring manager. Many companies encourage employees to help find qualified candidates by publishing job openings and by offering cash bonuses. If you add up the percentages in Figure 3-1 for both employee referrals and personal networking, you will see that some form of personal referral is the largest source of new hires. The message is clear:

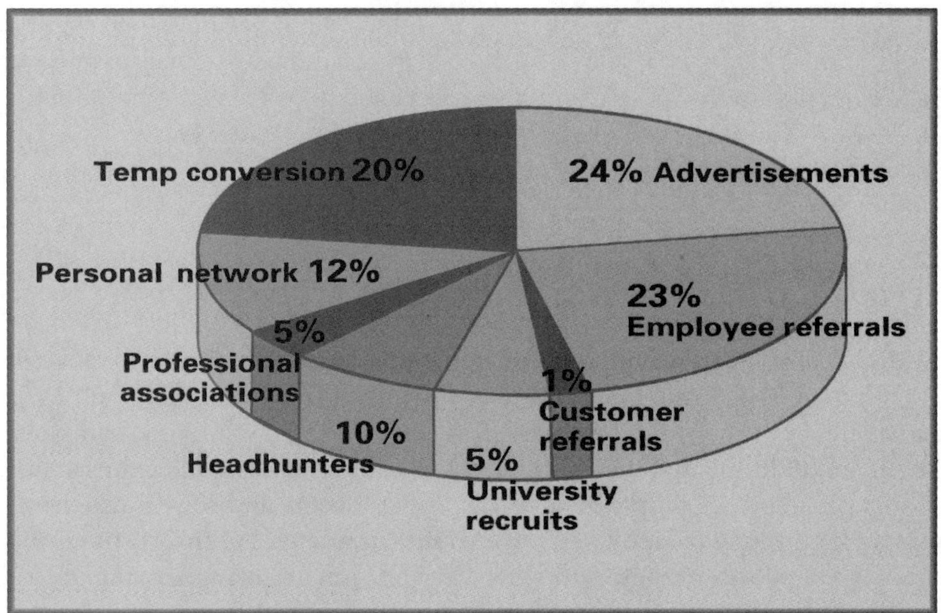

Figure 3-1 *Percentage of hires from various types of recruitment vehicles at a prominent software company*

Talk to your friends and to your friends' friends. Make contacts and let everyone know you're looking for a job.

Once you have experience, you can consider using a headhunter. Professional recruiters make their living by finding the right people to fill jobs at companies that are willing to pay their fees. However, professional headhunters are interested only in experienced programmers that can command the higher salaries because headhunters' fees are a percentage of the first year's salary of the employees they recruit. This percentage currently is approximately 20 percent.

If you're still in college, look for recruiters on campus. Many companies set goals for hiring a certain number of programmers right out of college. Companies typically interview candidates in their junior year and often recruit interns in their senior year. Interns at software companies do such jobs as testing or minor development in a work-study arrangement. Interns are paid a minimal wage and get to learn about their future occupation by actually working at it. By the time interns graduate, they likely have a job in place at a company they already know and like.

Go to trade shows aimed at programmers. Several occur regularly throughout the country like Software Development East and West, MacHack, ObjectWorld, and ObjectExpo.

Look Online for Jobs

Another way of finding open positions is through the Internet and other electronic bulletin board systems (BBSs). This is becoming one of the fastest and most dynamic ways of finding open jobs—and it's fun!

Electronic Bulletin Boards

For jobs in the Silicon Valley area, try the Bay Area Macintosh User's Group (BMUG), which has listings for Macintosh programmers. CompuServe forums for Symantec, Microsoft, IBM, Borland, WordPerfect, and other large software companies often have job listings. Ask who on a BBS knows of a job you might be right for.

Internet

Some particularly good sources of jobs on the Internet are us.jobs.offered, comp.jobs, and comp.jobs.offered. These sites list literally hundreds of open jobs.

Online Career Center (OCC) is a nonprofit national recruiting service on the World Wide Web. This service provides a graphical (see Figure 3-2), easy-to-use format, and it can really pay off. OCC was started more than two years ago by six companies. Now more than 3,000 companies participate in the service. The companies pay to post listings, but you pay no fee to respond to listings or post your résumé.

OCC works with the Internet, Prodigy, GEnie, CompuServe, America Online, and other national online networks to develop economical, effective ways to provide employment advertising, outplacement services, and communications via networks. OCC provides and manages an electronic delivery system for processing job listings among a cooperative of employers.

The American Job Bank (ajb.dni.us), an online service of internetworked state employment agencies, is another excellent source of jobs all over the country.

More than 15 million American homes have computers that can access online services, and this figure is growing at an annual rate of 30 percent. By the mid-1990s, 30 million homes will be able to access online services—one out of every three American households. Use of online services is currently increasing

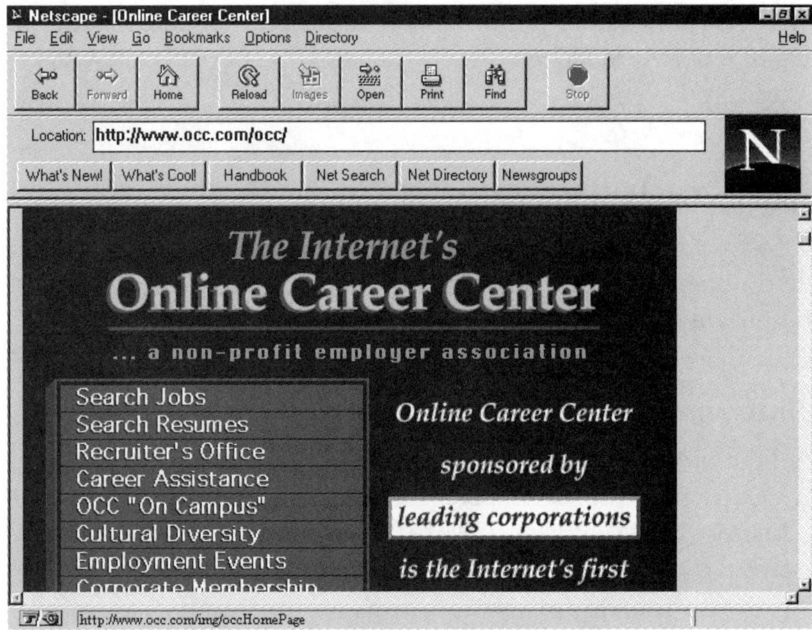

Figure 3-2 *Online Career Center's home page*

at a rate of over 1 million people per month, and networks are now accessible from more than a hundred foreign countries. Public and commercial networks are truly becoming one of the hottest areas of job recruitment and placement activity. See Appendix A, "Internet Job Search Fundamentals," for more information on surfing the Net and for a list of great sites to visit during your job search.

Experts predict that eventually the Internet will replace the more traditional means of recruiting applicants for jobs, but that day has yet to come. You still need to explore the other ways of finding jobs presented in this book, but don't neglect the Internet—for programmers, it's a natural!

The Perfect Résumé

Because programming requires a logical mind, close attention to literal details, and an ability to see through abstractions to the heart of a problem, many programmers have an aversion to common marketing tactics, and some even let that develop into an aversion to marketing itself. However, when you're trying to convince an employer that you are the right person for a job, make no mistake—what you are actually doing is marketing yourself. You are

Major Internet Sites for Jobs

- Online Career Center: **http://www.occ.com/occ**
- America's Job Bank: **http://www.ajb.dni.us**
- E-Span Interactive Employment Network: **http://www.espan.com**
- Usenet groups: **us.jobs.offered**, **comp.jobs**, **comp.jobs.offered**
- For jobs in the Silicon Valley and Bay Area, try **ba.jobs.offered**.

showcasing your accomplishments, highlighting your abilities, and positioning yourself as the best candidate for the job. In this effort, your résumé is your most important marketing tool. The perfect résumé opens the door to the position you want.

Your résumé is usually the first information a prospective employer receives about you, and it will usually be the one piece of information that convinces a hiring manager or HR representative to either spend time interviewing you or screen you out. Thus, it is critical that you spend the time and energy necessary to create a résumé that shows off your skills and history in relation to the particular job for which you are applying.

Creating a Résumé That Positions You in the Best Way

There are two general types of résumés. One is chronological and lists your education and job history by years. This type of résumé may also include some personal data or a list of skills, but its primary focus is on how your past few years of employment history apply to your career goals. This is the traditional form of résumé and also the most common. The chronological résumé is the safest choice unless you have very little actual experience, especially if you've just graduated and have never before held a job. In that case, you may wish to use the second form of résumé common today: the skills résumé. In this type of résumé, you list your skills in an organized way and provide only a brief chronological history. Figure 3-3 is a chronological résumé and Figure 3-4 is a skills résumé.

Brian Picard
722 Fourteenth Street, #750
San Jose, CA 95023
(408) 555-1439

OBJECTIVE

To obtain a position as a Windows software engineer with a growing company where I can make an effective contribution to a team.

EXPERIENCE

1993-present, Johnson Mobile Software, Palo Alto, CA

Senior Engineer: Designed and implemented Windows executables and libraries in C and C++ for mobile computing software applications. Provided support for designing, coding, and debugging of Windows applications using Microsoft Foundation Classes (MFCs) and other commercial libraries specific to the field. Performed self-tests of software before handing it off for quality assurance.

1992-1993, Silicon Valley Computer Works, Santa Clara, CA

Principal, Independent Consulting Firm: Developed software products and services for small businesses and professionals. Using my experience with the C++ language and object-oriented programming, created components that could be reused with modifications to meet specifications of individual clients. Developed a sales tracking database application and a variety of interactive marketing materials in C++ and 4GLs.

1991-1992, Detroit Health Strategies, Inc., Detroit, MI

System Administrator: Specified, designed, and programmed Lotus Notes applications. Implemented training and administered Notes servers at two company sites. Used C++ extensively and designed and coded a C++ Windows application to schedule work flow.

1990, Sizemore Academy, Steamy Hill, IL

Microcomputer Applications Teacher: Taught a variety of microcomputer applications and concepts in a lab environment. Began programming in C.

EDUCATION

1990 M.A. History and Philosophy of Science, Indiana University, 3.97 GPA

1987 B.A. Computer Science, University of Rhode Island, English Minor, 3.95 GPA

LANGUAGES, TOOLS, PROJECTS

Symantec C++, Microsoft Visual C++, Microsoft Foundation Classes, Visual Basic, OLE 2.0 (including automation), dBASE, Access, SQL, Lotus Notes, OBEX Enabling kit. Strong UI and prototyping skills, with presentation graphics background. Also skilled in Windows internals.

PERSONAL

Hard working and reliable with a solid work ethic. Father of two children. Involved in local politics and community affairs.

Figure 3-3 *Chronological résumé*

Martin Sulu
2431 Beth Place, Apt. 243
Boston, MA 02456
(201) 555-8954
msulu@ulink.cambridge.edu

OBJECTIVE

To obtain a position as a software developer and programmer with a good company in a growing field.

SKILLS

Languages Knowledgeable in the following programming languages: C/C++, Lex Yacc, SQL, Lisp, MIPS 2000, Pascal, Basic, and UNIX Shell.

Platforms Proficient on the following platforms: Windows 3.1 and newer versions including 32-bit NT and Windows 95, DOS and extended-mode DOS, UNIX System V, Macintosh OS versions 6.x, 7.0, and 7.5, and VME.

Network Architecture Extensive understanding of the architecture of peer-to-peer and client-server network models, familiarity with NetBIOS and SMB servers and redirectors, seven-layer ISO model with practical work done at top four levels.

New Technologies Thorough understanding of object-oriented programming principles and techniques, machine structures, and multimedia and some familiarity with 4GLs.

PROJECTS

Modification of an Operating System Took a preexisting OS supplied by course professor and modified it to support threads, a file system, user-level multiprogramming, a virtual memory system, and networking. Key aspects included synchronization and concurrence of multiple processes, process scheduling, memory management, and coordination of a group project.

Design of a Compiler Provided with an OOP language specification, developed a lexical analyzer, parser, semantic analyzer, and code generator to compile a specified language on a MIPS R2000 computer.

Windows Implemented a remote client station that acts as the primary interface to the server system through COM port communications. Client software required user-friendly GUI and graphical interpretation of data.

EDUCATION

B.A. University of California at Berkeley - 1994.

RELATED EXPERIENCE

Josephs Furniture, Alameda, CA - 1992-1993. Worked part time during undergraduate study. Showed consistent reliability and often received commendations from management on my ability to solve complex problems.

Figure 3-4 *Skills résumé*

The résumé in Figure 3-3 shows a chronological listing of Brian Picard's experience. Brian is an experienced programmer who has held several jobs, each of which has been a step up from the previous one. This type of history looks good on a chronological résumé, because it shows a steady rise in responsibility and in the importance of the projects Brian undertook.

Martin Sulu, however, has never held a programming job. He's straight out of college, so to position himself correctly he needs to show what skills he accumulated in his studies, what type of projects he worked on—to emphasize the skills he has acquired rather than his actual experience. Notice that Martin also included a synopsis of the major projects he worked on in school as well as a reference to a part-time job that had nothing to do with programming. Including the projects gives evidence of the skill set that Martin states he gained in college, and including a former employer shows a history of reliability, even though the employer was not in a related field.

Programmer's Perspective

What do I look for in an engineering candidate right out of school? Well, one thing is languages. Does the person have extensive knowledge of C? Now universities are also starting to teach C++, so I also look for that. Another thing is knowledge of fundamentals. Has the person taken classes in data structures? Does the person know operating systems? Most people in universities are not studying on Macs or IBM PCs; chances are they're working on VAXs or UNIX systems, so you can't take knowledge of operating systems for granted.

If you are applying for a job, find out what the employer is looking for and show the employer that. Also list the classes you've taken on the fundamentals. Use a similar logic to determine the best format for your résumé. If you have a good job history, use the chronological style. If you're straight out of college, you're better off using the skills style.

Enrique Salem
Architect, Peter Norton
Computing Group, Symantec

Matching Your Résumé to the Job Description

In almost all cases, before a company recruits candidates for a job, the hiring manager prepares a written job description, also listing the educational requirements, experience requirements, and salary range for the job. This information provides both the background for attracting the right candidates and the first hurdle for screening applicants The Human Resources department uses the job description to weed out applicants who don't meet the stated qualifications.

Your chances of getting an interview are vastly increased if either your résumé or your cover letter contains key words from the job description.

Remember that HR personnel are likely the ones doing the screening, and you can bet money that they know little or nothing about programming or the job for which they're screening applicants. They publish the relevant parts of the job description in a classified ad and then put the job description on the company's internal bulletin board or give it to a recruiter. When the résumés come in, the HR personnel sort them looking for matching key words in the résumé and job description. They also look for matches on experience and education, but the first qualifier is those key words. If your résumé lists some of the same skills the job description asks for, many HR people will pass the résumé on to the hiring manager even if your experience and education don't match exactly.

Consider the following job description:

> *Lead architect and programmer for designing, coding, and debugging of corporate vertical applications in a client-server environment. Must have thorough understanding of distributed database programming and LAN operations, including the SMB server-redirector model, NetBIOS, IPX, and ISO model, as well as SQL and C/C++ languages. Must be a strong team player. Two years experience and a BA in Computer Science desired.*

Now look at the résumés in Figures 3-5 and 3-6. They describe exactly the same person with exactly the same experience, but one of these résumés will likely pass the first round of HR screening and the other one may not. Dilbert Grundley's job experience is actually quite a good fit for the job, but the HR staffer doing the screening might not be aware of that from Dilbert's résumé in Figure 3-5. Look what happens in Figure 3-6 when he changes the résumé to include key words from the job description (underlined for the reader's reference).

Dilbert Grundley
6904 East Stone Lane
Phoenix, AZ 85497
(602) 555-1265

OBJECTIVE

To get a challenging programming job with growth potential in a stimulating environment.

EXPERIENCE

1992 to present **Allied Systems, Phoenix, AZ**

Systems Engineer Responsible for creating custom network-aware applications for use across disparate systems in an enterprise-wide environment. Applications included an internal messaging system and a calendaring program for use across wide-area networks using Novell NetWare and IBM PC LAN and LAN Manager NOSs. Extensive work at the transfer layer as well as the application and data layers.

1990 to 1992 **Symbiotic Synchronicities of Los Angeles, Inc., Los Angeles, CA**

Systems Analyst Duties included creating and programming multiuser programs for medical research and analytical engineering implementations. Applications centered around host-based minis with slave stations. Demonstrated reliability as individual contributor as well as good coordination and project management.

1986 to 1990 **Centipede Communications, Inc., Denver, CO**

Development Engineer Assigned to testing. Used MS Test to write automated test scripts and library functions to provide usability, performance, bug, and stress testing for API function calls of Windows voice messaging applications and audio information processing systems. Analyzed and reported hardware and software problems in voice mail systems. Maintained test case results and document testing report for the release of the voice messaging application.

EDUCATION

1982 to 1986 **University of California, Santa Cruz**

B.A. degree in Computer Science; Minor in Physics.

Figure 3-5 *Résumé written without attention to the job description*

The second résumé is much more likely to appear to the HR person to be a match than the first résumé, even though the two résumés describe exactly the same job history. Still, the job description said "distributed database programming," not "multiuser networked application," and it said "IPX," not "NetWare,"

Dilbert Grundley
6904 East Stone Lane
Phoenix, AZ 85497
(602) 555-1265

OBJECTIVE

To gain a position as an architect and programmer of vertical applications in a client-server environment.

EXPERIENCE

1992 to 1995 **Allied Systems, Phoenix, AZ**

Systems Engineer Responsible for the architecture, design, coding, and debugging of custom distributed client-server applications for use across disparate systems in an enterprise-wide environment. Applications included an internal messaging system incorporating distributed database programming technology and a calendaring program for use across wide-area networks using NetBIOS and IPX protocols with SMB server-redirector models using C++. Extensive work at the transfer layer as well as the application and data layers of the ISO model.

1990 to 1992 **Symbiotic Synchronicities of Los Angeles, Inc., Los Angeles, CA**

Systems Analyst Duties included creating and programming multiuser distributed database programs for medical research and analytical engineering implementations. Applications were client-server modeled with SQL. Demonstrated reliability as individual contributor and team player as well as good management.

1986 to 1990 **Centipede Communications, Inc., Denver, CO**

Development Engineer Assigned to testing. Used MS Test to write automated test scripts and library functions in C and C++ to provide usability, performance, bug, and stress testing for API function calls of Windows voice messaging applications and audio information processing systems. Analyzed and reported hardware and software problems in voice-mail systems. Maintained test case results and document testing report for the release of the voice messaging application.

EDUCATION

1982 to 1986 **University of California, Santa Cruz, CA**

B.A. degree in Computer Science; Minor in Physics.

Figure 3-6 *Résumé that uses key words from the job description*

and those who don't know the jargon may not make the connections. Many HR staffers are not technical people and will not know that you're a well-qualified candidate unless your résumé uses the exact words of the job description. The key words should match verbatim what is in the classified ad. If you come across a job in another way, then you would do well to ask for a written job description before submitting your résumé.

Aside from key words, HR personnel also use such factors as gaps in employment, inconsistencies, many jobs in a short period of time, and errors on a résumé to filter out candidates.

Gaps on your résumé cause the HR person, and often the hiring manager, to raise an eyebrow because they may indicate a lack of direction or commitment to your career. As already noted, it is expensive to hire someone, and no company wants to hire a professional who seems a poor prospect for continued employment. So if at all possible, you should structure your résumé to eliminate any apparent gaps. If you spent a year traveling around Southeast Asia on a fishing boat, be sure you state that in your résumé or your cover letter. If you were out of work collecting unemployment (or worse yet, had a job dealing burgers at a fast-food joint) for six months, then consider structuring your résumé using yearly increments instead of months. If you structure it right, you can completely skip those six months.

Similarly, if you've had a lot of jobs in a short period of time, using yearly increments could work in your favor. For instance, if you worked at Company A for six months from December 1992 to June 1993, then Company B for four months from August 1993 to November 1993, and then Company C from December 1993 to November 1994, you might eliminate Company B from your résumé by stating your history as follows:

1992–1993 Company A

1993–1994 Company C

Even this history isn't ideal—most HR people like you to stay at a company for at least two or three years—but it certainly looks better than it would if you listed all three companies and the months you stayed at each one.

Inconsistencies on a résumé are unusual enough to raise suspicions. Examples of inconsistencies are having a job title at an early job that sounds better than one held later, an education that has nothing to do with your job history, or a chronological history that doesn't seem to make sense. To avoid having your résumé rejected on the basis of inconsistencies, take an objective look at your history as you've outlined it. You may be able to explain anything that looks unusual or strange, but you'll never get the chance if you're screened out without an interview. So work on anything that may appear odd or inconsistent. Present the information differently or include an explanation right there in the text.

Analyzing the Sections of Your Résumé

Whether you arrange your résumé chronologically or according to your skills, you should examine each part separately to make sure it focuses on the job you are applying for. For instance, look at the following objective:

> ***OBJECTIVE:***
>
> To obtain a position as a Windows software engineer with a growing company where I can make an effective contribution to a team.

This is a fine objective if you're applying to a small, upcoming company that creates Windows software. If you're applying to Apple Computer, this objective will be enough to get your résumé rejected on first sight. Similarly, it would be inappropriate for a corporate programming job with a company that primarily operates in the UNIX environment or even with any company large enough to no longer consider itself "growing."

Of course, you wouldn't be so foolish as to submit a résumé that has an inappropriate objective, because by now you're aware of how important it is to customize the résumé you send for the job and company you're applying to.

But what about the experience or skills section of your résumé? Maybe you think this section simply requires reporting—that is, this part presents "just the facts," and there's no variation in a truthful reporting of the facts. Well, that's not exactly true, as you'll notice if you read the same news story in a right-wing publication and then in a left-wing publication. There are different ways of portraying the same facts, and there are different selection criteria for determining which facts to include and exclude.

There is a cultural bias in the United States against "tooting your own horn." Modesty is seen as a virtue, and in many cases it is. On your résumé, however, it is not. Look at the following description of a job that someone listed on a résumé:

> **1994–present, American Science Engineering, Inc., Sunnyvale, CA**
>
> Senior Engineer: Worked on Windows programs and libraries mostly using C. Provided support for designing, coding, and debugging of Windows applications using Microsoft Foundation Classes (MFCs). Tested software before handing it off for quality assurance.

This programmer pretty accurately described what he did at his last job. A potential employer would not be repulsed by this entry, but on the other hand, he or she probably wouldn't get too excited by it either. Look what happens when the programmer jazzes up the entry with accurate detail:

> **1994–present, American Science Engineering, Inc., Sunnyvale, CA**
>
> Senior Engineer: Designed and implemented high-performance Windows programs and libraries in C and C++ for mobile computing software applications. Provided first-line development efforts and team support for designing, coding, and debugging of 16- and 32-bit Windows applications using Microsoft Foundation Classes (MFCs) and other commercial libraries specific to the field. Created custom automated self-testing software and tested all code against this before handing it off for quality assurance.

The second entry is much more interesting than the first. It not only indicates a broader range of activities for which this programmer was responsible, it also gives the reader the impression of high energy and a drive for achievement. You'd be surprised at how much influence these subtleties have on a hiring manager. So don't be too modest in your résumé. Modesty is not a virtue when job hunting.

One caveat: although it is one thing to put your best foot forward and represent your abilities in the best possible light for the job you're applying for, don't go so far as to make up histories or fabricate job experience or talents that you don't actually have. If you do this, you will undoubtedly be found out and will either fail to get the job or lose it once it's yours.

Before sending any résumé, use a spelling checker, reread your résumé after it's printed, and ask a friend to read it too. Spelling checkers are programs, after all, and imperfect ones at that. They catch many errors, but fail to catch others based on context, for instance. Remember that your résumé is your primary means of marketing yourself: make it look professional. The HR people may not throw out your résumé because it contains spelling or grammatical errors, but they might, and the hiring manager may interpret errors as a sign of careless or sloppy work.

Also, remember that the most effective résumés are customized for the job you're applying for, so don't create a generic résumé and print vast quantities. Use your generic résumé to customize each résumé you send according to the examples in this chapter, and then print each one on a laser printer. (Don't use a dot-matrix printer—you're an up-to-date computer professional, after all.)

The Perfect Interview

Once the HR staff has whittled down the stack of résumés to a manageable pile, they'll send these to the hiring manager. The hiring manager will then do some more whittling and will usually select four or five candidates to interview. Sometimes the hiring manager will also do a bit of screening by telephone, so you should be prepared.

Preparing for Phone Screening

Phone screenings are not usually as thorough as in-person interviews, and they do not replace them. You won't get a job from a phone interview, but you may get eliminated from the running, so take phone interviews seriously. You must either be prepared to answer the phone at any time from 8 A.M. to 6 P.M. and talk intelligently and patiently about your qualifications for the particular job you've applied for, or buy an answering machine and let it always answer the phone during those hours. If you have applied for several jobs and think you may have trouble keeping them straight in your mind at all times, then you may want to choose the latter solution. If a hiring manager does leave a message for you, refresh yourself on the job and company and then call back as soon as you can. You can expect a conversation that lasts about 20 minutes and hopefully ends with the hiring manager inviting you for an in-person interview.

Preparing for the Interview

You've passed the résumé screening and maybe a phone screening and have been invited to an interview. At this point you have a good chance of getting the job if you keep up the effort. Remember that you're still not a shoo-in, but you have been able to convince the prospective employer that you're worth talking to, and you should proceed to the interview with confidence.

Investigate the company before you go for an interview. At least search for information on a BBS and, if you can, look at an annual report. Company annual reports provide a wealth of information. If the organization is a large public company, the local library may have its annual report; otherwise, you can call the main company number, ask for Investor Relations, and then ask the company to send you an annual report. Or if you have a stockbroker, ask him or her to send one to you.

Actually, it's better to do this research on the company when you send your résumé—don't wait until interview time. Really dig into what the company does, what its technologies are, and even who the major company players are. Figure out how your talents might fill the company's needs. Consider this to be an exercise that you owe yourself. After all, if you succeed in getting the job, you'll be spending the next several years of your life with the company. You need to know enough about it to see if it will be a good fit for you. It will also be much easier to convince the hiring manager once you know enough to justify the match to yourself.

Sources of Information on Prospective Employers

- Annual reports
- Knowledge Index
- Dunn and Bradstreet
- IQuest
- Computer Select
- Trade publications
- Your public library's index of periodicals
- BBS forums associated with the company
- Friends in the industry
- Internet

The Interview

The time for the interview has come at last. Getting the interview was hard enough; now you have to convince the hiring manager that you are the person for the job. How do you do that?

First, relax. This is easier than it sounds. You want the job, and you will probably be anxious and nervous about saying the wrong thing. Just take a mental step back. Remember that you are a valuable professional. You have the ability the company needs. They need you as much as you need them. Remember that there is a possibility that you may not be right for the job. You're there representing your own interests, and you need to make sure that this particular job fits your idea of what you want to do. Life doesn't end if you're not selected for a particular job. Another job that is right for you will come along. Keeping these things in mind will make it easier to have confidence in your own abilities, and that confidence will show.

If you're interviewing for a programming job at a company that makes shrink-wrap software, you don't need to show up wearing a suit. Developers at that type of company are very informal, and if you wear a suit you'll look like you may not fit in. In fact, most programmers don't wear suits no matter where they work. If the job is a high-level one or at a finance company or bank, for example, it may be a good idea to wear a suit. However, for many programming jobs, a clean, well-pressed shirt and pants are fine for the interview. If you're not sure what to wear, don't be afraid to call the Human Resources department and ask what's appropriate.

Programmer's Perspective

When I think back on interviewing programmers, several people stand out, like Leo Cohen. He had super high energy. He just jumped up to the whiteboard, diagrammed how Windows worked, and then sat back down. And what you could really see was that he was sitting on the edge of his chair. He was eager to answer every question. He was ready. It's important to show enthusiasm in an interview. You don't want to be obnoxious, but you want to be enthusiastic.

Enrique Salem
Architect, Peter Norton
Computing Group, Symantec

When you begin your interview, try not to be too aggressive or too withdrawn. The interviewer will usually start with a set group of questions. These will be open-ended, and the hiring manager will probably be hoping that you will take each question and run with it, volunteering information on the general topic and talking about your background, your achievements, and your interest in the particular subject and revealing your attitude about it.

"The most important rule is be positive."

The most important rule is be positive. Talk about your achievements. Smile, and be friendly and open about your interest in the job and the challenges it would bring. Do *not* complain about any other job or company or manager you've had in the past. Nothing turns off a hiring manager faster than hearing negative remarks about your past experiences. Dwell on your accomplishments and how they apply to the job you're interviewing for. Make each question an opportunity to talk about related work you've done successfully. Keep on track. Answer the questions and illustrate your answers with examples of what you've done along the same lines—accomplishments you're proud of.

Something else you should do in an interview is ask questions. You've studied the company and thought about the job. Now ask questions that relate to both your everyday tasks if you were to get the job and the strategy of the company overall. Relate your questions to what you know about the company. Use this opportunity to not only learn more about the job, but also to reveal to the hiring manager that you have done your homework, that you know something about the company and its products or line of work. Too many people don't bother to learn anything about a company before they come to an interview. Showing that you did research will set you apart from most of the other applicants.

A Few Questions You Should Ask Prospective Employers

- What is the exact nature of the job?
- What percentage of the work is new development and what percentage is maintenance of existing code?
- What is the size of the team?
- Does the company support flexible hours?
- Does the company support occasional telecommuting or working at home?
- Is continuing education available through the company?
- How is compensation divided between salary, bonuses, and other forms of payment?
- Are stock options available?
- What is the benefit plan?

Always be sure to convey a sense of interest and a high level of energy. The manager wants someone who will work hard and get a lot done. Be bright, be focused, and be sharp.

Second-Round Interviews

Often when you interview for a professional position, you will be asked to interview with several people. It is common in large companies for you first to have a one-hour interview with the hiring manager. Then, if the hiring manager likes you and thinks you can do the job, you will be called back for second-round interviews. Second-round interviews are usually scheduled on a later day and involve speaking to several people, all of whom have a particular interest in you because they would be working directly with you. Be prepared: Sometimes this can be a long day and a grueling process. It's not unusual to spend six or eight hours in second-round interviews. You'll meet many people, and you'll need to answer each and every one patiently and thoroughly, often times repeating the same information or stories over and over again. Try to reset your mental slate each time you move to another interview. Remember that none of the secondary interviewers has talked to you before, and you need to respond to each one—even the last one—just like you did in your first interview.

Programmer's Perspective

In an interview, I look for signs of openness: posture, curiosity, questions. For example, if I ask a question and the prospect doesn't know the answer but they know I know, then they pass the test when they ask me for help.

Never in an interview indicate that you aren't accountable for your own problems. When a candidate blames organizations or politics or the school, then you know the person isn't learning anything wherever they go, and I just say no. Don't blame other people in an interview. Understand what went wrong and explain it.

Jim McCarthy
Director of Program Management, Microsoft

After you leave, all of your interviewers will present their views of you to the hiring manager, who will make the final decision. The secondary people with whom you interview will have varying degrees of influence, depending on the company culture. Some companies hold a meeting in which all the interviewers give their opinions and discuss how they think you'd fit in. In other companies, the process is less formal. Usually none of the secondary interviewers has enough influence to get you hired if the hiring manager isn't convinced you're the right candidate, but usually even one has enough influence to ruin your chances if he or she feels strongly that you wouldn't be right for the job.

Thus, in second-round interviews you should try to get a feeling for who each person is and how you would work with that person. You should be pleasant, ask questions, and try to make all your interviewers feel that they would be better off if they were working with you, just as in the initial interview.

References

If you are seriously being considered for the job after the second-round interviews, either the HR person or the hiring manager is likely to ask for references. You will be asked for the names and phone numbers of people who can talk about you and their work experiences with you. Be careful about how you handle references. Before you use anyone as a reference, call the person, say that you're looking for a job, and ask if the person will consent to giving you a good reference. Don't use anyone as a reference until you have spoken to the person and are sure he or she will say glowing things about you. If a reference portrays you negatively, you can lose the job at the last minute.

Working with Recruiters

If you are new to the programming field, either because you've recently graduated or because you've switched from some other profession, then the chances are good that an executive recruiter won't be interested in working with you, and you should refer back to other sections of this book. Executive recruiters are commissioned by a company that is trying to locate a candidate for a particular job, and they're paid only if they successfully place someone in the job. If they do succeed, then they are paid a sum that is typically from 15 to 20 percent of the new hire's annual salary. Because of this pay arrangement, executive recruiters are not interested in spending their time finding jobs for people who make less than about $60,000.

However, if you've been in the profession for a while and have climbed the salary scale to the point that you're making enough money to interest a recruiter, they can be a huge help. Bill Donovan is one of the country's best executive recruiters specializing in the programming and high-tech fields, and he contributed quite a lot of information to this book on the subjects of career assessment and placement agencies. "If you're entry level, then you're wasting your time going to an executive placement firm," says Bill. "They won't touch you unless you have experience and are making a high salary. But when you reach that stage in your career where you are a successful upper-level manager, satisfied in your current position, you will probably be contacted by an executive recruiter at least once a year."

Once you've reached this level, you'll know it. The secret then is when recruiters contact you, as they will, be nice to them. Don't cursorily dismiss them because you're too busy to take time or are not interested in a new position. There will very likely come a time when you will be interested, and then you'll want those contacts in your back pocket.

If you're an experienced executive looking for a new job, then your challenge will be to convince recruiters that you're the type of person their clients will want to hire. Send your résumé to a few recruiters and write individualized cover letters. Make those letters specific. Tell recruiters why they should be interested in you. Remember that to a recruiter you are only as valuable as you are marketable. Be sure then to talk in your cover letter about any highly marketable skills you have. For instance, if you know C++, then mention it up front in the letter—don't bury it somewhere in the back of your résumé. The same holds true for any other highly sought skills, such as experience with internationalizing code, creating distributed client-server applications, or Internet programming.

How to Find a Recruiter If One Doesn't Find You

These reference books list recruiters and their specialties. Look in your local library for these books or call the publisher.

Directory of Executive Recruiters
Kennedy Publications and
Consultants Bookstore
Collins Pond Road
Fitzwilliam, NH 03447
(603) 585-2200

Executive Employment Guide
American Management Association
135 West 50th Street
New York, NY 10020
(212) 586-8100

When you've written your cover letters and have sent them with a résumé to recruiters, then forget about the recruiters you've contacted and continue your job search in your own way using the other tools and techniques listed in this book. Don't call the recruiter. This irritates them and makes them think you're desperate. Remember: Working with recruiters is a two-step selling process. You need to convince recruiters that they want *you* as a marketable professional whom their clients will also want. If several months pass and you hear nothing, then send another letter.

If the materials you sent interest a recruiter, then the recruiter will call you and do a phone screening. This screening is similar to the phone interviews discussed earlier, but in this case, the recruiter may or may not have a specific position in mind. In any case, you need to take as much care and thought in a phone interview with a recruiter as you would with a prospective employer.

Using Employment Agencies

There are a few high-tech employment agencies that can help you find a job if you're an entry-level or beginning programmer, but employment agencies typically are better for placing clerical workers and, to some extent, technicians (such as dental hygienists, secretaries, file clerks, and telemarketers). Contacting an agency that doesn't specialize in programming and high-tech jobs is practically useless because most employment agencies simply never get calls for programming jobs. However, a few employment agencies may be helpful. One way to find them is to contact the National Association of Personnel Consultants at the following address:

National Association of Personnel Consultants (NAPC)
1432 Duke Street
Alexandria, VA 22314
(703) 684-0180

Another way to find agencies in your local area that handle programming jobs is to call a few of the human resources offices at companies in your area that you know employ programmers. Ask if they ever use an agency to find programmers and, if they do, which one they use. You can even ask for a contact name—and you should, since there may be only one person at an agency that specializes in programming or high-tech jobs. If the company you call doesn't use employment agencies to locate programmers, then ask if they know of any agency that does specialize in that area, even though their particular company may not use the firm.

If you do locate an agency that you think can help you, then remember these tips from Bill Donovan when you're dealing with them:

- Screen agencies. Ask about their success rate in placing programmers with backgrounds similar to your own.
- Don't let them try to force you into taking any position. Go for the job that meets your job search objectives.
- If you don't hear from them for a few weeks, switch to another agency. Make sure they're responsive.
- Accept interviews even when they don't coincide with your goals. It's good practice.

A Preinterview Checklist

This chapter has talked a lot about how to create an effective résumé, how to customize your résumé and cover letter for each job, and what to do and not to do in an interview. No matter if you're interviewing with a recruiter or a prospective employer, you will find a preinterview checklist helpful. The idea of a preinterview checklist is Bill's, and his checklist, which follows, is one of the best I've ever seen. It may be helpful to use it whenever you think about going for an interview.

Before You Leave for the Interview:

- ❑ Do you know the job title?
- ❑ Do you know the interviewer's name?
- ❑ Do you know the interviewer's phone number in case of emergency?
- ❑ Are you sure of the time of the interview and the location and how to get there?
- ❑ Do you have five copies of your résumé to bring along?
- ❑ Do you have your research information to bring along and study as you wait for the interview?
- ❑ Did you think of ten questions to ask and ten questions you'll likely be asked?

Review Your Responses to These Commonly Asked Interview Questions:

- ❑ Tell me about yourself.
- ❑ What do you know about our organization?
- ❑ Why are you interested in this position?
- ❑ What can you do for us?
- ❑ What are your strengths and weaknesses?
- ❑ How have you prepared for this position?
- ❑ What are your outside interests?
- ❑ What salary are you looking for?
- ❑ What are your long-term goals?
- ❑ Describe your education and school activities and accomplishments.

Tips for the Interview:

- Don't smoke or chew gum during an interview.
- Arrive about 15 minutes early.
- Give a firm handshake. Smile. Be relaxed and confident.
- Project confidence and self-assurance.
- Be courteous and friendly to the secretary, human resources person, and everyone else you come in contact with.
- Ask the interviewer for a job profile as soon as possible.
- Don't be afraid to take control of the interview. Maintain a positive, self-assured attitude.
- Maintain good eye contact.

Questions to Ask the Interviewer:

- What are the specific job duties and responsibilities?
- What skills are required to perform the job?

- Is there any training required prior to starting the job?
- To whom will I report?
- How will my performance be evaluated?
- Who will evaluate my performance?
- What individuals and groups will I interface with?
- What is the growth potential for this position?
- What type of training programs are available?

Depending on your own situation, you may want to add to Bill's list. For example, you may want to know if there's any chance for geographical relocation either within the country or in a foreign country. You may wish to know the salary-to-bonus ratio for jobs similar to the one you're applying for. You may also want to know what languages are typically used in the applications that you'll be writing; for instance, if the company uses C, do they also use C++, and if so, how much of your time would be involved in writing C applications and how much would be involved in using C++?

How and When to Leave Your Current Job

Suppose you already have a job in programming. You've been with a company for a while, and you're wondering whether this is the time to move elsewhere. How do you know when to stay put and when to move on?

"That's a good question," says Bill, "and a tough question, too. Let's say you're not making any progress in your current company, you're being passed over, and others are being promoted. Then it's time to take a good look in the mirror. Maybe your supervisor has said that you should learn some new skills like programming in C++. Did you do anything to comply with your supervisor's request? Often the answer to why you're not happy lies with you. Take a look in the mirror and see whether or not you're supplying the skills your company needs."

Dilbert reprinted by permission of United Feature Syndicate, Inc.

Of course, if you do take Bill's advice and examine yourself honestly to see what you're doing (or not doing) to make yourself more valuable to your current company, then you can often find ways to keep your current position and correct whatever deficiencies that are keeping you from advancement. This level of self-awareness will both help you progress in your current job and improve your prospects for landing a new job that will provide you with a chance for significant advancement. After all, the skills that your current company wants are probably the same ones that similar companies will want. Thus, whether you stay or leave, being sure that you have the desirable skills will help you in your future career.

But sticking with your current company isn't always the answer, even when you do have the skills required or desired. "It all boils down to job satisfaction," is Bill's advice. "If you wake up in the morning and you don't feel like going to work, if you feel you're not going anywhere and there's no chance of change, or if your company is facing changes that might eliminate your position, then these are all indicators that it's time to start looking around.

"I know one person who works for a company that's cutting back. They're a British-owned company, and they've been closing offices in the United States and eliminating positions. This woman is a friend of mine, and I looked her right in the eye and said, 'Are you waiting until you show up for work one day and find the building locked? Then you're going to spend three months getting a new job. Are you prepared for that?' There's never any guarantees anymore with employment, and being aware of where your company is now and where it's going is crucial to knowing when to leave."

Leaving a Company

So suppose your current job position is starting to look shaky, or suppose you're not getting anywhere in your current job, you're dissatisfied, and you've decided to leave—what then? The smartest thing to do is to begin your job search while your current company is still paying your salary—and thus your mortgage, car payments, and so on. No matter how hard you work or what your hours are, you'll still have time at night or on weekends to craft that résumé, to scan the want ads in the local paper, and to contact some recruiters. Begin the search by sending out résumés on your own time and going to interviews before work, after work, or on your lunch hour. One thing to avoid is neglecting the job you have while looking for another, and another thing to avoid is the attitude that you no longer care about the projects you're working on.

When you decide to leave your current company, remember that they have been and still are employing you to do a job, and that doing that job to the best of your abilities and keeping a good relationship with the people at your current company is just as important as ever. If you are truly a professional, then this will be the only thing you can do, as it's the only professional way to behave.

Remember that your current supervisor is someone whom you'll need later on down the road for a reference even though you may not need him or her now to get a new job. It's actually highly unusual for a job candidate to let a prospective employer contact your current employer. Usually, employed programmers do not want their current employer to be contacted because it is a sure-fire tip-off that a person is looking elsewhere, and prospective employers almost always understand and respect this. After all, the new company may not offer you a job, and if they've contacted your current employer, then they've put you in a very awkward position. Most companies don't want to do that, so you won't need your current supervisor's reference to leave your current job. However, if you ever want to leave your new job (and most people work for several different companies during their careers), then you will likely want a good reference from your previous job.

Thus, it makes good practical sense to cultivate a professional attitude toward your current job and employer as you begin and follow through on your search.

Timing is sometimes a consideration in leaving a job. If you're close to an anniversary with your current employer, it may make sense to stick around until after then because anniversaries typically bring reviews, pay raises, and stock option vesting. If you wait until after your annual review, then you'll have a higher salary when you begin looking, and that means your new employer will have to beat or meet that salary rather than your prereview salary. You will also get some good feedback on your performance, on how you could improve, and on the possibilities that may be coming up at your current job. These all could be enough to keep you where you are, but even if they're not, you will get helpful information on how you've been viewed by your supervisor. Also, if you've been granted stock options that are worth something, they often vest after an anniversary. Leaving before significant stock options vest could cost you big bucks in some circumstances.

Of course, usually your leaving won't coincide with an anniversary, and the factors just mentioned won't be a consideration. However, there are still other timing considerations. For instance, you may have vacation time stacked up. If you do, then you could take off a few weeks between jobs and not lose any income. Conversely, you may decide you'd rather have the money. Remember that vacation time equates to money. If you leave a job with vacation time left, your employer will have to pay you for that time at your current salary.

In any case, you *must* give your current employer at least two weeks' notice before you quit. Often your employer may try to get you to stay longer—maybe up to a month. That's up to you and to the circumstances of your new employer. If your current employer wants more time to replace you and your future employer doesn't mind waiting *and* if it's comfortable for you, then you should grant your old employer's wishes to help make your transition out easier. Remember: this is a very small industry, and it helps a lot to make and keep friends, just as it hurts a lot to cultivate grudges and enemies.

The attitude to have when leaving a job is one of gratitude for whatever growth you experienced during your employment, of friendship for your co-workers, and of helpfulness toward your old employer so they can be ready to do without you. Keep these goals in mind, and you'll make a smooth transition out.

The Law in Hiring Practices

Like many other aspects of modern life, the process of landing a job involves legal issues. One of the ways the law constrains that process is through restrictions on discrimination.

In your job quest, it may be helpful to know your rights and how the law protects you against discrimination. Many groups in the United States are legally protected against discrimination in hiring. These include individuals who can be categorized on the basis of age, race, creed, sex, religion, national origin, physical disability, and various other medical conditions. Sounds like almost everybody, doesn't it? Because there are strict laws against discrimination in hiring, most companies have guidelines for interviewing candidates. It's helpful for you to be familiar with the general rules that might apply.

Basically, the courts will automatically question a selection process if

- It is subjective and nonstandardized.
- The content of the questions suggests bias.
- The lawfulness or reliability of the process is in question.

Companies implement nondiscrimination laws by defining basic types of questions that cannot be legally asked during an interview. In addition to the obvious questions—such as "How old are you?," "Do you plan to have children?," and "What country are you originally from?"—there are more subtle types of questions that the manager needs to avoid in the interview, such as

- Are you the head of household?
- How long do you plan to work?
- What clubs do you belong to?
- How are you planning to care for your children during the day?
- Are your relatives U.S. citizens?
- Where were you born?
- How did you happen to learn Polish?
- What are your feelings on civil rights?

This discussion isn't by any means inclusive and is presented here only to give you some idea of the law on hiring and interviews. See Appendix A for a list of more detailed books on the subject.

Another way the law affects how you get a job is through the rules on intellectual property. This is a bigger concern for you the higher up you go and the more specialized your work has been. Although your increasing skill is part of your personal "tool kit" that you can take freely from place to place, the law draws a line at special information and techniques that can be claimed as the trade secrets of your employer.

Figuring out where the line lies for you is not always easy, but take this as an example: you have learned over the years how to write code efficiently, and that skill is yours to use wherever you go. But suppose you develop a particular algorithm to solve a problem on the job or you have written a nifty module as part of a team project. These things, along with your knowledge of strategies and other information you know the company wouldn't want others to know, have to stay behind.

So in the interviewing process you need to respect this boundary and not discuss anything that is confidential to your current employer. Any company that might ask you to violate this trust probably isn't serious about the interview and isn't a place you would want to work anyway.

These issues stay with you even after you have made the decision to leave and are transitioning out of your old job. Do your best to tie up loose ends, hand off tasks that you are involved in, and help in any way you can. Cooperate in the exit interview process, and above all be sure that you bring in and leave at the company any papers, books, files (on disk or otherwise), or property (such as a computer) that may have been loaned to you. You should start at the new job clean and not bring with you anything that belongs to your former employer or that you developed while you were there. Sure, it's hard to give up the archives of your greatest handiwork, but it's best not to take the chance that an innocent decision to hold onto something may be misunderstood and cause trouble later.

Following Up

As soon as you leave the interview, sit down and write a follow-up letter. It should be to the hiring manager and should express gratitude for the time that was spent talking with you. Don't let your letter appear anxious, and don't get pushy. Don't ask the hiring manager to pass your résumé along to someone else (unless you're sure the interview was a flop and you are no longer being considered). Do restate briefly why you think you're the right person for the job and do be cordial. Use the sample in Figure 3-7 as a model.

Send the letter the same day as your interview and then follow up with a phone call about three days later. You may get invited back for another round of interviews with the manager and various members of the team, or you may be told that first-round interviews are still continuing. In any case, the fact that you bothered to follow up will be impressive. It's amazing how many people never do.

If you find out that the job was given to someone else and you're out of the running, then it's time to change your tack. At this point the hiring manager who interviewed you changes from a prospective employer to a source of information and a reference to other jobs. Ask why you weren't selected, but ask gently. Don't get angry whatever you do and don't argue with the decision.

Simon Shinewas
9476 Verde Vista Road
Del Rey, CA 90292
(213) 555-7823

March 22, 1996

Gina Rao
Coyote Computing
5364 North Point Avenue
Los Angeles, CA 90065

Dear Gina:

Here is just a short note to thank you for taking the time to interview me and for your consideration of my application for the Senior Programming Analyst position in your Windows group. After talking to you, I am even more excited about the job than I was when I read the ad. It sounds like a fascinating position with many challenges and the opportunity to work with a great team.

I'm very interested in the job and will be calling you in a few days to hear how your search is going. If you think of any questions that we didn't cover in the interview, please feel free to call me at the above number.

I look forward to hearing from you.

Sincerely,

Simon Shinewas

Figure 3-7 *A sample follow-up letter*

Explain that you feel this honest feedback will help you in the future. Remember that rejecting you is as awkward for the manager as it is for you, and the manager may beg off with a simple statement that there was a more qualified applicant. However, he or she may give you some substantive comments concerning your résumé or interview that will be valuable for the future. Whatever the manager says, be appreciative and ask about any other openings at the company in the same area. If there are none, ask if the manager knows of any other openings in the industry. Thank the manager again for spending time with you and be as positive as you were in the interview. Many a hiring manager has passed on the résumé of someone he or she really liked to another manager with a similar job opening.

The programming industry is wide and it is tall. It broadens each day into more aspects of our lives, from computers in cars to the World Wide Web. It breeds on logic and creativity, and it spawns specialists and unique opportunities. Programming is one of the fastest growing professions in the world. It is also one of the most rewarding. When you get the job, you're going to love it!

4 Seven Skills of Successful Programmers

Programmers are a breed apart from the ordinary person. Programmers for the most part are more logical, more literal, and more detail oriented than the population at large, and that's probably why they become programmers. "If you love puzzles, you're going to be good at programming," observes Gordon Eubanks, the president and founder of Symantec and a programmer himself. This comment reflects the intellectual foundation that forms the personality of most successful programmers. However, these basic traits aren't the only factors that spell success in the field of programming today. To get a few other opinions, I asked some of the industry's leading programmers and development managers to comment on what skills and traits programmers should cultivate to really succeed.

1. Underpromise and Overdeliver

Some programmers are amazingly successful. One legendary programmer who works for Symantec is Walter Bright, the original author of the high-performance Zortech C++ compiler and now a software architect on the

Symantec C++ team. Walter works from his home in a mansion on a lake near Seattle, Washington. Outside, across well-manicured lawns and next to his private lakeside dock, is his speedboat. His red Ferrari sits parked in the garage next to his other two cars. Walter telecommutes to work seven days a week, with an occasional visit to Cupertino, California, to meet with the rest of the Symantec developers. I asked him to describe the most important talent, skill, or trait that an excellent programmer should have to get to the top.

Walter's first response was "underpromise and overdeliver." "Almost nobody does that," he went on to explain. "It's almost always the other way around. When a manager or a private client asks for an estimate of how much time it's going to take to deliver some piece of software, the developer almost always promises more than he can deliver in the time frame. That's because programmers are human and we all want to be heroes. If what you promise is exactly what the manager wants to hear, then he loves you. But he only loves you until it's time to deliver on your promise. When that time comes and you can't do it, then the manager thinks you're incompetent, and that's the impression he's left with. But if you promise less than you think you can deliver in the time frame and then you get it done quicker or you get more done in the same time frame, then everyone thinks you're wonderful.

> **"If what you promise is exactly what the manager wants to hear, then he loves you. But he only loves you until it's time to deliver on your promise."**
>
> **—Walter Bright**

"You know it's funny, but if two programmers deliver exactly the same thing in exactly the same time frame, and the first one promised to deliver just what he did deliver while the second one would only commit to delivering less, the second one looks like the hero and gets all the applause."

Walter's advice is good, and it reflects an aspect of human nature that you should be aware of when you start thinking about jobs and making promises. People are always more impressed if you give them more than they think they're going to get. Of course, you shouldn't take this approach to extremes. If you regularly commit to much less than management wants or expects, they'll soon starting looking for other programmers to take the jobs.

Great programmers develop a keen ability to estimate accurately. They are able to reliably deliver their software components on schedule or even early. They are good at establishing concrete milestones and communicating all the interfaces to the rest of the programming team. This skill comes from experience, from soliciting the input of other key members of the team, and from breaking tasks into segments that are small enough to accurately estimate their completion time. You can't really know how long it will take to create an application until you've figured out what exactly you have to do. After you've broken the project into tangible tasks, subtasks, and dependencies, then you can add up the amount of time you will need to complete the entire project.

Some phases of the programming effort may need to be completed serially, and others can be done in parallel. Good project management software, such as Time Line, is available, and you should use it to help chart the time and resources necessary to complete any project. This software uses project management techniques to establish concrete milestones, clear hand-off points, and dependencies between the various developers on a programming team. The milestones are visible, and good programming management teams regularly review them to make sure they are reached and that the whole team is on track to meet the next milestones.

Code reviews also are required procedures of successful development teams. Members are invited to help each other through these reviews, and the whole effort is coordinated for the benefit of the project overall.

You, as an individual programmer, can use Walter's advice to "underpromise and overdeliver" to ensure that you and your efforts fit comfortably into the entire project, and teams of programmers can use Walter's advice to ensure that their programs don't become casualties of project slippage.

2. *Don't Put Bugs in Your Software*

I learned much of what I know about software development from Brad Silverberg, currently Senior Vice President of the Personal Systems Division at Microsoft. Brad is an incredibly talented software visionary and is responsible for two of the most successful software products ever: Windows 95 and MS-DOS. Windows 95 is now changing the face of computers around the world, and the development of Windows 95 applications is the fastest growing area in programming.

I worked for Brad at Borland when I was Director of Languages Research & Development, and I started the development of Turbo C++ when Brad was Vice President of R&D. Brad always had the slowest computers in his office, and he insisted on testing software on these ancient dinosaur machines. The reason he did this was to make sure that no one was being sloppy and writing software that depended on high-performance hardware to run well. I learned many things from Brad, but one piece of wisdom sounded so obvious that I discounted it at first: "Great programmers don't put bugs in their code." Really good programmers are meticulous about what they release.

I've heard that a bug costs ten times as much to fix a month after it's been injected into a code base, and a hundred times as much to fix after the code has been shipped, so it makes a lot of dollar sense as well as common sense to code software right the first time.

Again, does this sound too obvious? Are you now saying, "Of course, I don't put bugs in my software. No one puts bugs in their software." Well, no one may put bugs in their software consciously, but bugs do get into software, and they come from only one place—the person writing the code.

So how do you avoid bugs in your code? "Take care when you first construct your software" is Brad's advice. "Oftentimes, programmers will feel that they don't have time to 'do it right' to begin with, but they underestimate the time required to fix all the problems caused by a quick and dirty solution. It's up to you to be very careful when you first create the design and when you finally sit down and code the application."

Be wary of developing what is sometimes called the "cowboy mentality." Cowboys write code in a quick and dirty way. They work quickly—far more quickly than many others on their team—and so they see themselves as heroes. However, if the software they generate is full of bugs, and it usually is, or if the overall design of the software is flawed, then these cowboys have done nothing to help the team effort. They've only injected problems that other people will have to clean up.

A key word in Brad's comments is "design." You *cannot* create bug-free software unless you have a bug-free design. Too often programmers become so eager to start coding that they don't spend enough time on the architecture up front. Yet the design and architecture of a program are essential to the program's functionality. If you think of your programs as your children, then think of their designs as the skeletons that support everything else. Obviously, you wouldn't want to give your child a crooked spine, one leg shorter than the other, or three arms. Don't do this to the applications you create either. Spend enough time on constructing a good, solid design. Then as you write the code, give some thought to each function you

"Great programmers don't put bugs in their code."
—Brad Silverberg

implement. Think as you go. Don't just write like crazy and then hope to catch all the errors in the debugging sessions.

Another way to keep bugs out is to design usability in. Usability should not be considered secondary. Usability must be a primary goal if your software is to succeed with end users, because end users are who you're writing your software for. But not only does designing for usability keep the needs of the ultimate users in mind, it also helps you create software that is perceived to be more bug free. By considering the ways in which users will actually use your program, you can better anticipate the problems users may have with a particular design feature or feature implementation—and sometimes what the world considers a bug turns out to be nothing more than an inability to understand the way the software was designed to work. If you design with usability in mind, then you won't have to worry about this type of bug in your applications.

Another piece of advice I received from Brad Silverberg is "Design your program, no matter what it is, with quality as the first consideration." During the development of Windows 95, even though there was incredible pressure to ship the operating system, the priority given to quality delayed the release several times. Instead of shipping Windows 95 prematurely, a beta-test program involving more than a million early users was implemented to ensure that high-quality standards were met.

It is an intense dedication to quality that will get you into the ranks of the great and successful programmers. When you create a program, whether it's system software, a complex application, a class library, a utility, or whatever, you owe it to yourself and to your eventual users to create it to meet the highest standards you are capable of achieving. That means writing code that is sleek, elegant, functional, and readable. You *must* strive for this type of quality in everything you write.

A great way to improve the quality of your code is to actually read it. "Every week you should sit down on the couch with a printout of the code you've written and just read it," Brad used to tell some of his team members. "And read other people's code, too." Never was better advice given. Read code from other programmers to see how they've solved problems. Critique code that you read and try to figure out how the programmer could have accomplished the same thing in fewer steps or with less memory or with fewer lines. You'll be surprised at how much you learn through this exercise.

3. *Be Passionate and Hard Working*

Gordon Eubanks is a self-taught programmer who has risen to the very top of his profession. Gordon learned programming in Hawaii overlooking the ocean from his sunny apartment. "I learned a lot from reading and teaching myself," Gordon recalls, "I taught myself to write compilers from reading books." This isn't something just anyone can do; in fact, learning to write a compiler from reading a book is pretty astonishing. Yet Gordon is the kind of guy who makes astonishing things happen. Now after a successful career with such well-established companies as Digital Research and IBM, Gordon is the president and CEO of the company that he founded: Symantec. Symantec is one of the largest software companies in the world, and Gordon employs a lot of programmers.

I asked Gordon to share some of his thoughts on hiring programmers—on what kind of skills, habits, and traits he looks for when he hires someone to work at Symantec.

"Great programmers are passionate and hard working. They're very organized and methodical, they have the ability to structure things, but most of all, they're incredibly hard working."
—Gordon Eubanks

"Great programmers are passionate and hard working." Gordon believes, "they're very organized and methodical, they have the ability to structure things, but most of all, they're incredibly hard working. They immerse themselves in it. This is very difficult stuff. You have to be able to stay with it.

"If you're not willing to rebuild something when you get it halfway done because you see that while your idea was right, you haven't really put it together in the right way, then you're not going to be very good at programming. If you're not really willing to work with people on how things interact, you're not going to be very good at this."

Good programmers are meticulous in this way. They will search for perfection and go out of their way to achieve it. They are concerned about every detail, about making sure that everything fits well together, everything works, and everything is in a form that they'd be proud to show their boss.

Most programmers know that they need to break most applications into modules, and that often other programmers will work on some of these modules. Thus, a clear , well-organized approach to creating the modules is highly important so those modules can be logically divided. In addition, the interfaces need to be specified carefully and should be consistent throughout the entire project.

The meticulous programmer also selects established coding conventions and follows them throughout the entire program. Consistent use of conventions protects against common coding hazards. It adds predictability to low-level tasks and creates a standard for other programmers to follow in writing readable code. If your code follows clear conventions, then others will be able to read it more easily. If you format your code consistently, then others will be able to understand it. If you lay out the code so that all the loops are indented a certain number of spaces, all the parameters are ordered in the same manner, and other types of formatting are used consistently throughout the program, then you will create a piece of software with far more value to other programmers than sloppy code.

And don't forget to add comments to your code. Adding comments is something many programmers overlook or just don't take the time to do, and yet it is one of the most powerful ways to make your code more understandable. Next time you're tempted to just code on without comment, think of the last time you tried reading a piece of code and how much happier you would have been if some of those cryptic lines had been illuminated by comments.

Strive to cultivate a high level of organization in yourself and in your work. Organize your thoughts so you can create logical architectures and designs. Organize your projects to complete them on time. Be meticulous in your coding, and the benefits to you and to others who read and use your programs will be bountiful.

4. *Know What You Don't Know*

Every software development project is affected by unknowns. These can be external factors such as changes in a new operating system or in other software packages that your project depends on, or they can be internal factors such as illness in a team member and changes in management's objectives or priorities. Your software project will always be subject to unknowns, and identifying and planning around them is crucial to success.

People who manage projects, and that includes almost all software developers to some extent, are well aware of the impact of unknowns on the applications they're creating.

Jim McCarthy is Director of Program Management for the Visual C++ product at Microsoft. Jim fell in love with software in 1971 when he bought a Radio Shack TRS-80. He later taught himself programming by reading Kernighan and Plauger in a camper in the woods. Jim was a natural at programming and in a few weeks taught himself everything he needed to know. Then he wrote a program called LogicGem, which he went on to produce all by himself. He not only wrote it, he also tested the software, arranged beta-test sites, designed the packaging and marketing materials, and got his product into software distribution channels. After that, he worked at Whitewater Research, then at Bell Labs, and finally at Microsoft. Jim has a lot of experience with the process of creating software and has some insight into dealing with unknowns.

"Knowing what you don't know is what we call 'lucid ignorance,'" says Jim. "Programmers in my group get more points for cognizance of unknowns than they do for knowns. The unknowns are the things that are going to get you in trouble, so realizing what they are is extremely important."

I asked Jim to elaborate on how to identify unknowns in a project and how to deal with them.

"You start off by acknowledging them," was Jim's advice. "An unknown, for example, is when we don't know when we're going to be done with something. If we recognize that, we know not to say when we're going to be finished. I'm amazed at the number of people who accept completion dates from those who know even less about a project than they do. If you don't know when it is, then your boss certainly doesn't know.

"Programmers should be like doctors. Say you go to the doctor with a tumor the size of a basketball on your neck, and you say, 'Am I going to live?' Then he says, 'These things are always uncertain.' So you pay him $100, and you're happy. There's always uncertainty in the case of doctors, and programmers have to be more like doctors. We need to push the uncertainty out of the development organization and into the rest of the organization so the rest of the organization can get better at making adaptations to changing situations."

So what things are unknowable?

"There's a certain relationship between the time before a deadline and its unknowability. The farther out a date is, the more unknowable it is. Things that are a month or two months out are usually pretty certain. That's why we work on a milestone basis. We just look to the next couple of months. When you calculate your project, you can think of three variables: resources, features, and time. What combination of those three things will yield the desired product at the desired time and cost? It's hard to know. All three of them are somewhat unknown. You can be finished at any time, but the project may not have the features you want and may cost you more.

"Things are also uncertain because of all the variables underneath you. All programs are somewhat experimental. Nothing like it has ever been done; nothing like it has ever been tried. It's on a new platform, on new hardware, it's got new operating system components in it—it has a host of dependencies that are likewise unknowable. Your goal should be to make the correct decision every day, not to make the correct decision once and then stick to it.

"For example, every day you get new information, so you have to reevaluate your existing application of the time, features, and resources triangle. That triangle, shown here, is what you're working with as a project manager. So every day when you find out some dependency did something unexpected, or that you suddenly have additional funds to apply to the problem, or that the operating system you're creating an application for just slipped, you reapply the triangle to come up with a 'do-able' plan.

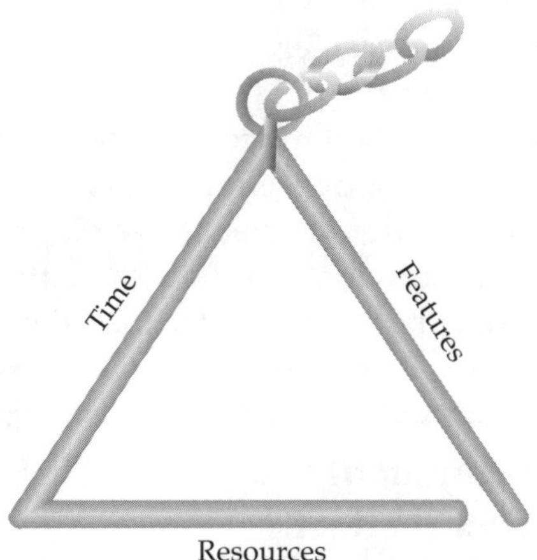

The Three Major Factors in a Development Project

"When there are variables, and there always are, the first thing is to admit that there are things you don't know. Then you nose down into the subparts. What are some of the things that if you did know would give you more certainty toward the end of knowing the whole thing? Even when you know things, you don't know them. Probability isn't bankable. If you have too many uncertainties, you need to sacrifice some of them. You need to choose which uncertainties to lose. That way you don't give all your resources to all of the uncertainties and get none of them resolved. Make everything certain except that which is uncertain. That'll smoke out uncertainties you didn't think of."

Of course, what Jim is implying is that you should have contingency plans and milestones. You need to set deadlines by which time specific uncertainties must be resolved and then stick to those deadlines. If the time comes and an uncertainty still exists, then you need to eliminate the feature or capability and proceed with your Plan B. But the first step is remembering that every project contains uncertainties and that identifying and dealing with them is tremendously important.

5. *Work Well with Your Team*

There was once a time when a developer could create a program from start to finish entirely alone, but that time is gone. Today's applications typically are far too large and complex for a single person to tackle. Now virtually all but the most elementary programs are the result of a coordinated team effort. Thus, fitting into a team is essential, and working well with your team is a skill that will significantly advance your career.

Ike Nassi, a vice-president at Apple Computer, is well aware of how team dynamics work and how important it is to find good team members. "Software development is a coordinated group effort," says Ike. "No matter how good individual programmers may be, they need to work well with the other development team members or they won't be effective. Software development is an activity in which the whole becomes greater than the sum of the parts, so at Apple we foster an atmosphere that encourages close cooperation among development team members, and we promote the team approach whenever possible."

> **"Software development is a coordinated group effort."**
> **—Ike Nassi**

Being on a development team is fundamentally the same as being on any type of team. You need to give and to take and have an honest feeling of camaraderie with your team members. You have to be able to give help when another member needs it. You have to be able to receive help, and sometimes constructive criticism, when a team member gives this to you. You need to be able to set aside your ego and pull together when the going gets tough. If you take care of the other members of your team, they'll take care of you. Also, psychological studies have shown that people appreciate and like you more if they feel they have been of help to you. So acknowledge help whenever you get it, and make your team members feel that you are truly aware of their contributions to your efforts.

Being a constructive member of a team isn't something that happens automatically. It takes work, and it often takes some restraint on your part. You can also read books on the subject. Quite a few exist today, but the old favorite is Carnegie's *How to Win Friends and Influence People* (New York: Simon & Schuster, 1981).

As a developer, you will undoubtedly have conflicts and disagreements with other developers on your team simply because in programming there is always going to be more than one right way to approach and solve a problem. Often two team members will disagree, and obviously only one will see his or her methods or ideas implemented. This is inevitable. However, disagreements don't have to damage development teams. In fact, they can strengthen the relationships within the group and lead to a better understanding of each individual's viewpoint and way of working. Usually new ideas surface when divergent opinions are compared, and that is healthy for everyone as well as for the project you're working on.

To make teamwork work, you need to check your ego at the door. You need to not be defensive about the code you write. Many programmers are reluctant to let anyone look at their code. It's good to hold yourself to a high standard but don't be afraid to let others see what you've done and give you some feedback. And you must be willing to listen to this feedback. When you offer feedback, be careful to make it constructive and not derogatory. You need to present it as a positive thing. You need to use tact.

Disagreements do not cause rifts in the fabric of a team if everyone stays positive. Keep in mind that all of you have the same goal. You're all trying to create a program that will meet certain objectives defined well ahead of the actual development effort. Don't take disagreements personally. Don't let your own ego get wrapped up in any difference of opinion. It will only sour your feelings for the group and cast a cloud over your own working conditions.

When you do have disagreements, don't write flame mail. Whenever you work on a software team, you will undoubtedly do a lot of communicating through electronic mail. E-mail gives you the ability to "speak" to virtually anyone or any group of people in the company you work with at the same time. It's great for sharing information among people who ordinarily would be hard to assemble all at once. It's a wonderful tool for fielding ideas to a large number of people and then getting opinions or a consensus. Unfortunately, it also provides an easy way to vent opinions that may be clouded by anger. Writing an angry or accusatory e-mail message and then sending it to one team member and copying everyone else may sometimes be tempting, but it will inevitably get you into trouble, create bad feelings in the person you are criticizing, and make others who receive a copy think badly of you.

A good rule of thumb to follow when you write e-mail containing criticism is to let the note sit on your machine for at least 24 hours before sending it. Such a cooling off period can help prevent ill-advised flames from poisoning the team atmosphere.

Another good rule for getting along well with your team is "Stay out of office politics." Politics are not as common in development groups as they are in other corporate areas, but don't be fooled into thinking you're not subject to politics just because you're a developer. Politics are subtle, and you can find yourself mired in them before you even realize you're getting involved. How do you avoid getting involved? Concentrate on your work, forget your ego, and try not to align yourself with any particular group or person. Try instead to shoot straight, treat everyone with equal respect, and concentrate on doing the job at hand.

Don't forget an obvious but often overlooked fact: your boss is also a member of your team. Remember that your boss is responsible for the overall project and may also be responsible for budgets, timelines, presentations to upper management, and so on. Your boss relies on you to deliver, and you rely on your boss to knock down obstacles, set rewards in place, and arbitrate disputes. Promote your boss, and your chances of being promoted yourself rise in proportion.

6. Follow Through to the End

Jerry Barber is one of my long-time friends. In 1984 we cofounded Gold Hill Computers, a company that pioneered new technology in the realm of artificial intelligence. Jerry also founded the Object Management Group and created the first ObjectWorld trade show. Now he is the Director of Technology Integration at Adobe Systems. Jerry believes in initiating new projects and following through until the goal is achieved. He recently flew his Cessna 182 from Seattle to Russia across the Bering Strait, wearing a survival suit at all times, because it's virtually instant death to go down in the icy Arctic waters off Alaska. Since Jerry keeps going until his goal is achieved, whether it's starting a worldwide organization like OMG or flying to Russia, I asked Jerry to comment on the ability to follow through on projects as a skill needed by programmers.

"Following through to the end is a very important skill. When you interview someone for a job, one of the things you look for is actual participation in a team that has delivered a product, because that's a unique experience and it shapes one's perspective.

"Beginning programmers tend to think that when the basic design issues are done and the implementation is over, most of the job is done. I think what surprises a lot of people is the number of different cases that need to be taken into consideration to make sure that a program actually works. That's when the finishing detail and polish need to be applied in order to create something that can work in the real world. This is the one area where follow-through is critical."

Jerry certainly is correct about this. Setting up an initial design for an application and making the first coding pass is only the beginning of a long process. Even when the code is complete, the feature set frozen, and the project passed along for testing, much still remains to be done. Debugging is an intense activity that is absolutely crucial to any software program. Good quality is critical, and achieving it isn't quick and easy. Refining and optimizing the program are equally important.

"Performance considerations are the other side of the picture," says Jerry. "Usually you get the architecture in place and make sure it's right, and then do the optimizations later. Premature optimization is the hobgoblin of small minds. From an engineering point of view, you don't want to optimize prematurely. On the other hand, you need to start thinking about optimizations in the pre-beta or even pre-alpha phase. This is something people typically don't spend enough time on. Usually a new programmer will think things are done, but you've got to do the optimizations also.

"To get a product out takes an incredible amount of focus and a terrific amount of work," Jerry goes on to observe. "One of the things that Adobe believes in is having small teams, because as the teams get larger, the amount of communication needed increases exponentially. So in the final phases of the software development effort you're much better off having small teams of people that will work the long hours together to get things done."

"When you interview someone for a job, one of the things you look for is actual participation in a team that has delivered a product..."

—Jerry Barber

Whether you work in a small team or a large one, the fact is that creating a finished piece of software is a long and arduous process. Good programming requires fine craftsmanship, and really fine craftsmanship can never be rushed. Your project is almost certainly going to take more time and effort than you imagine when you first start it, but to deliver really good programs, you have to be willing to follow through to the end.

7. *Keep Up with Emerging Technology*

The software industry changes faster than any other industry in the world. Yesterday's news is tomorrow's obsolete technology. Our technological horizons are expanding exponentially, and this is particularly true in software development as the information age arrives. It's not enough to be good at what you've been doing for the last few years or even to be a freshly minted graduate with a thorough knowledge of your field.

"Knowing your stuff" won't carry you far unless you're also aware of the changes taking place in the industry. You need to know what's going on so the code you write will tie in successfully to the world of today and maybe tomorrow. You also have to keep up with the changes in the computer field so you can mold the growth of your own career.

Enrique Salem is the chief architect of the Norton Utilities. Keeping up with technology is one of Enrique's primary concerns. He assumes that programmers naturally try to keep up with technology.

"Great developers are people who are hungry to learn," says Enrique. "They're people who are really charged up about new technologies and really want to know about them. They feel bad when something happens and they don't know about it. They really want to understand.

> **"Great developers are people who are hungry to learn."**
> **—Enrique Salem**

"Everybody knows Windows is hot today, and Windows will continue to be hot. Windows, Windows 95, and in the longer term, Windows NT, will all be important. I think the x86-based processors will continue to be important. It's going to be Intel. PowerPC is interesting, but I don't see that happening because Intel is so dominating. Also, because of all the miniaturization, you're going to see more hand-held devices like message pads. Wireless technology is also going to be tremendously important. Some of the things that General Magic is doing are nice, but they're still missing the connectivity. When the cost of connecting comes down, you're going to see a whole lot of growth in that. I think that's going to make wireless much more affordable and the hand-held devices much better connected.

"The current version of NT is Daytona, and that will transition, probably in early '97, into Cairo or some derivative of Cairo. The direction and future of NT is Cairo, so that really makes sense. Taligent is a neat concept, but there's not enough market share and not a compelling reason for people to start switching, so I don't think it's going to be a huge success.

"Other technologies that people need to be thinking about are OLE and OpenDoc. Instead of building whole new applications, you've got components that are parts of other things. Really understanding OLE and OpenDoc is the key. Neither system has been successful. Microsoft is pushing OLE, which is making it pick up steam, but the requirements of OLE still present obstacles. OLE requires a really fast processor, plenty of RAM, and some pretty heavy hardware requirements to bring up two applications and have them run in sync and not bog you down. But every year the price-to-performance ratio of processors is getting better. You've got to believe that this trend is going to continue and that technologies that are currently hardware intensive will be more accessible to larger audiences. OLE is one of the technologies that will really gain from that."

So how should you keep up with emerging technologies to spot trends like the ones Enrique mentions? For one thing, you should read. If you're like most programmers, you probably log on to the Internet regularly. Tap into some of the newsgroups and user groups to get a grass-roots feel for what's current. Subscribe to one or two of the weekly general computer industry weekly newspapers such as *PC Week*, *InfoWorld*, or *ComputerWorld.* They cover mostly the same news, though each slants its overall editorial coverage toward a slightly different market, and that market may change over time. Currently, *PC Week* is the leading general industry newspaper. *InfoWorld* and *ComputerWorld* cater to a more exclusively large-company and MIS-department crowd, so their stories are aimed more at corporate programmers. In addition, numerous publications such as *NetWork World* and *InterActive* address specific audiences. All of these are great sources of news about the industry. Read a few issues of every one you can get your hands on, and you'll soon figure out which covers more of the subjects that interest you. You'll probably want to subscribe to both a weekly newspaper with broad coverage and one that focuses on a specialty. Subscribe to one or two of each and read them every week.

For more in-depth coverage, subscribe to some of the monthly publications. *BYTE* and *Doctor Dobb's Journal* are the best established programming journals, but there's also *Microsoft Systems Journal*, *Embedded Systems Journal*, *Windows Tech Journal*, *C++ Report*, *Journal of Object Oriented Programming*, and more. Your employer will likely pay for any trade publication you wish to subscribe to, and taking the time to read these will be well worth your while.

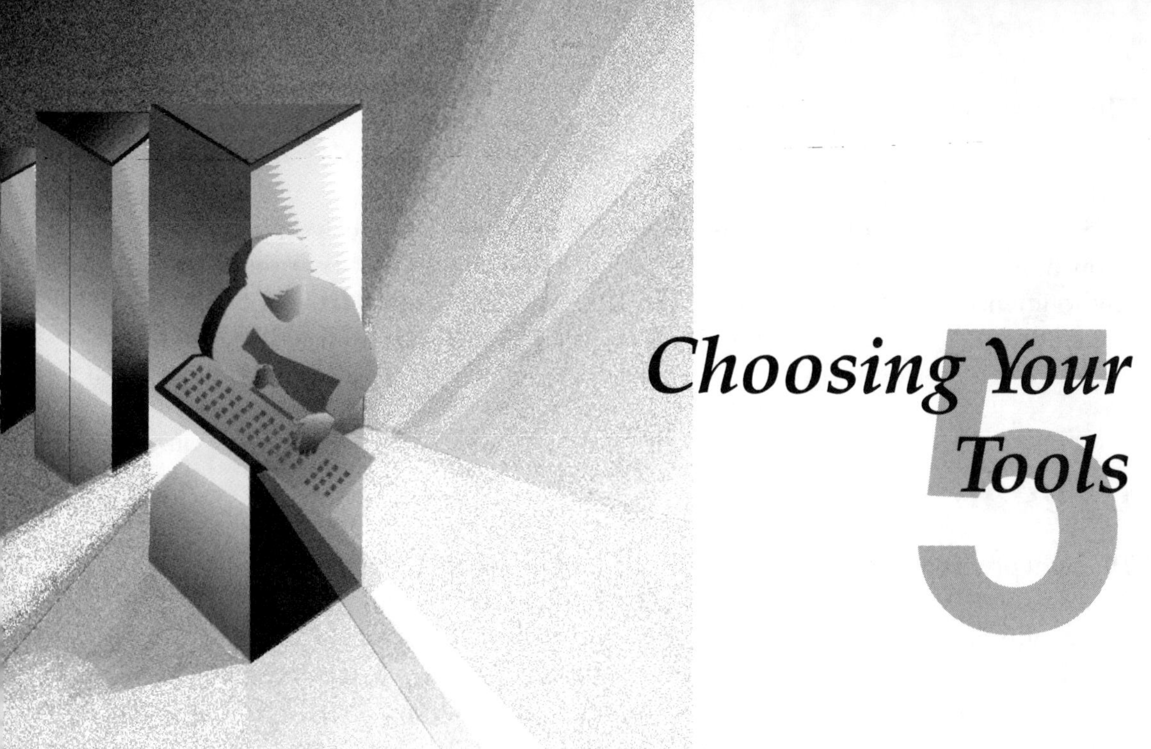

5 Choosing Your Tools

If you're going to be successful, you'll need the right tools. Tools are a factor in the success equation that was introduced about the time humans first came out of the cave. They were the original catalysts in the technical evolution of mankind. Just as we have evolved through the use of tools, so the tools themselves have evolved, and with this evolution has come specialization. Now there are special tools to help us do virtually anything, and it's become extremely important to have the right ones to do the job—especially in programming.

Just as a great painter needs the right paints and a great sculptor needs fine clay, a master programmer needs the best development tools. Writing high-quality programs requires software craftsmanship that can be enhanced using development environments and tools that give you more control and better insight into your application.

Today's programming tools provide a rich set of features and capabilities that make you more productive and thus more valuable to prospective employers. Taking advantage of tools such as automatic code generators, application frameworks, class editors, hierarchy editors, version control, optimizers, profilers, and testing tools enables you to deliver high-quality code in a reasonable period of time.

So what are the tools that are essential to your trade, the ones you'd better know how to use before you try to get a job? They are languages, programming environments, object-oriented editors, debuggers, visual tools, class libraries, 4GLs, and all the other tools that have been created to make your life easier and your software more polished.

Languages

The right programming languages are one set of tools that is essential to master. Since different languages are created with different design objectives in mind, the capabilities of languages vary. Languages also vary depending on where they are in the "evolutionary scale." For instance, COBOL was created quite a long time ago for the job of creating business applications. FORTRAN is a language that was created in a similar time period but customized for the scientific community. Both of these languages today are old in terms of software technology, and they are being replaced in the mainstream by the more modern C++ and 4GL tools.

As software advanced so did the sophistication and power of languages. C and C++ have risen to the top of programming popularity because they offer much more flexibility and productivity than did older languages. The majority of the modern Microsoft operating systems, like Windows 95 and Windows NT, are written mostly in C, which greatly enhances the relative value of the C language for programmers. Other building blocks of modern applications, such as the Microsoft Foundation Classes (MFC) application framework for creating Windows user interfaces, are written in C++. There is, in fact, an overwhelming move to the C/C++ language among top system and application programmers today. Of course there are still many lines of old COBOL code out there, so COBOL application maintenance is still a viable career, at least for the short term, but it's not a highly desired one or one that will likely take you all the way to your retirement. If your plan is to write serious applications or system software in the future, then you'd better learn to use C or C++.

While C and C++ are far and away the most popular languages in mainstream programming, there still is some need for assembly language programmers, especially in the area of embedded systems. Embedded systems applications sometimes use assembly language to maximize performance and minimize memory requirements. Since assembly language is lower level and much closer to actual machine language, it is also faster than any higher-level language. However, assembly language is also much more difficult to learn and use. Not many people have a knack for assembly language programming, but if you do, look to embedded systems for a good field in which to exploit your talents.

BASIC is a popular language that many people learn in high school and college. It's a good language to learn even for people who never intend to write programs for a living but would like to know something about programming. Since BASIC is such a simple language, it's easy to learn; however, its simplicity limits its power for professional programming. Microsoft's Visual Basic has become very popular simply because it's good for prototyping, for creating small applications, and for use in systems where performance is not an issue. If you plan to develop a career in MIS or management, BASIC may have some appeal for you.

C++, the object-oriented extension of C, is continually evolving. Object-oriented programming brings with it features such as reusable software components, inheritance from parent classes, polymorphism, templates, and more. But the object-oriented features of C++ aren't everything. Enrique Salem, of Symantec, is an ardent believer in the C++ language and the benefits it provides apart from OOP. "I think everybody should use C++," he says. "There's no reason not to. You get better type checking and default parameters. Instead of putting your declarations in some specific location, you can declare a variable as you need it, which brings your scope much closer together and makes your application easier to read. With C++ you get function overloading, which allows you to have two functions with the same name but different parameter lists. C++ gives you more readable programs that are easier to extend and maintain than programs written in non-OOP languages."

"I think everybody should use C++."
—Enrique Salem

Of course the extent to which you can use the features of any language depends on how well your compiler supports language standards. Up until recently, many compilers did not support C++ templates. Now they all do. However, not all of the compilers support C++ exception handling and run-time type identification. These are the kinds of issues to be aware of when selecting a compiler. The ANSI standards committee X3J11 issues specifications for the C++ language. When selecting a compiler, it is a good idea to get a copy of the C++ language specification and compare it with the compiler's capabilities.

Integrated Development and Debugging Environments

Most modern compilers are not sold in a stand-alone format. They are typically included in a development environment that includes various supporting tools like editors, browsers, debuggers, project managers, and automatic code generators that are integrated into that environment. Don't underestimate the importance of the development environment. It's not just a pretty face. It's a pretty face that you're going to have to look at for eight to ten hours a day. It's also a key factor in how productive you can become. You'll find that you'll either save or lose time depending on the quality of your development system's supporting tools and how well they are integrated.

Look at the screen shown in Figure 5-1. This shows the integrated development and debugging environment of Symantec's C++ product for Windows 95, Windows NT, and Windows 3.1. In this environment workspaces act like virtual desktops represented by tabs. These workspaces can be customized to optimize a particular job, like browsing or editing, and then saved and used over and over.

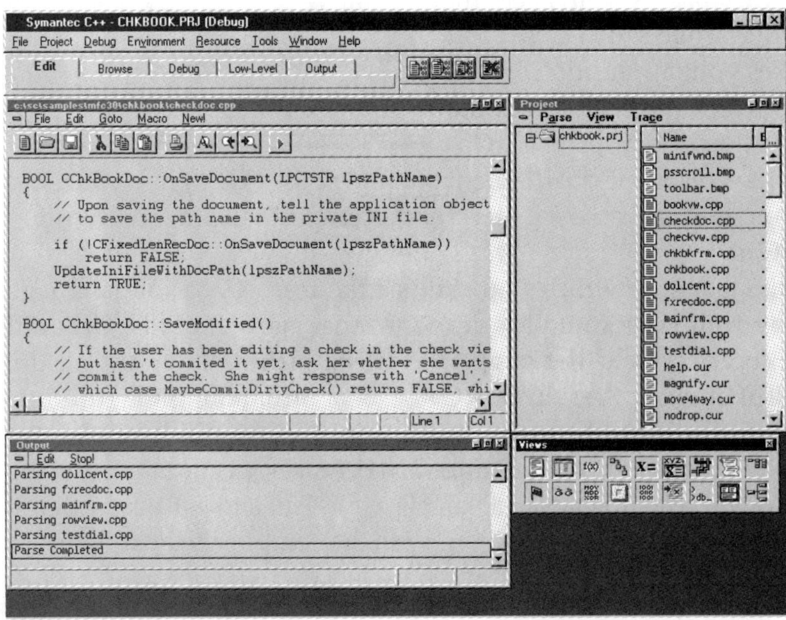

Figure 5-1 *Symantec C++ integrated development and debugging environment*

Project Management System

A major component of any integrated development environment is the project management system. The project manager simplifies your work by helping you to organize your code and your projects. This is particularly important for large projects.

Ironically, many project managers do not adequately support large and complex projects and instead force programmers to use command line tools whenever they need to deal with large projects. For example, many project managers can't support generating multiple dynamic link libraries in addition to an executable during a build process. However, this is not true of some project management systems, such as the one in Symantec C++. Since the project manager is a very important part of the development system, be sure you look for a professional system with a project manager that can support all your requirements.

Other Tools to Make Your Build Process More Efficient

Easing the build process is one of the important functions of a project manager, but other tools are also available to aid in or speed up the process. Symantec's NetBuild, shown in Figure 5-2, is a distributed build feature unique to Symantec C++. It allows a build to be automatically distributed across multiple computers on a network, thus reducing compilation time by factors.

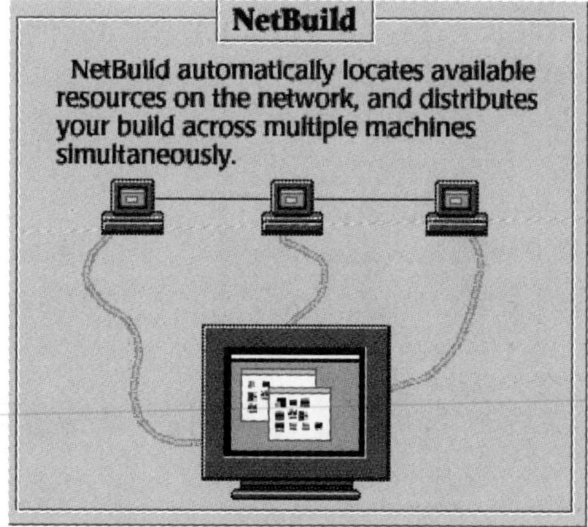

***Figure* 5-2** *Symantec's NetBuild tool*

Object-Oriented Editors and Browsers

A new breed of editing tools has arrived that is far removed from traditional editors. These object-oriented editors give you capabilities that were never available before. They are dynamic tools created for C++ programming that give you instant insight into your class hierarchy and class structures, no matter where you are in the build process, by parsing your C++ code as you are entering it. Object-oriented editors and browsers such as the one in Symantec C++ (see Figure 5-3) let you locate and zoom in on any piece of code you wish and edit the code right there without switching to any other tool. Some also give you the ability to graphically manipulate the relationships and inheritances of the classes in your application with a few movements of your mouse, at which point your code is automatically updated to reflect the new hierarchy.

At Symantec we developed the Class Editor and the Hierarchy Editor to help programmers navigate through and manipulate their code. With these editors you can edit classes in the three-pane browser, quickly find any class implementation in your program, and even graphically manipulate the structure of your class hierarchy.

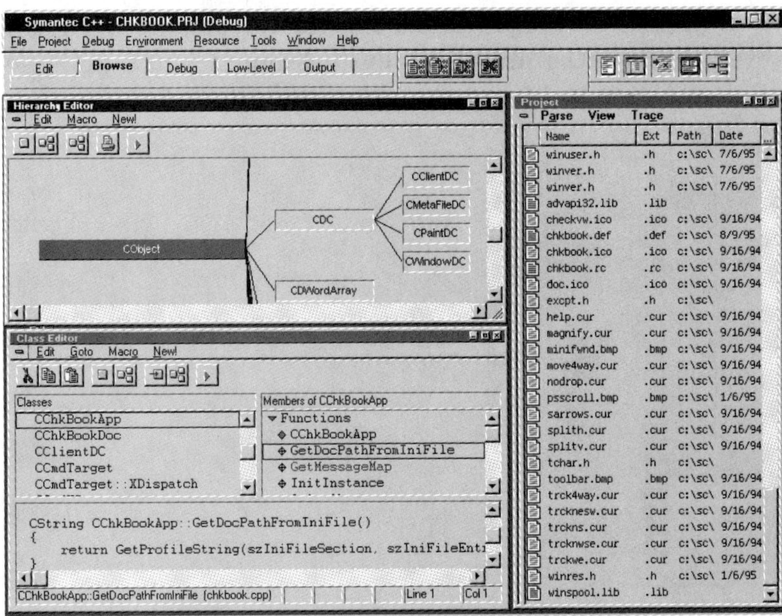

Figure 5-3 *Symantec C++'s object-oriented browser and editor*

Debuggers

If you're like most of the programmers in the world, writing an application is not a one-pass exercise. There's a lot of iteration on each code module, a lot of moving back and forth from the editor to the debugger. You will almost certainly spend as much time with your debugger as with any other tools you use. The debugger is critical to success, and if you place a lot of importance on selecting a good debugger, you'll be serving yourself well.

Don't settle for less than a graphical debugger like the one shown in Figure 5-4. The days of character mode debuggers are gone, and good riddance. Today's graphical debugger should support both high- and low-level debugging, 16-bit and 32-bit debugging, and drag-and-drop. Useful features include the ability to freeze and thaw threads, set hardware breakpoints, and view variables using a wide range of data types.

One good debugger for Windows is Periscope's WinScope. It captures API calls, messages and hooks, as well as tool help notifications and debug kernel messages. WinScope also traces time-sensitive software such as TAPI, TSPI, and multimedia.

A useful debugging tool is Bounds Checker from NuMega. This tool helps catch many boundary condition errors.

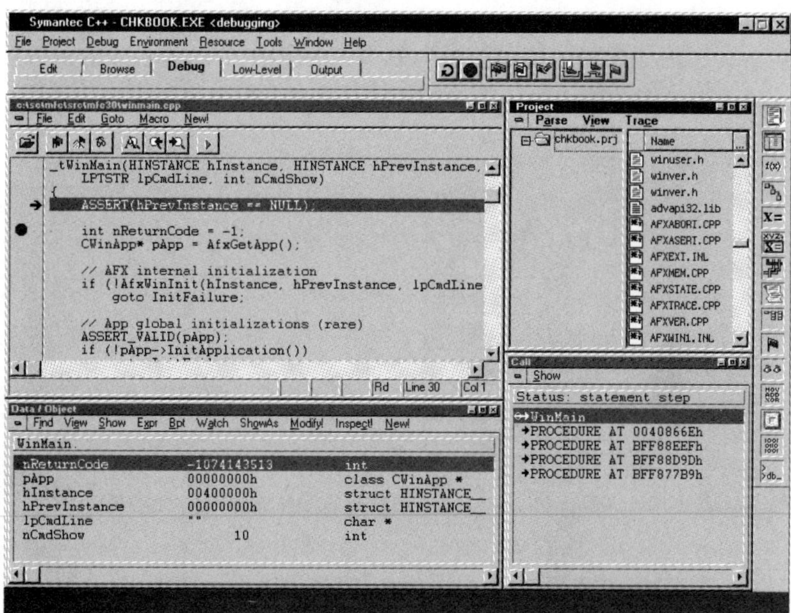

Figure 5-4 *Multithreaded debugger included with Symantec C++*

Visual Tools

Another innovation that you should master is visual tools. Visual tools eliminate many hours of tedious coding chores by letting you "draw" your user interface and resources and then automatically generating the code. This process is illustrated in Figure 5-5.

With Visual Architect you literally draw all the elements of your user interface and automatically generate the code for windows, menus, dialogs, and more. In addition, you can easily set all the attributes of the user interface elements, such as which commands they generate.

Visual tools first became popular for Windows programming, and consequently there are several very good resource editors around to choose from. Borland's Resource Workshop was a particularly popular resource editor for drawing the user interface and was sold successfully in a stand-alone version for several years. Now resource editors are included with most development environments, so you are not nearly as likely to want to purchase one separately.

AppPolish, from Encore Development, is a slightly different tool for working on the visual elements of your user interface. AppPolish is a rather remarkable tool that performs 45 different checks, including a complete spell check to find user interface errors in any executable, library, or resource file; a check for correct use of mnemonics in menus; and checks for duplicate captions, duplicate strings, and optimum alignment size. I highly recommend AppPolish for any programmer who can't afford to have his or her user interface appear amateurish.

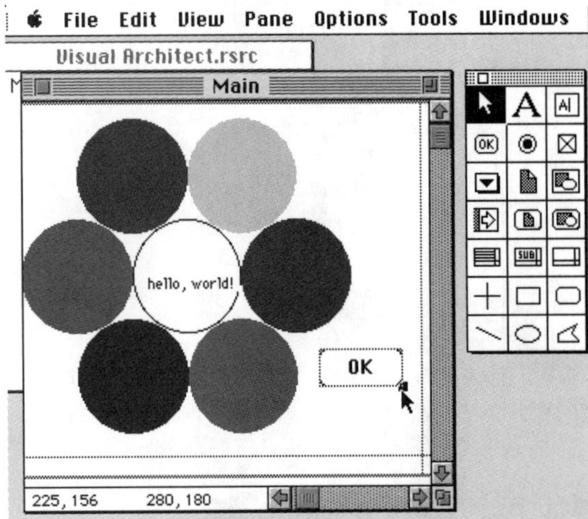

Figure 5-5 *Symantec's Visual Architect, from Symantec C++ 8.0 for Power Mac*

Stand-Alone Editors

You spend a lot of your time in your editor and the way it works is probably very important to you. I have found the one tool that programmers feel most strongly about is their editor. And everyone's tastes in editors is different. Almost every development environment sports its own integrated text editor, and stand-alone editors are popular add-on products.

To support your particular needs, an editor should be extensible. It should be fast and easy to use and should contain capabilities such as support for user-defined macros, color syntax highlighting, column selection, cutting and pasting between multiple windows, and multiple undo and redo. Almost all editors have these features and some have others that may or may not appeal to you. Pick the editor you start with carefully and be sure that your chosen editor is from a company that you feel has lots of longevity, since once you get used to it you'll be reluctant to switch to another one.

BRIEF used to be one of the most popular editors around for the DOS environment, but it was late in supporting Windows and has mostly lost favor with developers. A popular editor for the Windows environment today is CodeWright.

BBEdit is probably the most popular stand-alone editor for the Macintosh environment. BBEdit now runs on the Power Macintosh as well, and it takes advantage of the enhanced performance of the Power Mac processor. BBEdit supports Applescript, Frontier, and other OSA-compliant scripting languages. If you're looking for a Mac editor, try this one.

Class Libraries

One more very important element to the whole development tools mix is class libraries. Many libraries are supplied with the development system, and some are sold as stand-alone add-on products. These are invaluable tools and should always be building blocks in your program's design.

A few years ago, when the complexity of Windows 3.1's GUI interface and event-driven architecture were causing programmers to pull their hair out, the concept of a class library that could serve as a foundation for Windows development was born. Both Borland and Microsoft released class libraries that served this purpose. These libraries were so comprehensive that a developer could use them to literally create a working application in just minutes, and so they earned a special name. They were called *application frameworks*, since they actually supplied the framework for a finished application.

Borland's ObjectWindows Library (OWL) was an early application framework for the Windows platform, but it was a proprietary one. It provided the benefits of an application framework; but Borland has lost a lot of ground in the C++ market, and today OWL is an endangered species. At the same time OWL came out, Microsoft released the Microsoft Foundation Classes (MFC). MFC is now the industry standard class library for Windows development, and it is included in a number of compilers, including Symantec C++. MFC supplies the crucial foundation and user interface elements that you need to build Windows applications and has become a "must have" in any Windows developer's tools arsenal.

While application frameworks are a relatively new development in the PC world, where user interfaces have traditionally been the much simpler character-mode, the Macintosh has long featured a GUI interface and also a corresponding application framework, called MacApp. MacApp allows you to use library classes to quickly build applications on Apple systems. MacApp is being superceded by the OpenDoc Parts Framework (OPF) from Apple, which is built using pieces of Bedrock, a joint development project between Apple and Symantec. MacApp and OPF from Apple are joined by popular frameworks such as the THINK Class Library (TCL) from Symantec, a de facto industry standard for Macintosh class libraries, as well as PowerPlant from Metrowerks.

Bristol Technology is a company that is addressing the needs for cross-platform applications by providing efficient, effective tools for Windows-to-UNIX cross-platform development. The Bristol Technology family of Wind/U products offers developers compatibility between Windows and UNIX/Motif. This excellent product line includes a Windows-to-UNIX portability toolkit, a UNIX online help system, a Windows printing library, and ForeHelp for UNIX—an easy-to-use UNIX help authoring tool. Bristol Technology licenses MFC and has implemented a version that runs on UNIX. As a standard, MFC is expanding beyond Windows to embrace platforms such as UNIX and Macintosh.

There are other important class libraries. TOOLS.H++ from Rogue Wave is an indispensable library with many high-performance components such as bags, sets, heaps, linked lists, and more. Check out MATH.H++ from Rogue Wave if you are writing computation-intensive numeric applications.

Both Zinc and Inmark sell popular application frameworks that allow developers with more specialized needs—such as the ability to create cross-platform applications that run on multiple operating systems—to create applications with the same ease that MFC affords to more mainstream developers.

The Zinc Interface Library is an object-oriented, multiplatform, internationalized class libary that supports Windows, OS/2, DOS, UNIX, and other platforms. It is particularly useful for creating applications with worldwide ambitions, since it has been optimized for internationalization. It supports both single- and double-byte character sets, runtime configuration of system and error messages, and locale initialization.

In addition to application frameworks, there are several other types of libraries that fill specialized needs. Communications libraries support building applications that can communicate using modems, fax cards, or other remote communications means. For instance, Greenleaf Comm ++ provides a hierarchy of classes for asynchronous serial communications under DOS, Windows, and OS/2. A different type of library is a graphics library like the AccuSoft Image Format Library. This is a toolkit for adding support for all standard raster formats to applications. The GIF Toolkit from Genus Microprogramming provides a high-compression format for incorporating images into applications. Other types of libraries include libraries for network applications, memory management, math implementations, databases, and more. As the number of ways that we use our computers increases, so can you expect the types of class libraries to increase.

Fourth-Generation Language Tools

We have been talking mostly about tools for third-generation languages (3GLs). However, as fourth-generation languages (4GLs) become more and more sophisticated, programmers are starting to adopt tools for 4GLs.

Rapid Application Development (RAD) tools are basically another name for 4GLs. RAD tools not only provide high-level and therefore quick-and-easy application development, they also usually support database elements and techniques such as a business model repository, automatic transaction processing, object-oriented abstraction, optimistic concurrency, and seamless connectivity to major databases.

Client/server 4GLs should offer scalable, distributed decision-support application construction capabilities, and object-oriented 4GLs offer the opportunity for creating distributed applications with reusable object components. Transaction-based application builders support the construction of high-volume distributed transaction processing systems for online transaction processing (OLTP). The complexity and functionality of the application that client/server tools can create is largely a function of the tool's ability to deliver an integrated business application with complex logic and support for different database and connectivity features. Scalability relates to the tool's ability to support a number of concurrent developers, often through a design repository, as well as the ability of the tool to create applications that can support a large number of users.

One important feature of client/server tools is the ability to easily partition applications for distributed processing. Older-style tools allow client-side processing with access to server-based database procedures. However, the evolution of these tools will soon bring the ability to support easy placement and assignment of application processing between the client and one or more servers.

Symantec's Enterprise Developer offers a high level of scalability, which provides client/server applications with the default ability to handle multilevel master-detail processing, cache retrieved data, partition queries, optimized SQL generation, and optimized commit processing to ensure multiuser concurrency. Enterprise Developer also features an active business model repository where programmers can create and store business rules in one central location. If a rule changes, Enterprise Developer automatically enforces it on both the client and the server. This product also offers a high degree of database support and connectivity.

Enterprise Developer provides a new architecture called SCALE that speeds application development in several ways. The SCALE architecture includes the SCALE business model repository, which centralizes data models, data locations, and business rules. The SCALE transaction processor automates the processing of client/server transactions and provides data links that optimize access to major database engines.

Borland, Gupta, and PowerSoft also make 4GL tools. The most recent addition to the 4GL lineup is Borland's Delphi. Anders Hejlsberg, who created the first Borland product—Turbo Pascal, also masterminded Delphi. Delphi is excellent technology; it is fast and has some great features, but the fact that it's based on the Pascal language is a failing that few programmers will be able to ignore. Though Pascal will probably always have some die-hard followers, the majority of programmers have already jumped ship in favor of C or C++.

Add-Ons to 4GL Tools

Momentum's XIPC product is an add-on for 4GLs that allows applications to communicate on a process-to-process level with application components built in C, C++, or other tools. These application components may reside on the same system as the application or across the network on any of the over 30 operating systems supported by XIPC, allowing highly scalable and portable three-tier or multi-tier applications to be developed. XIPC provides the full complement of interprocess communication (IPC) mechanisms normally provided by sophisticated multitasking operating systems, including message queues, shared memory, and semaphores (for process signaling).

SILVERRUN-Enterprise, by Computer Systems Advisors, is another great 4GL supplemental tool. It is an integrated business modeling workbench. Fully scalable from departmental to large corporate development teams, SILVERRUN-Enterprise is designed with a powerful, multiplatform common repository that is ODBC compliant and provides concurrent access for modeling teams. SILVERRUN-Enterprise enables customers to build, manage, and exploit an enterprise's entire portfolio of models, including business process, conceptual, logical, and physical data models; application packages; and even a model and metamodel of a corporate data warehouse.

Version Control Tools

Team tools, such as version control tools, are usually also add-ons. Intersolv makes PVCS, the world's best-selling version control software for use in a network environment. It keeps track of who on the team has what version and automatically keeps files on a build server up to date. I once managed a team of developers who used an old beer bottle as a version control device. Basically only one person was allowed to check files out of the build machine at a time. When someone had a file open and was working on it, they also had possession of the empty beer bottle. That worked, but only because the team was very small and everyone worked very closely together. Today, controlling the versions on a modern build server in that way is unheard of. Modern source code control software takes care of the job much more efficiently.

Testing Tools

One last area of development tools are those that automate testing. While automatic test tools will never replace good old-fashioned beta testers and Quality Assurance engineers banging on the code, they do go a long way to improving code quality, speeding the development and debugging cycle, and catching errors instantly that otherwise might have taken a human operator quite some time to come across. Segue Software makes one of the most popular automated testing programs in the industry—QA Partner. QA Partner supports parallel testing of GUI and client/server applications on multiple platforms and across client/server networks throughout the development cycle. It automatically captures information on your application, and it can record object-oriented scripts of the steps required to drive your application through its test cases. This goes a long way toward helping you create well-tested bug-free software.

Choose Your Tools Carefully

Once again the importance of choosing your tools wisely can't be underestimated. Keep up to date with the latest product releases so that you can be as prolific and productive as possible. Push yourself to evaluate new tools as they are released and new language features as they are defined. Don't be caught in a rut with five-year-old tools. Keep learning!

If you're stuck programming in FORTRAN or COBOL, be sure to master object-oriented C++. This language will give you more power and flexibility and will harness the new features of operating systems such as Windows 95.

Decide on your primary development system based on the quality of the integrated development environment and the tools that are integrated into it. Make sure the environment is dynamic, interactive, fast, and built for C++ development.

Be familiar with the best editors and class libraries. Master the ones that come with the development environment or buy stand-alone ones that are more specialized. Learn 4GL tools for rapid client/server application development. Use version control systems to coordinate your programming team and automated testing tools to save time and improve software quality.

Look ahead to the future. Stay on the cutting edge and continually be on the lookout for new tools as they are born. Each year some tools vendor makes a breakthrough and brings a tool to market that has the potential to change the way you work. Be ready for these new tools and the increased productivity they bring. Stay on the leading edge with vendors you can trust, and your career will evolve right along with your tools.

6 Hot Technologies for Programming Careers

The high-technology industry is evolving at an increasingly faster rate. Today, an avalanche of new technologies is pouring forth, and picking the right ones to focus on is key to programming success. Looking at the time line in Table 6-1, you can see that about 120 years elapsed from the invention of the first computer to the introduction of the vacuum-tubed IBM 701 in 1953, with the first stored program. Twenty-two years later, MITS shipped the first personal computer, the Altair 8800. I remember spending many enjoyable months as a kid assembling an Altair from a kit, then programming the computer by setting eight toggle switches, and then toggling a ninth switch to load a program—one byte at a time. Who would have believed that six years later, in 1981, when IBM introduced the IBM PC, an entire multibillion dollar industry would be born.

Today there are over 6 million programmers in the United States alone, and the number continues to grow. Each year the number of new software technology implementations compounds. So how do you select which field to specialize in today so your future career goals will be realized? Keeping up with all the new trends and predicting which ones will stick is enormously challenging. Sometimes promising technologies fail. For example, artificial intelligence was a hot field in the early 1980s, but it fizzled out without fulfilling its potential.

Year	Event
1833	The first analytical engine (and first rudimentary computer) is introduced by Charles Babbage.
1944	IBM and Harvard University complete work on the first Mark I relay-based computer.
1946	The electronic numerical integrator and computer (ENIAC), weighing 80 tons and spanning 100 feet, was created.
1953	IBM ships the vacuum-tubed 701 computer, with the first stored program.
1954	John Backus at IBM creates the FORTRAN language.
1959	COBOL is first defined as a computer language.
1968	Intel is founded by Gordon Moore and Robert Noyce.
1969	Nicklaus Wirth writes the first PASCAL compiler.
1973	The C language is invented at Bell Laboratories by Dennis Ritchie.
1974	Intel produces the 8080 8-bit microprocessor.
1975	MITS introduces the Altair personal computer, its name derived from a Star Trek episode.
1977	Apple Computer is founded and introduces the Apple II personal computer.
1981	IBM introduces its first personal computer.
1982	Sun Microsystems is founded.
1983	Symantec Corporation is founded.
1984	Apple introduces the Macintosh.
1988	The Open Software Foundation is formed by IBM, Digital Equipment Corporation, and Hewlett Packard.
1989	The first battery-powered laptop computers become fully functional, and Intel moves up to the first 80486-based microprocessor.
1990	Microsoft introduces Windows 3.0.
1991	IBM introduces OS/2 version 20 and ships 1 million units, the same year that Microsoft introduces Windows 3.1 and ships 10 million units.

Table 6-1 *History of Computing*

Year	Event
1993	Symantec ships Norton Utilities 7.0 and Microsoft ships Windows NT.
1994	The Internet is dubbed the "information superhighway" and has more than 20 million users.
1995	Microsoft introduces 32-bit Windows 95.

Table 6-1 *History of Computing* (continued)

Other technologies are slow to catch on, but then explode. Robotics technology was hyped early in the '80s but didn't catch on. Now it's making a quiet comeback in vertical market areas like medical robotics. The Year of the LAN was heralded throughout the '80s and early '90s, and strong growth in networking continues unabated. Today, one of the hottest areas is the Internet as organizations everywhere race to establish a presence on the information superhighway. Knowing what's hot and what's not is important if you want to maximize your opportunities to work in the high-growth areas of the future.

In this chapter, I'll predict the areas that will be hot throughout the next few years—the technologies that show the brightest promise for growth and innovation and that should provide excellent careers. In every case, these are technologies that not only solve problems for users today, but also lay a foundation for a pathway into the future.

Dilbert reprinted by permission of United Feature Syndicate, Inc.

Windows 95 Programming

The Windows 95 operating system from Microsoft creates one of the biggest job opportunities for programmers. Organizations everywhere are struggling to convert their applications to the Win32 API to take advantage of the benefits of Windows 95—its support for plug-and-play, drag-and-drop, multitasking, and long filenames, as well as its better network support and superior desktop metaphor. A recent *Computerworld* study showed that 83 percent of the corporate MIS audience that reads *Computerworld* is planning to upgrade at least some of their users to Windows 95 within 12 to 18 months of the new operating system's ship date.

Today, more than half of professional program development is performed using the C language rather than its object-oriented sibling, C++. However, the benefits of reusability, extensibility, and interchangeable components depend on object-oriented C++. Mastering Windows 95 and Windows NT programming is a huge undertaking, and one that can be made simpler by using the built-in functionality offered by the MFC application framework. MFC is one of the most productive and useful foundations for Windows programming today. The ability to program for Windows in MFC and C++ will continue to be a highly sought skill. Will the other systems—OS/2, the Macintosh operating system, and UNIX—disappear? Probably not, but the most common platform will be Windows.

Programmer's Perspective

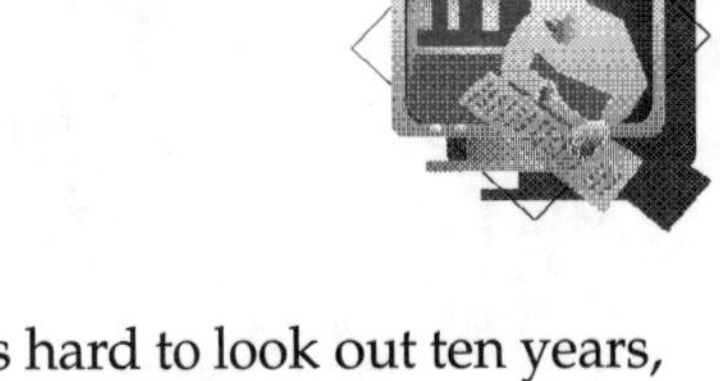

"It's hard to look out ten years, but certainly for right now the Windows architecture is going to continue to dominate. Expertise in MFC, Win95, and the Win32 API is important, and how to develop and architect programs for that environment is incredibly valuable. If I were a student one year from graduation, I would be immersing myself in understanding MFC and the WIN32 API and how to use it."

Gordon Eubanks
CEO, Symantec

Object-Oriented Programming

Object-oriented programming (OOP) is the new programming paradigm that is rapidly replacing structured programming as the way to build applications. The three cornerstones of OOP are encapsulation, inheritance, and polymorphism. Encapsulation involves combining methods and data to create objects with clear programming interfaces. Inheritance involves deriving objects from other objects, thereby reusing much of their functionality. Polymorphism allows different objects to respond to the same message in a manner appropriate to their type. OOP allows software to be created quickly and reliably and eases the task of software maintenance.

The popularity of OOP will continue to increase as the backlog of yet unwritten programs rises at large businesses and software houses. Today, applications are becoming larger and more complex. As the size and complexity of applications increases, so does the number of person-years required to complete a project. The result is that projects will be either stretched out over years and completed by the traditional small teams (impractical), or more programmers will be added to projects, along with the associated problems of coordination and integration. One of the few proven methodologies for handling this increase in complexity is object-oriented programming.

Most organizations that have moved toward object orientation have focused on application development technology. Object-oriented networking and database technologies are also beginning to spread. Making these three types of software solutions work together seamlessly and successfully depends on the ability of the vendors for each piece to adopt the same standards for structure and interoperability.

"Programmers with OOP expertise today are commanding a premium, with salaries typically 28 percent higher than average."

With organizations moving to both reduce their software backlog and adopt standards for interoperability within heterogeneous environments, OOP will become even more important to the computing infrastructure of the twenty-first century. Programmers with OOP expertise today are at a premium, commanding salaries typically 28 percent higher than average.

Multimedia Programming

Remember when your monitor displayed nothing but small block characters in green or amber on a black background? Back in the old user-hostile days, computers were popular only with programmers, scientists, and a few hardy souls who dared to venture into the land of bytes. All that has changed.

Today multimedia has come into its own, and the enigmatic C:\> prompt has given way to animation, sound, and new ways to interact with the computer. Multimedia combines audio, video, text, graphics, maps, telephony, connectivity, and other emerging forms of computer technology to achieve a user interaction with the computer that is much richer and more powerful than anything ever seen before. As expertise in this area grows, so will the sophistication of programs and the demand by users for more vivid personal experiences with their computer systems.

"I predict the demand for multimedia technology in business software will accelerate over the next few years, making multimedia programming a great career specialty."

Right now, multimedia is one of the few areas of computer industry growth being led by the consumer rather than the business market. For instance, fun products such as Delrina's Echo Lake allow home PC users to create digital photo albums in an easy-to-use multimedia authoring environment. But there is an emerging multimedia opportunity in business software. I predict the demand for multimedia technology in business software will accelerate over the next few years, making multimedia programming a great career specialty.

The interest in multimedia will likely shift to the business arena as business applications of various multimedia components become more mainstream. Market Vision recently projected the top-ten business applications of multimedia (see Figure 6-1). Training is a natural. Remote collaboration, information management, and telephony are also areas of expected high growth.

One of the hot developments coming very fast in multimedia is digital video. I asked Jerry Barber, Director of Technology Integration at Adobe Systems, to comment on this technology, since Adobe is expert in this area.

"Digital video gives you movies on your computer. Macintosh has a popular implementation called QuickTime with a well-designed architecture. Microsoft has a system called Video for Windows, which has a very simple design. It's

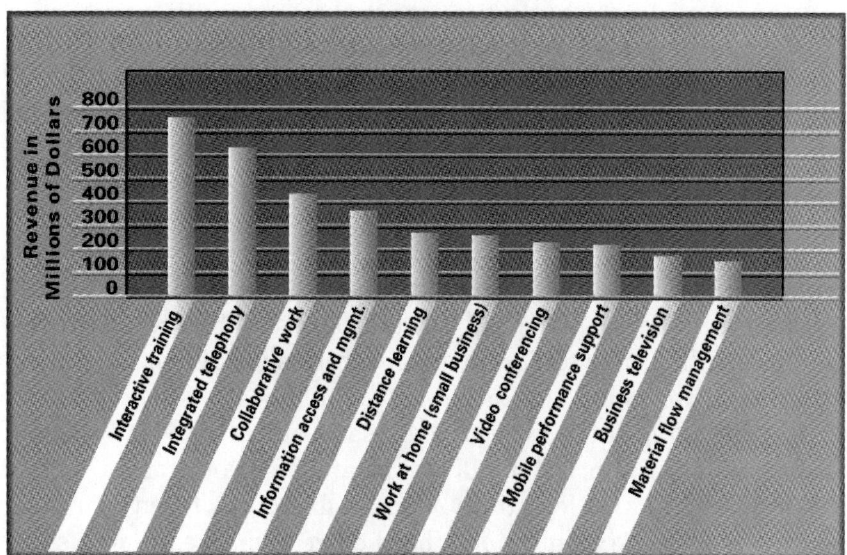

Figure 6-1 *Projected top-ten business applications of multimedia*

going to take time, but more and more people will be creating their own digital home movies. Right now the focus is on getting the performance of the machines up and the compression of the algorithms down to where a person can create full-screen video.

"As time goes on, handling time in graphics and in the computer is going to be a key skill because putting video on your computers is only a start. The direction you want to go is interactive video—being able to interact with the movies or the training session directly."

It's no secret that Microsoft is actively getting into interactive TV and multimedia applications, and for good reason. "Multimedia is going to be a hot thing in the next five years," says Jim McCarthy, Microsoft's Director of Programming Languages. "Anything that enables software to bond closer to humans is going to be a good bet. I would bet that multimedia with a special emphasis on virtual reality will be one of the strongest specialties that any programmer could go into at this time."

> **"As time goes on, handling time in graphics and in the computer is going to be a key skill because putting video on your computers is only a start."**
> **—Jerry Barber**

Multimedia technology is hot right now, and it will be hot throughout the '90s, as applications migrate from boring text-

> **"It's not too strange to imagine that in ten years time you may be a senior programmer in charge of 'world design.'"**
> **—Jim McCarthy**

based interfaces to more appealing interfaces with high-fidelity color graphics, digital video, animation, high-quality sound, a wide range of fonts, context-sensitiveenvironments, and eventually, support for speech recognition and vision. Within the next ten years, you will see some real breakthroughs in this area. Jim goes on to say, "Soon we will be able to design virtual worlds inside our computer, so having expertise in designing worlds will be a skill that's in real demand in about ten years. You should strive to be an impresario of worlds. Not only will it be good for your imagination, but it will also be great for your career." In the computer industry, ten years is a long time. After all, think back to ten years ago today. Network servers were 20-megabyte hard drives the size of large shoe boxes that could be partitioned into shareable volumes. Today, a 500-megabyte drive easily fits in a pocket and is so inexpensive that everyone has his or her own. As Jim says, "It's not too strange to imagine that in ten years time you may be a senior programmer in charge of 'world design.'"

Digital Cameras and Graphics

My daughter Gina's elementary school in Palo Alto, California, has installed a QuickCam digital video camera on each of its Macintosh computers. These cost only $85 each and can be used to take movies or digital photos. The kids really love having their pictures taken and being able to take home a hard copy to show their parents. It's nice when software can be used to make people happy. There will be a continued strong demand in the home for multimedia software driven by interest in new versions of best-selling games such as Myst and Doom and, in the future, by interest in interactive TV.

Digital photography and imaging will be among the linchpins of the whole multimedia explosion. Multimedia technology will be enabled by more sophisticated software delivery formats such as MPEG, with its superior compression and playback capabilities.

Programming for the Internet

Communications is an area of huge growth, and it will continue to be strong well into the future. The information superhighway is here, and it's creating career opportunities for programmers everywhere. As more and more companies reach out globally and the need for instant communication becomes more pressing, most corporations will realize that the kind of wide-range communications they require can only be provided electronically. Companies around the world will want to plug into the Internet and set up Web servers to promote their organizations, communicate with other companies and remote offices, and even sell their products.

Web content, although graphical and informative, lacks interactivity. "The key to the Web of the future is a high degree of interactivity," says Daniel Putterman, President of Maximum Information, Inc. "Interactivity means usability—and that's what is going to make electronic commerce on the net a reality."

Programmer's Perspective

"One of the important technologies near term, by the end of this year or next year, is color. What's driving it is the near-term availability of printers for the home that are basically photographic in quality yet are affordable (in the $500 range). Making digital versions of chemical photographs is getting less expensive, and digital cameras are going to start hitting the mainstream. But what people don't realize is that the ability to take a color image and print it with faithful skin color and so forth is very complicated. Anyone involved in graphics is going to have to understand color in a big way. The support for this is arriving in the operating system, with Color Synch 2 on the Macintosh and Image Color Management on Windows."

Jerry Barber
Director of Technology Integration,
Adobe Systems

Interactive Web development companies like Maximum Information are creating their technical resource pool from developers with UNIX programming experience. This is primarily due to the fact that the majority of Web servers are UNIX based. "It's hard to find the right programmers for interactive Web development," says Mr. Putterman. "Most of today's developers are focused on GUI development for Windows. In reality, Web programming means rolling up your sleeves and going back to the days of true cross-platform compatibility."

> **"The key to the Web of the future is a high degree of interactivity."**
> **—Daniel Putterman**

The multitude of UNIX platforms and the increasing number of Windows NT-based Web servers is creating a need for code that truly runs on multiple platforms. In essence, Web development is creating a new reason for developers to come out of the woodwork and display their talents.

Data Security

As commerce over the Internet matures, developing the fail-safe systems that guard the treasure chest and accurately execute transactions will be key. The Internet, which currently has more than 25 million addresses, will increasingly be used for intra-enterprise communications and transactions. But its lack of fail-safe security currently makes the Internet imperfect for important transactions involving money or valuable data. As the means for providing secure electronic transactions become available, organizations everywhere will move quickly to add this electronic channel to their distribution portfolios, creating many job opportunities for programmers who can implement fail-safe security systems.

Security in the information technology industry is the key to commerce over the Internet. Creating secure methods of transferring money (either through credit card information or through some other type of monetary unit exchange) is of paramount importance. Basic security systems must provide the following:

- The ability to authorize or deny access to users, usually at a point of granularity that allows distinctions among groups and individuals regarding rights such as read-write and read-only and that allows these rights to be applied to specified data and program objects
- A method of user authentication

- A method of transferring data securely from one physical location to another without risk of violation during the transfer

For the Internet to fulfill its promise of easy global commerce, the problem of making transactions safe must be addressed. However, the Internet is not the only area in which security is an issue. Virtually every local area network (LAN) has some type of security need, as do wide area networks (WANs), large organizations, schools, banks, and the government. The U.S. government, in fact, has helped fund technology development to provide secure information. Companies such as Rivest, Shamir, Adleman (RSA) have pioneered effective software algorithms for encryption, transmission, and authentication of users. There are great career opportunities for programmers specializing in the creation of corporate or commercial applications for communication over the Internet or other networks that are designed with security in mind and that implement new methods of user authorization and authentication.

Electronic Commerce

The Internet provides an exciting avenue for new growth in electronic commerce. In electronic commerce, businesses or individuals trade with each other by means of electronic communication and transaction processing. Electronic data interchange (EDI) describes routine information exchanges between computer-based processes. The most common partners in EDI are businesses and their customers. For example, generating a customer's purchasing system for transmission to a vendor's sales order-entry system is an application of EDI. Another example is a vendor's billing system that prepares invoices directly for a customer's accounts payable system.

EDI is prevalent in the transmission of messages throughout the business world through e-mail within corporations and across public-access data networks such as the Internet. Though e-mail is not usually considered in the electronic commerce mix, it is often associated with the arrangement of business transactions and in this way is important to electronic commerce. More frequently, however, EDI is associated with transaction processing and the completion of sales transactions. As the use of the Internet for commerce increases, so the need for secure and efficient programs for electronic commerce will increase. The Internet and electronic commerce and all that these imply will stimulate a huge need for programming implementations.

Digital money, or e-cash, is coming and will change the way people manage financial transactions. E-cash is money transferred across electronic networks instead of through the traditional banking system. Currently, e-cash comes in many different forms and is based on a variety of values—currency, gold, and so on. With e-cash, you simply "download" an amount of money to a personal computer and then send that "money" over the Internet to merchants who then send you whatever product you've ordered. The U.S. Commerce Department projects that by the year 2000, more than 1.6 billion dollars worth of commerce will be conducted with e-cash, and that this amount will rise to almost 3 billion dollars by the year 2005 (see Figure 6-2).

More traditional communications will also flourish as the old tried-and-true phone and cable companies rush to join the flood toward home banking, home shopping, interactive TV, and other technologies just on the horizon. Regional telephone holding companies and cable companies will most likely begin providing services such as local video service, local voice and data access outside their areas, and interexchange carrier services. These companies have the luxury of revenues from traditional voice and data services that they can use to fund their initial efforts on the information superhighway and in interactive television and other home-oriented electronic services. In addition, the transmission infrastructure is already in place.

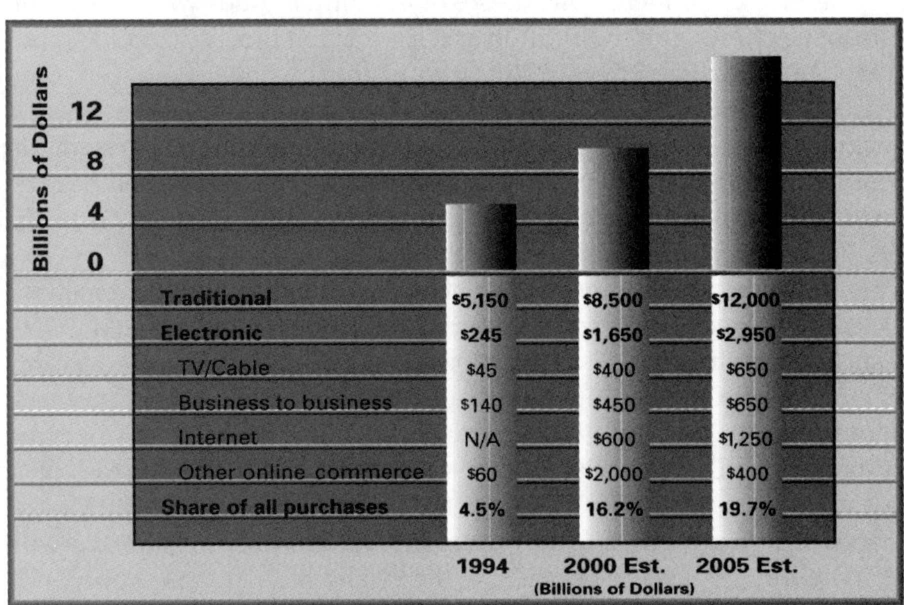

	1994	2000 Est.	2005 Est.
Traditional	$5,150	$8,500	$12,000
Electronic	$245	$1,650	$2,950
TV/Cable	$45	$400	$650
Business to business	$140	$450	$650
Internet	N/A	$600	$1,250
Other online commerce	$60	$2,000	$400
Share of all purchases	4.5%	16.2%	19.7%

Reprinted from the June 12, 1995 issue of Business Week by special permission ©1995 The McGraw-Hill Companies, Inc.

Figure 6-2 *Where e-cash will take off*

Networking

The Internet grew out of an Advanced Research Projects Agency (ARPA) project sponsored by the U.S. government and has since spread into the public and business sector. Local area networks (LANs), by contrast, arose in corporations around the world and grew into wide area networks (WANs) and finally into global networks. Now they form the cornerstone of the workaday world. The need for applications that can take advantage of network services, for applications that can be logically distributed around a network, and for network operating system software and utilities is tremendous, with no slowdown in sight.

Both proprietary and standards-based networks abound in the global corporate world. Ethernet, for example, developed at Xerox's Palo Alto Research Center, gained such tremendous popularity that in the 1980s the IEEE established a set of standards for LANs, with Ethernet being one of them, along with IBM's token ring network and 10-base twisted-pair networks. At about the same time, the International Standards Organization (ISO) instituted its seven-layer model to describe software communication in a LAN environment. Novell's NetWare, on the other hand, is a proprietary network operating system, but it is so popular that it also exists as a de facto standard.

"In the future, programmers with expertise in NetWare engineering and Windows NT networking will be in high demand."

In 1994 the LAN server market increased 28 percent in worldwide shipments and 27 percent in worldwide revenue. IDC predicts that the market for LAN servers will continue its phenomenal growth well into the future (Susan Frankle, IDC).

As of mid-1995, Novell, the leader in networking, had installed about 6 million NetWare nodes worldwide. Novell's vision is a "billion user network"—a vision likely to become fact sooner than most people think. LANs and WANs will crisscross the world and start penetrating third-world countries as they gear up technologically. The budgets for LANs continue to increase at virtually every major corporation, and so do jobs related to them. Meanwhile, Microsoft is mounting a serious challenge to LAN software vendors with Windows NT finally becoming a viable networking solution. In the future, programmers with expertise in NetWare engineering and Windows NT networking will be in high demand.

Expenditures for both hardware and software for wide area internetworking are increasing at an equally fast rate. The Gartner Group predicts that the number of Internet routers used in large corporations to connect LANs across long distances will increase 24 percent during the next three years. As a result, the number of WAN ports will grow, and the corporate network will become an internetwork of routers, hubs, and switches. Long-distance links will either be provided by public carriers or established as an extension of corporate LANs.

Although the much-heralded Year of the LAN didn't arrive with the bang that LAN vendors had hoped, now virtually every year is a Year of the LAN. This means lots of opportunities for programmers who are interested in and knowledgeable about creating network-aware applications, distributed applications, network utilities, transport optimizations, drivers, and so on.

"Excel in network programming or administration and you are sure to have no problem finding a job anywhere."

Symantec, for example, has developed the Norton Administrator for Networks, which allows network administrators to perform a variety of tasks across a network, such as installing software, inventorying hardware and software, and monitoring network use, from their own consoles. This product is an excellent example of an application that runs on heterogeneous networks and exists because of the huge proliferation of networks. Excel in network programming or administration, and you are sure to have no problem finding a job anywhere.

Mobile Computing and Wireless Communications

Today, laptop computers are the fastest growing part of the PC market. When mobile computing was first introduced, it was an instant hit with users such as salespeople who need to keep in touch with clients from the road. Salespeople can now transmit orders from the field in real time. They can print electronic copies of data sheets and leave them with clients. They can download demonstrations and pricing information. But salespeople are not the only ones who can use this technology. Today, mobile computing is in high demand by everyone.

In addition, LANs and WANs are offering tremendous career opportunities for programmers in a new area: networks without wires. According to the Gartner Group, although the use of wireless networks is moderate today, it will really start picking up steam over the next several years and will probably be an area where new jobs will start appearing. According to author S. MacAskill (*The Wireless LAN Market: A Snapshot*), annual growth rates of between 40 percent and 65 percent will be seen in 1996 and will continue through the end of the decade as the technology matures and applications are developed to take advantage of the growing personal digital assistant (PDA) market.

Although so far I have been disappointed with PDAs such as the Apple Newton, I believe that once PDAs really start enabling easy communication, such as allowing users to send faxes and e-mail from anywhere, the market will finally take off. When successful hardware technology arrives, so will software designed to exploit wireless remote communications.

The wireless LAN market includes hub-, internetworking- and radio-based devices for extending Ethernet and token ring LAN connectivity to remote users and locations via wireless links. Pen-based products as well as mobile and cellular digital packet data services are part of the overall wireless market, but not included in the LAN-based space.

Software developers will find the following types of applications in demand for wireless communications:

- Sales automation systems like ACT! that connect mobile salespeople to the corporate office
- Software that facilitates recovery from a catastrophic event, such as an earthquake or flood, which knocks out traditional communications
- Applications that help automate the connection of remote users to a LAN
- Applications that automatically pick up and send mail, data, graphics, and so on

The combination of mobile computing and wireless communications is compelling. Someday, tiny portable devices that support wireless communications will allow anyone to communicate inexpensively at any time from anywhere. Wireless communications is not a big field yet, but it is growing significantly every day and will probably be a hot technology well into the next century. The DataQuest chart in Figure 6-3 shows the projected increases in wireless communications. If you're interested in the growing market for wire-

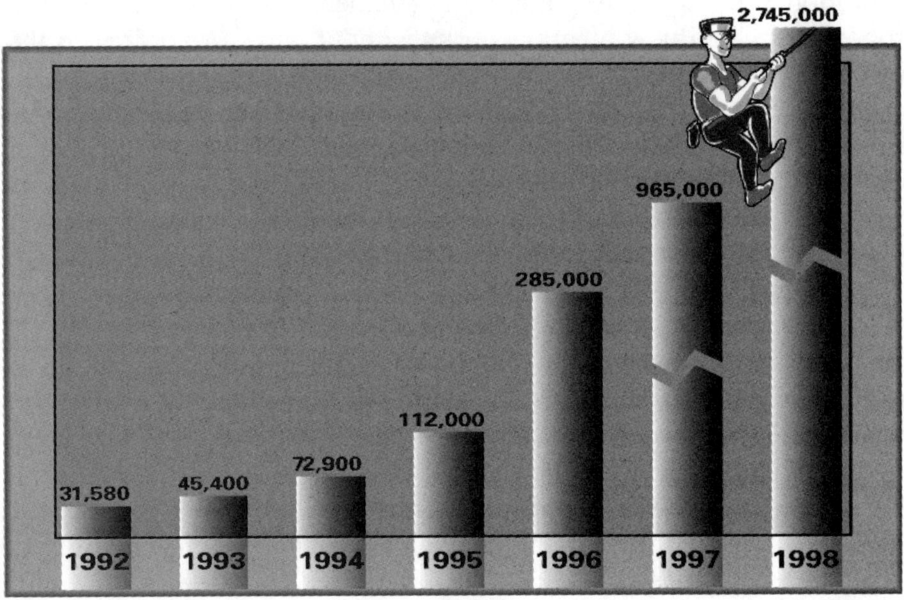

Figure 6-3 *Worldwide total wireless LANs*

less communications, check into some of the major innovators. Currently, these are Apple, AT&T/NCR, Motorola, Sony, General Magic, and Xircom.

Client-Server and Distributed Computing

The next logical step up from network-aware applications is distributed applications. Distributed applications divide computing tasks across multiple machines on a network to optimize overall network performance and efficiency. In the future, many more programmers will be employed to develop distributed applications that run across a network and communicate via a series of remote procedure calls (RPCs). This strategy is also called client-server computing and is one of the biggest growth areas for future employment.

The typical client-server application has the following three types of components:

- **Functional** The actual algorithms that perform operations on the data
- **User interface** The elements with which users interact
- **Data management** The storage of the information the application processes

Clients make requests of servers, and servers satisfy those requests. The user interface almost always runs on the client, and the data management component usually resides on the server. The actual functional logic that performs operations on the data may be located on yet a third system. This three-tiered client-server architecture will increasingly become the adopted approach for Fortune 1000 companies.

Client-server programming is one of the hottest career opportunities open to a broad base of corporate programmers. If you are currently supporting old legacy systems, you should learn all you can about client-server computing and head your career in that direction as quickly as possible.

Most of the client-server development tools on the market by their nature limit the scalability of the applications that can be generated. Applications that work well in test environments or with a limited number of users tend to fall apart when deployed throughout a large enterprise. New products, such as Symantec's Enterprise Developer, have lately arisen to solve these problems, and you can expect big advances in the client- server area in the very near future. Next-generation client-server development tools will combine the rapid application development (RAD) environment of today's popular 4GL tools with the performance and flexibility of C++. The best way to become indispensable in client-server programming is to spend the time necessary to thoroughly master client-server development tools.

"The best way to become indispensable in client-server programming is to spend the time to thoroughly master client-server development tools."

Many companies, such as PeopleSoft and Vantive, have focused on building prepackaged client-server applications that perform a particular function, such as human resources or customer information management, extremely well. This type of niche software also provides opportunities for building an interesting career.

Companies that focus on a vertical market and develop best-of-class client-server applications probably represent a great employment opportunity. Or perhaps you have the right idea for the next big killer client-server application and should start a company to build it.

7 Component Programming

Component programming represents a revolutionary change in the fundamental way we write programs. It's a new way of creating software, and it's a method you'll need to master if you want your programming skills to be in demand as our industry progresses. A solid knowledge of the theory and implementation of component programming is critical.

With component programming the benefits are significant:

- Complex or distributed applications can be broken into discrete parts, or *components*, and thus dealt with more easily by various teams of programmers.
- The components can then be reused or even sold as parts of different applications in the future.

Because of the ability to reuse components and thus to build on pieces of code that are proven and predictable, reliability is improved, interoperability between applications is enhanced, and applications overall are higher in quality. Component programming also reduces the development time of subsequent projects and allows easier implementation of a common look and feel across applications.

Object-Oriented Programming

The cornerstone of component programming is object-oriented programming (OOP). I've been a leading proponent of OOP for many years now, and nothing has altered my opinion about OOP and its impact on the future of programming. OOP is a change in the way applications are created, designed, and even conceptualized. The era of OOP is dawning, with every mainstream operating system vendor including Microsoft, Apple, Sun, and IBM now promoting OOP as the best way to interface to their operating system. OOP is a true paradigm shift that will impact this industry in the same way that the industrial revolution changed the nature of manufacturing. What we're emerging from now is an era in which application programs are all crafted from scratch and by hand.

Programmers of the past 20 years were like the master craftsmen of two hundred years ago. They made all the components of a program and made them to fit together into a whole. That's like a carpenter who builds a desk by planing all the panels and forging the iron handles and even the wood screws. That's the paradigm that we've been working under with procedural languages. But as OOP takes off, we will have reusable objects that can be purchased and simply plugged in or customized to fit virtually every need. With OOP the programmer is freed from the need to create every detail and instead can concentrate on what the application is going to do and what benefits it is going to provide to the user. Because of OOP we're going to see a tremendous flowering of creativity and productivity among programmers, just like we did in the 1800s, when the availability of standardized parts like wood screws gave birth to a virtual explosion of productivity and new inventions.

Not surprisingly, most of the industry leaders I interviewed for this book have strong feelings about this new revolution in programming and have spent lots of time thinking about all the strengths it offers, as well as potential obstacles it might create as it comes into its own. Gordon Eubanks, Symantec's president and CEO, hires hundreds of programmers and is very vocal on the subject of components. Of course, Gordon has lots of experience himself with designing efficient applications, and his early work with operating systems has led him to some interesting observations.

> **"One of the great advantages of object-oriented architectures is that they really make reusable components practical."**
> **—Gordon Eubanks**

"Building reusable components is something that has been recognized for 20 years as a logical thing to do," says Gordon. "People who construct buildings buy two-by-fours at the lumber yards and they don't go cutting down their own trees to make lumber. There are standard sizes to bricks as well as many other things. People have learned to use the standardization in these components effectively.

"Programming is a little more complex. While the concept of reusable pieces has been around for a long time, I think we've recognized that we haven't really had the technology to apply reusable pieces effectively. One of the great advantages of object-oriented architectures is that they make reusable components practical. The ability to use reusable components is extremely important in object-oriented architectures. For the last 20 or 30 years programmers started with subroutine libraries and then wrestled with how to reuse code. The problem becomes increasingly complex as more people try to use the same code applied to different problems. When you have both of those factors—more people and more different kinds of problems—code reuse becomes extremely difficult. And if you then try to put on top of that a requirement like cross-platform support, where the underlying environment the application runs on can vary, then code reuse becomes almost an impossible problem. But object-oriented technology makes this much more practical than did an architecture around procedure calls."

Gordon isn't the only one who sees the importance of object-oriented programming. Other industry leaders also see the huge potential for components today. Jerry Barber, from Adobe, explains the shift away from single applications that operate on their own to programs that need to interoperate both with other applications and with parts of themselves. Jerry sees OOP architectures as offering a great way to customize tomorrow's applications.

"With component programming you can have small groups working on the components, which takes less people and goes much faster. With no dependencies, what you can do is get a product to a certain state, ship it, and then a month or two later ship an additional component that gives it additional capabilities."

—Jerry Barber

"From the business model perspective, component programming allows you to customize the software even after it gets to the customer."
—Jerry Barber

"Component programming is going to be the fundamental structuring technique for future architectures," Jerry observes. "It involves building whole systems of components that give you the functionality of a monolithic program. Component programming is important from the perspective of the software developer because it gets away from these huge monolithic pieces of code where you have to have large numbers of people developing things and, therefore, a lot of dependencies among the group. With component programming you can have small groups working on the components, which takes less people and goes much faster. With no dependencies, you can get a product to a certain state, ship it, and then a month or two later ship an additional component that gives it additional capabilities. Without the concept of components, you just can't do that. You finish a program and the next time you can change its functionality is in the next major upgrade, which is 12 to 18 months later. Of course what that implies is that you've got the people in place who can break down the program into components and get the interfaces right."

"From the business model perspective, component programming allows you to customize the software even after it gets to the customer. And it allows the users to customize the product themselves, but I personally don't think that's going to happen very much. What will happen is that as the product moves through the distribution channel, the channel will add more functionality as it gets closer to the user. A good model is the automotive industry. You can buy all sorts of options when you buy a car, but very few people do that. What really happens is you go to a dealer and they have chosen a collection of options that fit their geographical area. I think software users are asking for solutions rather than features. Component programming allows the software industry to move to a solution-based approach. I think this will happen first in international distribution. As you get to a component-oriented approach, features specific to the Japanese market, for example, can be added by the distributor in Japan."

Jerry's vision of where component programming is going is highly significant. It changes not only the way we write programs, but also the way that users see programs and see their options. Adding on components to existing software is a powerful concept and one I'm sure will come to fruition.

And aside from the huge benefits of object and component technology, the complexity of systems and APIs make using components a necessity. With the backlog of programs today and the increasing need for more programs as well as more complex programs that can interact with each other, it is no longer possible to use the old methods.

> **"We're componentizing our products and implementing object-oriented programming practices."**
> **—Bruce Brereton**

The average programming backlog at large corporations is increasing every month. The Standish Group estimates that more than half of all software projects overrun their initial cost estimates, which costs U.S. companies over $59 billion annually. To understand the gravity of this situation, Bruce Brereton, who is in charge of software engineering within the Novell Business Applications division, offered the following example. "When we moved our WordPerfect word processing product from version 3.x to version 4.x, it took approximately 20 man years to develop. Moving to version 5.x took about 200 man years. If things continued along the same lines, it would have taken us many years to complete version 7 of WordPerfect. This is why we're componentizing our products and implementing object-oriented programming practices. We couldn't do without it!"

The WordPerfect product is just an example of what's going on everywhere applications are being built. Clearly we can't continue on the current track we're on. We *have* to move to a more efficient way of creating applications. We *have* to use components.

Of course, OOP is not a cure for all evils or a solution for all technical problems. It still requires great design and great implementation. Enrique Salem, who heads one of the wildly successful Peter Norton development teams at Symantec, puts this point in perspective. Enrique says, "for a class you are developing to be worth anything, it has to be what people call 'minimal and complete,' meaning the interface to that class has to have the right number of functions that a programmer needs to use and has to be complete, with all the services someone would expect. What all that implies is that someone has spent a lot of up-front time thinking about what the class or the object is going to require and, because of that up-front planning, has taken into account more of the things people are going to need and in turn has made it more reusable."

Happily, today we have some powerful component programming solutions and emerging OOP standards like Microsoft Foundation Classes (MFC), Open-

Doc, the Object Linking and Embedding standard (OLE2) from Microsoft, and the Object Management Group's Common Object Request Broker Architecture (CORBA).

Microsoft Foundation Classes (MFC)

Microsoft Foundation Classes (MFC) is the de facto standard for writing Windows applications. Microsoft sometimes refers to MFC as "the C++ API for Windows." MFC has become a popular tool for creating Windows applications because it is extensive, efficient, and has a low program overhead. MFC was developed by Microsoft as an open standard for Windows user interfaces and is licensed by several vendors, including Symantec, that supply C++ development tools.

MFC is an object-oriented application framework that you can use as a foundation for your application. In fact, if you use MFC you can write a fully functional application by adding just a few lines. That will give you a pretty rudimentary application, but it provides a great starting point. And MFC applications can automatically be generated using code-generation tools such as Microsoft's AppWizard and Symantec's AppExpress. This further saves coding time and guarantees the generation of bug-free code.

The MFC framework offers a considerable leg up when building Windows 95, Windows NT, or Windows 3.1 applications. Following are the main categories of classes into which MFC is divided:

- Root Classes
- Application Architecture Classes
    - Application Classes
    - Command-Related Classes
    - Document/View Classes
    - Threading Base Classes
- Visual Object Classes
    - Window Classes
    - View Classes
    - Dialog Classes
    - Property Sheet Classes
    - Control Classes
    - Menu Classes

  - Device-Context Classes
  - Drawing Object Classes

- General-Purpose Classes
  - File Classes
  - Diagnostics
  - Exceptions
  - Collections
  - Template Collections
  - Miscellaneous Support Classes

- OLE 2 Classes
  - OLE Base Classes
  - OLE Visual Editing Container Classes
  - OLE Visual Editing Server Classes
  - OLE Data Transfer Classes
  - OLE Dialog Box Classes
  - Miscellaneous OLE Classes

- Database Classes

- Macros and Globals

Even though MFC provides substantial functionality, most of its implementation represents only a thin layer on top of the Windows API. I talked to Mansour Safai, General Manager of Symantec's development tools division, about the advantages of this approach. "MFC was designed to add very little overhead to your application. Overhead has been a weakness in other class libraries to date. Another advantage of MFC is that its similarity to the Windows API makes it very appealing to C programmers. If you want to take advantage of the latest system technologies in the Microsoft operating systems, MFC is the way to go."

Object Linking and Embedding (OLE)

Object Linking and Embedding (OLE) from Microsoft started as a simple concept to support documents that contain or reference other documents. OLE has now evolved into a base component of Microsoft's Windows 95 and Windows NT operating systems and has emerged as an industry standard for application integration. OLE facilitates application integration by defining a set of standard interfaces, groupings of semantically related functions through which one application accesses the services of another. The way OLE exposes functionality through interfaces makes it an open, extensible system. It is open in the sense that anyone can provide an implementation of a defined interface and anyone can develop an application that uses it. It is extensible because new or extended interfaces can be defined and integrated into existing applications without requiring changes to existing code.

OLE has improved over time in both performance and reliability. For example, while OLE1, the first version of OLE, did provide for updating the objects contained within the container document whenever the linked object was updated in its original application, this mechanism was less than robust and would fail if the original file was moved. Also, OLE1 didn't allow the user to make changes to the embedded object without first leaving the container document and its application and then opening the application that originally created the object.

With OLE2 the linking aspect was improved so that links do not break when files are moved. This is accomplished by means of a *moniker*. A moniker allows tracking of objects and nested objects, as well as storage-independent links. *In-place activation* was also introduced in OLE2. With in-place activation, whenever you want to make a change in the contained object, you simply double-click on it and the entire tool set of the application that created the object is laid over the frame of the application that you're currently working in. Thus you can make your change quickly and easily.

OLE2 also added the powerful notion of OLE Automation. Using OLE Automation an application can expose an interface to internal objects. The application can then be driven by another application or a scripting language such as Microsoft Visual Basic or Symantec Basic. This allows applications to be totally customizable in the field, implementing functionality never thought of by the original programmers.

You can easily see why OLE2 is popular with users. It gives them a lot more flexibility and is a lot easier to use than OLE1. For programmers, however, OLE2 means more work and more learning. OLE's future success is being driven by the vast number of vendors who are eagerly rushing to adopt the OLE standard and architecture.

"OLE is a complicated technology from Microsoft, and programming it in C can be a nightmare," said Mansour Safai. "The good news is that OLE's functionality has been encapsulated inside MFC. Now, providing the capability of in-place activation in your application is as simple as setting a check box in AppExpress."

"OCX's are going to revolutionize software programming as far as speed of development and overall quality of the application."
—Mansour Safai

The emergence of OLE custom controls (OCX) is one of the most exciting aspects of OLE. OCX allows you to encapsulate a component and standardize its external interface in a language-independent fashion. This means that applications can be built out of previously developed standard components using a variety of tools. While a similar functionality existed in Visual Basic Controls (VBXs), OCXs offer superior support for both 16- and 32-bit operating systems. "Software programming is becoming more and more similar to electronic design, where engineers can simply open an electronic component handbook and pick the parts they want to use," said Mansour. "OCX's are going to revolutionize software programming as far as speed of development and overall quality of the application."

OLE fits into Microsoft's Common Object Model (COM). Enrique Salem is quite excited about the benefits that component programming through COM delivers, because he can now use commonly available building blocks to boost the productivity of his team—something that's critical in the commercial software business.

"The whole Component Object Model (COM) is the way of the future," says Enrique. "If I can use a spreadsheet like Excel or 123 that's already on the market to manipulate numbers instead of having to create one, then that's what I want to do. If I want a paint program, let me use something from Corel or the guys who do Designer. I'm not going to recreate it."

"The idea is similar to reusable classes," Enrique goes on. "The idea of COM is that there's a specific way for an external program to ask you for your interface. That's what COM talks about. I can actually say, 'I want to interact with you, how do I do that?' COM is just a defined way of doing it. With reusable classes a programmer can say, 'Here's my interface. Here's how I'm going to hide my data. Here are the functions to access it.' Using a class is a better way of packaging code

"The whole Component Object Model (COM) is the way of the future. If I can use a spreadsheet like Excel or 123 to manipulate numbers instead of having to create one, then that's what I want to do."
—Enrique Salem

because it gives the author of that class more control over the way people look at the data. OLE and COM use many of the same techniques and they also give you a defined interface for finding out 'how do I access your data?'"

OpenDoc

Apple, Borland, IBM, and Novell have formed a standard for document exchange and creation, called OpenDoc, that competes with OLE. Though not as popular as OLE, OpenDoc offers broader cross-platform support, including Macintosh, Windows, UNIX, and OS/2. OpenDoc is based on IBM's System Object Model (SOM), an object-oriented interface that provides cross-language support.

OpenDoc enables distributed cross-platform components to be created with source code that is freely available without licensing requirements. It changes the way we think of documents. Traditionally, a document has been created as one monolithic structure tied to an application that users must use for editing, viewing, and so on. OpenDoc documents are instead created of smaller components, such as text components, which contain characters; graphic components, which contain lines and drawings; and video components, which contain digitized video, etc. A component carries with it the ability to edit itself, and thus components can be easily "mixed and matched" to fit a particular need. This is similar in end result for users of OLE2, but the structure of the technology is different.

OpenDoc's cross-platform compatibility, along with the fact that it is embraced by several standards organizations, including CI Labs and the Object Management Group, makes it attractive to many people.

It used to be that OLE and OpenDoc were "religious" in that people would be staunch believers in one technology and not the other. However, it now looks more like they too will both exist well into the future and that they will probably coexist quite nicely.

OpenDoc Services

OpenDoc consists of a series of services:

- A compound document service that manages display and user-interface aspects to create a unified document model that supports multiple data types

- Component services that support the integration of components into documents and applications
- Storage services that allow OpenDoc technology to store and exchange compound documents and media
- Management services that provide a dynamic linking mechanism based on the CORBA-compliant SOM standard
- Automation services that support scripting
- Interoperability services that allow interoperability with other technologies, including OLE2

Common Object Request Broker Architecture (CORBA)

Imagine what would have happened if we had come up with the idea of using components for building houses but never figured out how to create those components in a standardized way. What if you couldn't be sure that a bolt from one vendor would fit into a nut from another vendor? It would be chaos.

"CORBA 2.0 provides interoperability among ORBs as well as language independence and network independence."

Obviously, in order for components to be useful in a broad sense, they need to be standardized so that you can be sure they'll work together. This is where the Object Management Group (OMG) comes in. OMG was formed out of a consortium of leading software, hardware, and end-user organizations to define and promote standards for object interoperability. I am currently serving on the OMG board of directors and am happy to be a part of this important effort.

The OMG has recently agreed on version 2.0 of the Common Object Request Broker Architecture (CORBA), which defines the makeup of messages passed between objects, known as object request brokers (ORBs). CORBA 2.0 provides interoperability among ORBs, as well as language and network independence. This is a product of one of OMG's main missions, namely to create a standard for developers to follow that allows an application to delegate the responsibility for executing computations to other computers that return them contained in an "object." Thus objects become a type of Remote Procedure Call (RPC) with data contained in them. Vendors can implement CORBA-compliant object solutions on their network of choice, including TCP/IP and NetWare, and be assured that they will be able to interoperate.

The OMG has had a very important influence on the industry. Serving as a focal point, it brings the new technologies and the vendors that create them together, allowing for contact and discussion to further the goals of interoperability. In addition to CORBA, OMG has been involved in Microsoft's Object Linking and Embedding (OLE) standard, as well as OpenDoc, espoused by Apple and IBM, and IBM's System Object Model technology. When IBM created the SOM object standard, it made sure that SOM was CORBA compliant.

System Object Model (SOM)

IBM's System Object Model (SOM) is a CORBA-compliant object that was created to solve several problems. The first problem is that objects usually are tied to the languages that were used to create them. A C++ object cannot easily be used with a different language, and neither can a SmallTalk object, an Actor object, and so on. Language independence is required for truly reusable "mass production" objects, and that independence isn't supported by most of today's methodologies.

Another problem is the fact that many objects are not truly discrete. Often implementation details are unavoidably compiled into the programs that use class libraries, resulting in tight "bindings" between the class library and the application in which it is used. Applications must often be recompiled any time a change is made in the class library. This problem is particularly acute when the class in question is in the form of a Dynamic Link Library (DLL). If a base class in a DLL is changed, it is necessary to recompile the entire application that uses it. This is an expensive process for producers of commercial applications; and even for in-house development teams, recompilation and redistribution of an application is burdensome.

A third problem is that no binary standard for C++ objects exists, so class libraries created by one vendor often cannot be used with tools from another vendor.

SOM, and its distributed version DSOM, address these problems. First, SOM is language neutral. This is due to the fact that SOM interactions are based on standard procedure calls. In addition, SOM preserves a large degree of language independence by supporting multiple method resolution devices and by providing bindings that can vary widely from language to language. Language independence is a goal that few technologies have aimed for prior to SOM, and one that SOM has largely achieved.

SOM also addresses the problem of the requirement for recompilation of applications whenever modifications to an integrated class library are desired. Because SOM accommodates changes in implementation details, recompilation of applications using particular class libraries is not required when changes are made to those libraries.

SOM is fully CORBA compliant, and of course, through the promotion of an industry-wide standard for binary objects, SOM also addresses the problem of vendor interoperability.

The Future of Component Programming

As you can see from the above, there are still several standards out there vying to become the one that everyone uses for components. There are also still a lot of existing applications that were created with a procedural structure and more that are continuing to be created in that way because of the constrictions of language usage or even managerial disinclination to change. While we at Symantec have begun to create and use several different components across applications, true component programming is still something we're striving for and haven't quite yet reached.

While we still have a way to go, the future of programming is, in my opinion, component programming. Components are undergoing a lot of change today and will be rapidly adopted as they mature through the rest of the decade. Figure 7-1 shows META Group's prediction for how component software eventually will evolve. It starts at the operating system level, and eventually the use of components branches out to include virtually all types of software.

The Pasta Theory of Programming

To end this chapter, I would like to introduce a theory that I read while surfing the Internet. A fellow by the name of Ruby from SoftTeach was describing the "pasta" theory of programming. It goes like this: as developers, we all know of the trials and tribulations of "spaghetti" code. Spaghetti code (see Figure 7-2)

Programmer's Perspective

"I think that components are something that get a lot of talk and components are one of those things that a reasonable person who is experienced in computer science can understand. It's so logical and makes so much sense, and it seems on the surface to be a very easy problem, but in fact the problem with reusable components is sort of like getting to the end of a rainbow. It's very difficult because every time you make a step forward you uncover a whole new set of issues with real reusable components. I don't believe that the world will immediately change into one where people are buying objects and just plugging them together. It's much more complex than people realize.

One of the most important issues in reusable components is getting the component granularity right. This is a tough problem. Another issue is with versions. This is where different applications need slightly different versions of the same component to run correctly. In the end, there isn't a version that works with everything. That's another hard problem, but one that you quickly run into.

I think if you look in terms of ten years, we've made real progress. If you try to look in terms of one year or two years, we're still learning. It's like chess. It takes an hour to learn chess but a lifetime to get good at it. Reusable components are very complex and subtle. And we're not there yet."

Gordon Eubanks
President and CEO, Symantec

is horrendous; nobody likes to debug a spaghetti code application, because it is poorly organized and because trying to understand and unravel the interdependencies within your application can be a nightmare.

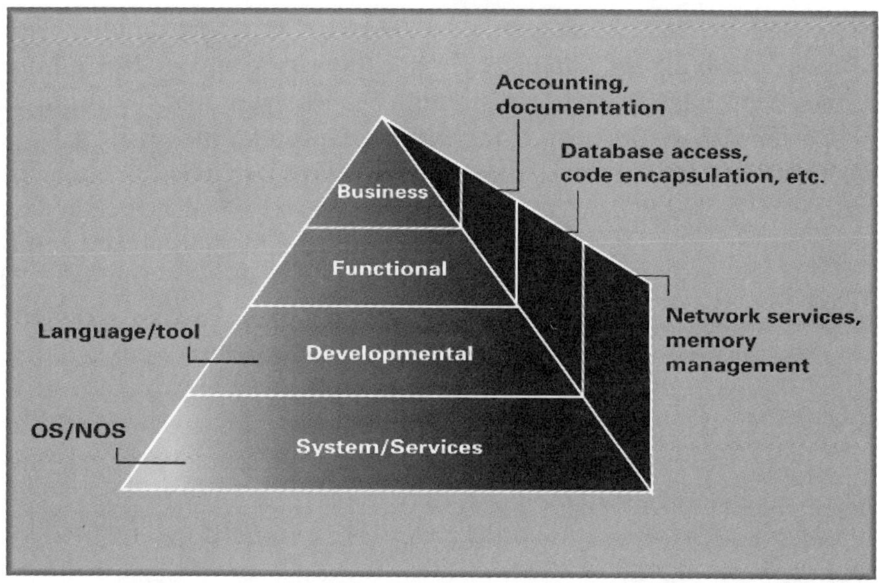

Source: The META Group

Figure 7-1 *Component software hierarchy/evolution of services*

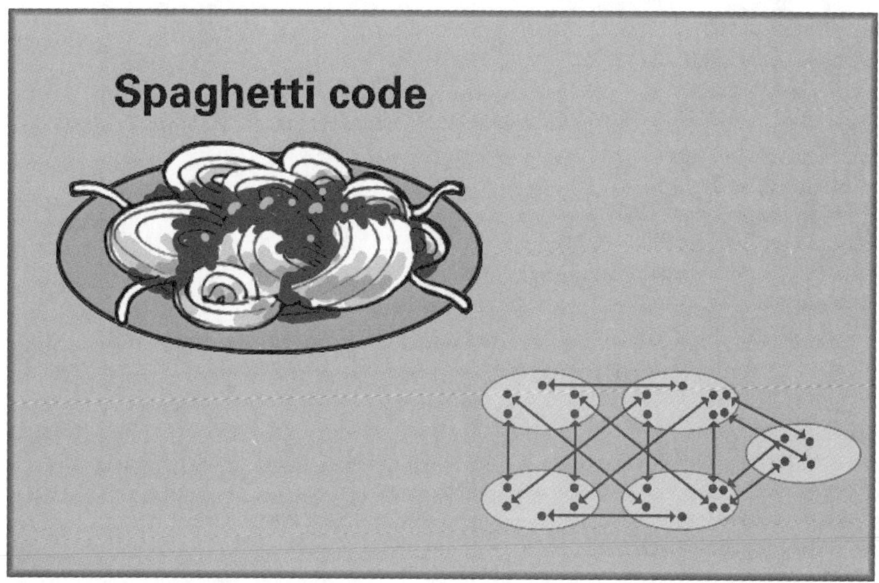

Figure 7-2 *Spaghetti architecture*

Some pioneering spirits invented a new approach to programming called "lasagna" code, which is better than spaghetti code. Lasagna code (see Figure 7-3) is organized in layers so that the interdependencies within your application are better specified, more organized, and better architected. Maintaining lasagne code applications is a far simpler task, but of course lasagna code has a big weakness: it is inflexible in that you tend to inherit a whole mass of code that you may not want or need. So your application becomes larger and more difficult to evolve as you add new functionality.

That is why great programmers have invented the right approach—"ravioli" code! Ravioli code (see Figure 7-4) is programming using a components-based architecture, meaning you use only what you need. It is organized so that self-contained objects include all of the good things they need directly in themselves. Unnecessary dependencies between the different layers are eliminated. Your application gets all the benefits of the layering architecture introduced by lasagna code without inheriting all of the overhead necessitated by that type of approach.

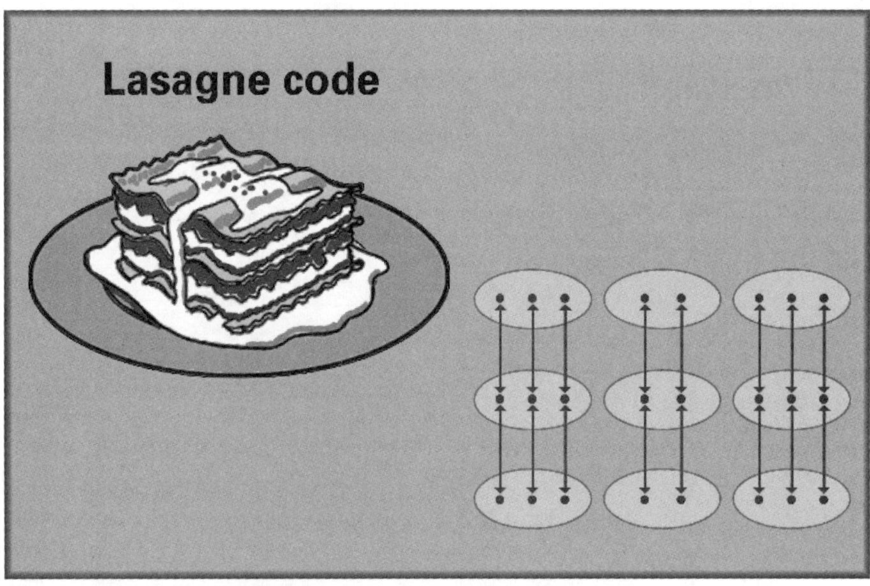

Figure 7-3 *Lasagna architecture*

Figure 7-4 *Ravioli architecture*

Great programmers know that what the world really needs is more ravioli code, because it creates better architectures for better applications.

Optimizing the Software Lifecycle 8

Developing great software is an art and a science. Most people would agree that shipping high-quality software on time is a good thing; the challenging question has always been how to do it. Why is it that some software projects that are staffed with great programmers, backed by lots of resources, and committed to a realistic schedule nevertheless end in failure? Although there is usually more than one factor, typically the root of the problem is a breakdown in the development process. The efficiency of the software development process can make or break any project—and along with it, the development team.

One of the best strategies for ensuring software success is to adopt an optimized software development lifecycle. This lifecycle consists of well-defined phases that each software project proceeds through, with concrete and measurable milestones throughout the entire cycle. At Symantec, because we live and die by the software we create, we've adopted a product lifecycle to manage our software projects to success (see Figure 8-1). This lifecycle can be applied equally well in a corporate setting. The eight phases of the Symantec software lifecycle are concept, proposal, definition, build, test, master, ship, and maintain.

Successfully adopting a standard software lifecycle has many benefits for the development team, the whole organization, and you. Here are just a few examples:

- The team members develop a common understanding of the project status and terminology. For example, arriving at the beta milestone has more meaning when everyone in engineering and quality assurance agree that this point has been reached, and the precise definition of "beta" is well understood.
- The software ship date is more predictable because the schedule is re-planned at each milestone. Other groups in the organization that set their schedules based on the software release date can make more accurate projections.
- Product teams have higher morale when they successfully deliver software on time.
- Each participant feels a sense of accomplishment when a product ships and is well received. Being part of a successful project is great for each member's résumé and career development.

The adoption of a software lifecycle process not only improves predictability but software quality as well. By "high-quality software" I don't just mean software with very few bugs—I mean reliable software with high value to the user. High-quality software helps users get their jobs done efficiently and

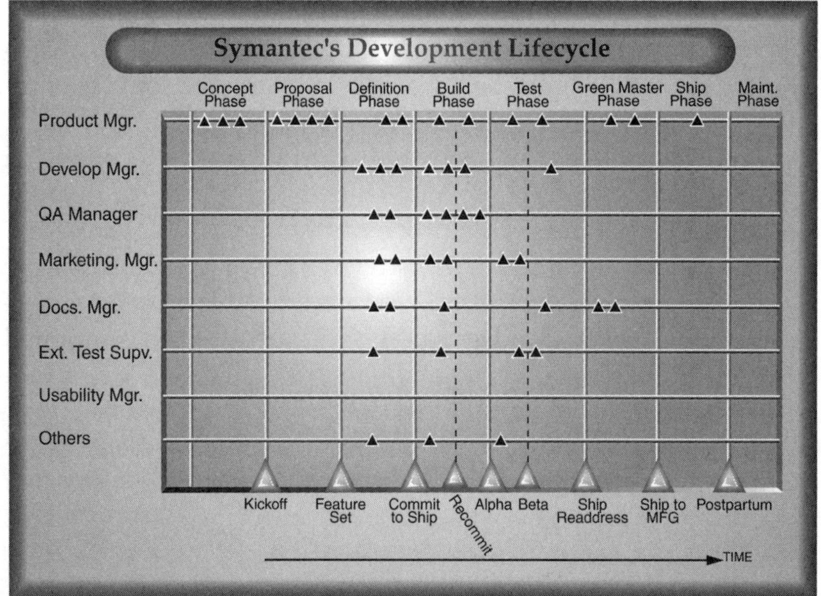

Figure 8-1 *The eight phases and nine checkpoints of Symantec's software development lifecycle*

intuitively. All too often in software development, every programmer is working hard, but the software that is produced in the end fails to satisfy the user. It fails the quality test because what the user needs to accomplish was not clearly understood by everyone on the project team or focused on through every phase of the development cycle. This lack of understanding results in incoherent development, where everyone is hard at work on little pieces of the application instead of concentrating effort on the high-value items that translate into quality software for the end user. What is needed is a model of coherent development, where the team focuses its attention on the most important features and functions to produce software of high quality to the end user.

Building quality into software requires a comprehensive planning phase early in the lifecycle of the product followed by a focus on fulfilling the key user requirements in all the subsequent phases—from designing the program to creating a solid product specification to actually coding the program to assuring quality and so on. No phase in the development cycle can be safely skipped or neglected. Each is important. The remainder of this chapter explores each phase of the software lifecycle, describing the objectives and deliverables of the various phases.

Concept Phase

Whether it's commercial software or internal corporate applications, embedded systems or low-level communications drivers, all software has exactly the same purpose: to fill a user's needs. The better you can identify and specify the needs of your users before you start a project, the more effective and desirable your software will be. During the concept phase you need to pinpoint the user's problems that you're trying to solve and determine the best way to meet the user's needs.

There are many ways to approach understanding your user. The following list presents some of the most popular methods.

Tools for Understanding Your User

- Rapid prototyping
- Customer or user interviews
- Written or phone surveys
- Focus groups
- User needs analysis
- Quality function deployment
- Advisory councils
- Competitive analysis
- Analyst's reports

User research that identifies needs can range from formal exercises to simply talking with end users informally. In a corporate setting, user needs are sometimes stated via internal memos, MIS requests, and similar reports. In the corporate world, software analysts typically are responsible for this critical task. In the world of shrink-wrapped software, product managers perform this job.

Focus groups are small groups of carefully screened users who are asked to discuss their needs with a moderator in a group setting. Typically, 10 or 12 users are gathered in specially designed rooms that have one-way glass so the development team can watch the group's reactions without influencing them. A usability engineer leads the users through typical usage scenarios. Learning how to conduct usability testing will be a widely sought skill as organizations realize the importance of implementing intuitive user interfaces in their software.

Focus groups are valuable for getting a general picture of users' perceptions of their needs and the applications available to solve those needs. Often you can get a good idea of what users are concerned with and how they view their options. Sometimes you can get unexpected insight into user problems that hadn't occurred to you before. Focus groups are also useful for trying out ideas to see how they may be received. Focus groups are great for stimulating ideas and for gaining insight into how your users think. However, they are seldom large enough to be statistically significant, and so drawing hard conclusions from focus groups alone isn't valid.

Focus groups are a tool of *qualitative* market research. To get data that is statistically significant, you need to perform *quantitative* research. Surveys can provide quantitative answers to questions regarding user needs and attitudes. Often they're used to validate ideas developed in focus groups or to ascertain trends important to your development efforts. Phone and written surveys are the most common survey types. At Symantec, we also use trade publications to assess popular opinion, we talk to end users at trade shows, and we do an in-depth analysis to understand what the competition is doing.

Rapid prototyping is a useful technique for refining your software design and validating your user interface directly with users before committing to months of coding. Using tools such as Visual Basic, you can quickly construct screens that approximate the look and feel of the final application. Then you can see what users think of the interface and gain valuable insights. If you have artistic talent, you may want to consider rapid prototyping as a specialization. This will be an increasingly important programming task in the future.

Quality function deployment is a system for analyzing customer needs and developing plans to improve customer satisfaction. Quality function deployment was pioneered in Japan in the automotive industry and provided a competitive advantage for those companies that adopted it. Today, many software companies are looking at QFD as a methodology for improving management systems to more efficiently deliver high-quality software. QFD helps organizations improve communication between customers and the programming team by using well-tested tools and techniques.

Getting inside your user's skin and viewing problems from his or her point of view is critical, but it's not the only way to figure out how to create the optimal solution.

Imagine how successful your program would be if it not only answered the stated needs of the end user, but did it with breakthrough technology. This

Programmer's Perspective

CCC is a large corporation in the Midwest that develops software to provide accurate estimates for automobile repair. Githesh Ramamurthy's group provides sophisticated CD-ROM–based collision-estimating software. Githesh's division employs about 150 programmers.

Since Githesh's applications need to address a host of issues, I asked him how he went about identifying the needs of his users.

"We've probably been through about 40 different software projects in the last 15 years, and I can only remember one or two of them not being successful. Many of them generated hundreds of millions of dollars in revenue.

"If I look at the pattern, it comes down to a very basic formula: truly understand what your users' needs are. This sounds simple and everyone pays lip service to it, but not very many people do it. For instance, if a farmer in 1902 wants a more productive farm, what do you do to address his need? If you ask the farmer, he's going to say that he needs a horse that eats half as much, that goes twice as far, and that doesn't need to sleep. He's not going to tell you he needs a tractor because he hasn't heard of the technology. He doesn't know he needs it. If you implemented his stated requirements exactly, you would have to take the path of genetically engineering horses rather than creating a tractor. So therein lies understanding user needs.

"What we do is tear apart the problem at the front end. What is the business problem? What is the user trying to do? What are his issues? What are the challenges he's facing? We tear it down into lots of detail, and then we typically spend a lot of time on the problem, and we do design walkthroughs, code walkthroughs—we do a lot of walkthroughs. They're a pain, they're frustrating, but they pay off in the end."

Githesh Ramamurthy
President, Product Development Division, and Chief Technology Officer, CCC

brings up an important point: Often users don't actually know what would best solve their problems. You can find out what their problems are, and you can find out what they think would solve them, but it's up to the programmer or project manager to actually come up with the solution.

There are many ways to identify user requirements. Once you're convinced you know your user well enough to understand his or her problems and attitudes, then you need to plan your software application to provide the solution.

Proposal Phase

Once the user needs have been identified, the next step is for the team leader or project manager to meet with the programming team to generate a proposal that outlines the scope of the project and resources required. A good deal of brainstorming usually transpires regarding how to provide the best end-user solution. This is where creativity plays an important role. Consider the story that Githesh mentioned earlier about the farmer. This anecdote points out that you can't simply assume that what users think they need is what they do need. Sometimes it takes a radical new approach to solve a chronic problem. If you and your team are lucky enough to have a project that gives you the opportunity to break new ground and create a new and more effective solution to an existing problem, then you will be well on your way toward a fat and happy retirement.

There are a few questions that you should answer about each project that will help you define the application and the development effort required to produce it. Answering these questions in a group will help all team members gain a common vision and provide further insight into the project and the effort it will require.

Common Questions for a Development Project

- Who are the users for the software and what are they trying to do?
- How much time and budget do we have?
- What expertise do we need and what resources do we have? Do we need additional resources?
- What platforms will this application support?
- With what systems does the application need to integrate?
- What existing components can we reuse for this development effort?
- Will the application be translated into different languages? What other localization issues (such as 2-byte character support) are there?
- Will this application be network aware? If so, should components of the application be distributed across the network?
- How will we test the application?
- What are the documentation and online help requirements for this project?

Once you have a clear picture of what you're trying to accomplish and how you're going to meet each requirement, you need to create an overall project plan with clear insight into the nature of the project, the resources it will require, and how long it's going to take. At this point, it's wise to be conservative in estimating how much your team can accomplish within a given time frame. Remember Walter Bright's advice to "underpromise and overdeliver." However, time is also a resource, and not a limitless one. If you're working in a commercial software company, the time you have to bring your product to market is limited by market trends and by your competitors. A commercial application released a year after competitors have already solved the users' problem is going to be at a severe disadvantage. If you're creating software for internal use in a corporate setting, you have the time constraints imposed by the needs of the corporation. In almost every case, when you consider the overall project plan, you're going to have to make some trade-offs in features and functionality versus time for completion.

Coming up with the right proposal that balances the needs of the user, the capabilities of the team, and the time for completion is one of the toughest challenges in software development. Everyone wants to make the best possible software. The goal is to propose the right initial design for the software that provides the highest quality and greatest value to the user within the framework of the time and resources available.

The final step in the proposal phase is to get your project plan approved by management with realistic and achievable expectations for the development team. In this step, it's important to perform a cost-benefit analysis in advance. Management always wants to know where costs can be reduced without affecting quality or time to market. Knowing where these areas are in advance will make this step proceed more smoothly. In addition, the total cost of the project must be justified by clear organizational benefits. If all goes well, your project will be approved. However, it's much better for projects to be canceled at this early stage rather than down the road after lots of money and effort have been expended.

Definition Phase

Once the project is initialized and the software team has been assembled, it's time to clearly define the road ahead. This phase is sometimes called the "fuzzy front end," and if you are not careful, a lot of time can be wasted trying to determine the scope of the project and the time and resources required. Guidance on how to best design your software is beyond the scope of this book. However, Albert Einstein has some very relevant advice: to "keep it as simple as possible, but no simpler."

In the definition phase, the end-user needs must be prioritized and transformed first into architecture and design specifications and then into functional specifications. Everyone has a different wish list for the software feature set, so synthesizing all the input and clarifying the fuzzy front end can be a tremendous challenge. However, selecting the right design point, choosing the best architecture, writing comprehensive functional specifications, and developing a clear and shared vision of the software project across the entire development team are critical to successful software development. The definition phase should focus on producing these deliverables as cleanly as possible.

"Usability engineering is an interesting specialty that can offer a great software career path."

Ideally, usability testing should be performed during this phase to validate design decisions (though more typically, usability testing is conducted during the beta cycle, and by then it's too late to make major modifications to the software based on user feedback). Using rapid prototyping or sequences of screen shots drawn on paper, users should be walked through the application. Usability engineering is an interesting specialty that can be a great software career path. More and more organizations are building in-house programming teams that evaluate software from a usability standpoint and focus on improving it from the user's perspective. Whether usability testing is performed in-house or by an outside company, you need to start early. You should consult a usability professional as soon as plans for the user interface begin to take shape.

During the definition phase, a set of documents needs to be developed that will serve as guideposts for the rest of the software lifecycle. These documents should include the following:

- A product plan with descriptions of the user, user environment, and feature set. This plan is basically a high-level description of who the software is for and what the software will do and how it will do it.

- An architecture and design document that outlines the major components of the software and their interfaces.
- An engineering plan with a list of tasks and the time allotted for each and the resources assigned to the project, including programmers, QA engineers, technical writers, and usability engineers.
- A quality assurance plan that describes how the software will be tested and any test scripts to be developed for automated testing.

"Selecting the right design point and best architecture, writing comprehensive functional specifications, and developing a clear and shared vision of the software project...are critical to successful software development."

- A documentation plan that describes documentation, tutorials, online help, and readme files.
- An international engineering plan if the software is to be localized for the international market.
- Detailed product specifications that describe the operation of the software for programmers, quality assurance engineers, and technical writers.

These documents will continue to evolve throughout the software lifecycle.

The tendency of most development teams is to rush into the build phase and start coding. However, achieving reliability in software development requires knowing what you are doing ahead of time, not inventing as you go. Redesigning software after you've spent months coding is ineffective and demoralizing. No matter where you are working, your main responsibility during the definition phase is to define as completely as possible the code you are about to write.

Build Phase

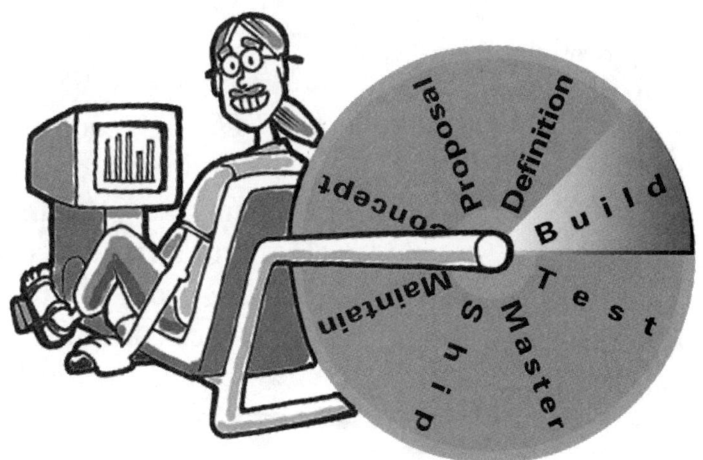

During the build phase, the product is actually developed. Two excellent books from Microsoft Press discuss the build phase in detail: *Code Complete* by Steve McConnell and *Writing Solid Code* by Steve Maguire. These and similar volumes provide advice on coding practices that is beyond the scope of this book. However, consider these rules of thumb:

- **Practice active software project management to keep the build phase on track.**

  A number of activities should occur in parallel during the build phase, such as building the user interface, developing the application logic, developing the test tool and test bed, and writing the initial documentation. Most applications today are so large and complex that they require a team of programmers to work on them. There are many job roles within the programming team for you to specialize in.

  Dividing the work load intelligently among the team members and integrating all components smoothly into the overall application is important to optimizing the build phase.

- **Avoid feature creeperia.**

  In most of the projects I have been involved in, there has been a tendency to add cool features midway through the project. Because each additional feature by itself frequently is not a big programming challenge, unplanned features creep in and cause problems. Feature creeperia can cause integration problems, increase testing time, lead to erroneous documentation, and throw off the product design. Of course, sometimes the right thing to do is add features and delay the schedule. However, it is important to make these decisions consciously, and grudgingly, and clearly communicate any changes to all parties concerned.

- **Pacing is critical.**

  To determine where you are at any given time, you have to be able to evaluate your progress against milestones. When the project begins, you should have concrete milestones that describe tasks to be completed and time frames, and you should compare your own progress against these milestones as you proceed. If you think you may miss a milestone, spend a few extra hours right then to get back on track. Don't put off the effort with the thought that you'll catch up later. If you must miss a milestone, then adjust the master schedule right then. Otherwise, you will wind up with way more work than you can possibly accomplish at the end of the project. In the shrink-wrap software business, if your pacing is off, you can ruin your marketing plans by not delivering what you announce or not synchronizing your marketing programs with the release of the software.

- **Risk management is an important method for getting back on track.**

  As you get into coding, if you find your original estimates are way off, you may want to make some midcourse trade-offs between implementing features and saving time. Each project will be different, and you will likely have some tough choices to make. Dropping risky features early is one good way to bring in the schedule. There isn't any universal advice that you can apply when evaluating whether or not to drop a feature to make a date, but you should consider the questions listed here:

  - ❑ How hard is the feature to implement and how long will it take to do so?
  - ❑ Does the feature address one of the critical needs of the user? Is it significant in the sense that considerable functionality or usability will be sacrificed if the feature is excluded?

- ❑ If the feature is implemented within the required time frame, will it be substandard in comparison to either the other features of the product or similar features of competing products?
- ❑ Is the feature in line with the overall objectives of the application?
- ❑ Is the feature necessary as support for other features?
- ❑ Does the feature have any dependencies that could adversely affect the feature's functionality or finish time?
- ❑ Would this feature give the product a substantial advantage over competing products?

As you progress through the coding cycle, remember to keep quality foremost in mind. It is far harder and much more expensive to get bugs out of the software once the application has solidified and moved to alpha testing, so be careful when you're coding the first time around. Consider all the other parts of the application that your code may affect, think about what you're doing as you do it, and test the code to whatever extent you can as you go along.

Remember to Expand Your Horizons

If you are working on a large project and are assigned to a team developing a specific part of the application—for example, the user interface—then you can expect to concentrate on that one area until the entire project is completed. However, when the time comes to do the next project, try to get assigned to something you haven't already worked on. This is a simple but highly effective way to expand your expertise, and it also helps to keep you interested and challenged. Just as actors try to avoid being stuck in a niche, so should you. You may like being the RPC king, but your value as a programmer goes up when you expand your horizons and continue to become proficient in different areas of programming.

- **Get rid of time wasters.**

  One of the most important attributes of a programmer is the ability to deliver high-quality work on schedule. So how do you keep on schedule? And how do you avoid being thrown off and working 72-hour days at the end of the project to complete it in time?

  Avoid interruptions when you work. Create an environment for yourself that is conducive to thought, concentration, and focus on the task at hand.

  Use your time wisely. Divide your work into three categories: must do, should do, and would be nice to do. Finish your must-do list first before moving on. Consider taking a time management class to improve your efficiency. Use an electronic organizer such as ACT! to plan your daily activities.

  E-mail is a typical disruption for programmers. I have seen people spend entire days doing nothing but generating and answering e-mail messages. Don't do it. Keep e-mail short and sweet—and don't get involved in e-mail disputes. These not only waste your time and that of others on the distribution list; they also create bad feelings, sometimes bad enough to throw you or someone else off stride all day.

Meetings are another potential time waster. Work hard to make the meetings you attend run efficiently and generate results. Your team should have regular meetings for code reviews and so on, but keep these to a minimum. Let the project manager worry about coordinating all the team members, and ask that he or she avoid scheduling too many meetings. If you have a manager who enjoys meetings, it might be helpful to point out how much time they require.

The major goal of the build phase is to complete all the coding and produce a fully featured application for alpha testing. When the alpha version of your program is ready, you move into the test phase.

Test Phase

In the test phase, the main objective is to squeeze all the bugs out of the program, get performance up to snuff, and master the software. Once a program reaches the alpha stage, its features and functions are complete, and it is perhaps two-thirds of the way to shipping. Opinions vary considerably as to when a software project should be considered in the alpha stage. Some feel it's best to wait until all features are operational and performance is in range. Others advocate entering the alpha stage much earlier than that.

Of course, reaching the alpha stage early doesn't imply that you will ship early. There still may be many months of testing before your project is ready to move into the beta test stage.

Quality assurance and usability go hand in hand. Often what may appear to a user to be a bug is actually just a feature with poor usability. Usability testing should continue through the alpha stage, and the software should be fine-tuned to be as intuitive to end users as possible.

There are many logistics to work out to ensure smooth implementation of the test phase. Issues include identifying who will test which version of your software, how you will send the software to the testers, how testers will report bugs, and how fixes will get out to the field. There are job opportunities for test coordinators who administer these programs effectively.

The criteria for moving a project into the alpha test phase should include the following:

- ❑ The code is complete; it is written and stable for the major functional areas of the project. All core functionality at this stage should be complete, and the program should substantially conform to the user interface in the product specifications or definition.
- ❑ The bug database connecting Engineering, Quality Assurance, and the alpha test sites is up and running.
- ❑ Alpha documentation is ready.
- ❑ The QA test plans are complete and have been reviewed by the development team to make sure that all areas of the software are covered.
- ❑ The test tools are in place, with all testing tools including batch files and any automation scripts, and all tools are accessible in a common area. Lab machines should be configured and ready for testing. To ensure maintainability and reproducibility, all files related to the test tools should be managed using a version control system.

The key milestone in the test phase is the beta test. During beta testing, the software is moved into the user community for real-world testing. Beta testing is crucial because it is impossible to think of all the different ways in which end users will use the software. When the software is in the hands of end users, you can be sure it will be tested in ways you never imagined.

As for the alpha stage, several criteria must be met before software is moved into the beta stage:

- ❑ The beta software should be stable enough to use successfully. Sending software that cannot be installed or that immediately crashes frustrates users.
- ❑ The user interface must substantially conform to the specifications. All buttons, list boxes, check boxes, and other controls that will be present in the final version should be present in the beta-test version, and no user interface components should still be scheduled for later inclusion.
- ❑ A variety of beta sites should be selected, ideally to exercise the software in different ways, and the users involved in the testing should have various degrees of expertise.
- ❑ A simple and clear process should be established for sending feedback from the beta sites to the programming team and for getting new beta versions from the team to the beta sites. The beta sites must be willing and able to report bugs in a timely fashion and in a manner that makes them reproducible.

After beta shipment, the key activity is systematically finding and fixing the bugs. When all open bugs are either closed or deferred for the next release, you are ready to master the software.

Master Phase

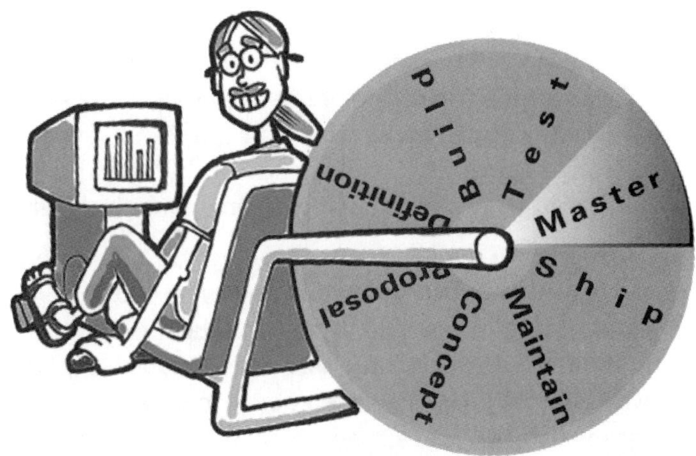

When creating commercial software, releasing a high-quality product is critical. Your customers won't forgive you if the software they purchase is buggy, unstable, or cannot be installed, and investors won't forgive you if the quarter's profits go toward fixing a buggy release. With internal corporate applications, it's a bit easier to provide your users with a fixed version. However, first impressions are still very important. The master phase is a final checkpoint for ensuring that your software is high quality.

At Symantec, we typically have a two- to four-week period where we test a final release candidate to make sure it is highly reliable before we ship it.

Ship Phase

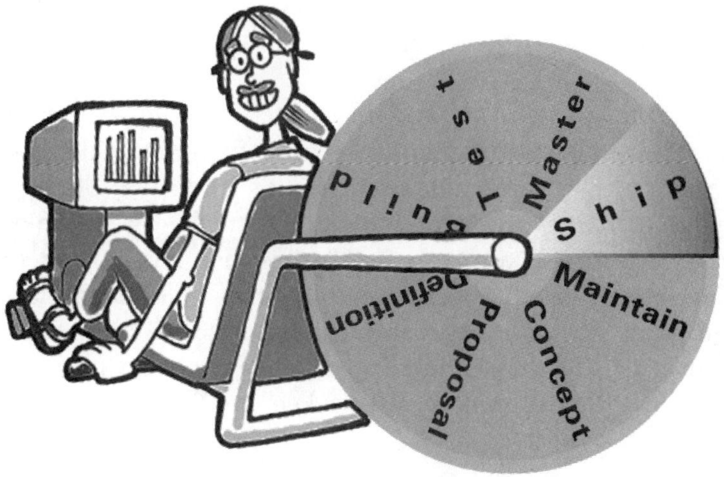

Finally, all the hard work pays off. The software is done, the documentation is complete, and the product is ready to ship—it's time for a big team celebration. However, don't forget to have a postmortem meeting to discuss what went right and wrong with the project. This meeting might take half a day and be attended by all the team members. During the meeting, it's expected that people will complain. This is the ideal time to learn what to do differently in the next project. Someone should take good notes and try to come up with concrete suggestions for improvements for the next project. Managers should try hard not to respond negatively to any comments so the atmosphere of the meeting is open and allows all participants to speak their minds.

After the post-mortem meeting, make sure to relax and recharge your batteries so you're ready for the next project. Software development is tough work, and it's important not to allow yourself to get burned out.

Maintain Phase

It's important to plan a maintain phase for fixing bugs discovered by users. Every piece of software contains bugs. It's important after you ship to be responsive to fixing problems that arise, but this is possible only if some members of the team are assigned to this task and not off on vacation or building the next version. Although this is the end of the cycle, this phase is a very important one, as Intel's disastrous episode with the flawed Pentium chip taught all of us. The proper handling of bugs is a tricky business and must be done in a professional manner, always keeping the end user's needs in mind.

Optimizing Development with a Software Lifecycle

This chapter described a software lifecycle designed to optimize software development. Adopting a software lifecycle does not require bureaucracy, time-wasting activities, and interruptions. Rather, it requires proactive approaches to identifying and avoiding problems. Most important, it requires the team to replan the project at each phase based on the most current accurate data.

At Symantec, our teams work hard to successfully manage our software projects through these phases, and it's a big reason why we are able to ship world-class software that wins reviews and meets the needs of our users. You can do it, too!

9 Selecting the Right Company for You

Congratulations! You made it to the final chapter. By now you've seen what a great career programming can be and how much promise it holds for the future as a continuing source of challenge, excitement, and rewards—both personal and financial. You've seen what some very successful programmers have achieved in their professional lives, and you've read tips from those programmers on how to enhance your own career. You've studied the programming job market to see where the jobs are, how the pay rate varies by industry and geography, and what the various types of jobs are that you might be interested in pursuing. You've looked at some of the hot technologies of the future that you can get into today and how those technologies are destined to pay off handsomely in the years to come. You've also gained some insight into how to evaluate your own wants and needs and how to apply this information in your job search. Finally, you've learned where to look for jobs, including how to surf the World Wide Web.

By now you should know not only the seven hottest technologies but also the seven skills that will help you most to succeed in any programming career. You should know what factors to consider when determining whether to leave your current job. In addition, you should now have all the information you need to go out and capture the job you most want by crafting your résumé and cover letter and honing your interview and follow-up skills to gain a competitive edge. This last chapter provides specific advice on narrowing down the field and selecting the right company to work for.

Seven Tips to a Successful Career

Since we're thinking in sevens, I will summarize here what I consider to be the seven most important tips for a successful programming career. These tips are important not only from the standpoint of developing your overall career, but you can also apply them to find the right companies to target.

Specialize in a Platform with a Future

The first tip for a successful career is specialize in development for a platform that has a good future. Don't target a company that specializes in creating software for a platform that was popular five years ago. The ideal platform is one that's both popular today and has great future potential. Windows is the platform that most readily comes to mind as the most promising for PC development work. Windows fits all the criteria for a good platform choice: it's wildly popular today, it has the greatest possible future potential, and it's a product of the market leader in systems and software. Target a company that creates applications for the ever-evolving Windows platform, and you'll have a huge advantage for continued career growth.

The Macintosh is another established platform that continues to grow in popularity as it moves from the 68K processor to the PowerPC. Also consider the embedded-systems market, which will continue to grow as smart appliances, from TVs to cars to phones to microwave ovens, increasingly gain acceptance. Look, too, at the personal digital assistant market, which is small today but will grow over time.

Companies that are tuned in to the marketplace have the most chance of success, and a good indication that a company is tuned in is the platforms for which the company creates applications. A good company usually has chosen a winning platform as part of an overall strategy of catering to the customer. Jeffrey Tarter, editor of *Softletter*, a prestigious newsletter for top management at the leading software companies, gives the following advice:

"If it's not a broad-based and important technology that is the focus of the company, then that's a danger sign. In programming, as in everything else, people tend to pigeonhole you based on your résumé, so the first job you have may be the one that defines all your jobs in the future. Even worse is winding up in a company that specializes in a technology that isn't going to grow or that is going to become obsolete."

Being on top of market trends also involves being aware of what other people in the market are doing. As Jeffrey puts it, " If a company isn't paranoid about the competition, then it's a dangerous place to be. I see companies that either feel they truly have no competition or that denigrate the competition. In reality, they need to be thinking about what the competition is going to be able to deliver two years into the future. I think the best companies out there are absolutely driven by fear of the competition. Microsoft is an excellent example of a company that's always been driven by a fear of the competition."

Master the Right Tools

The second tip is pick the right tools and master them. Tools are essential to programming, and with the right tools you can achieve far more than you can without them. By mastering the tools of the trade—which include compilers, application frameworks, 4GL environments, testing tools, and version control systems—you can dramatically increase your marketability.

Object-oriented languages are the languages in high demand today, and they will continue to be hot in the future. C++ is the right choice for a language that will open more doors in your career than any other. Proficiency in old-fashioned COBOL, FORTRAN, Pascal, and mainframe languages might get you a job today at some companies, but you probably won't be paid as much, you'll have difficulty finding companies that still require those other languages, and your future won't be nearly as bright as it would be with an object-oriented language. So look for companies that do most of their development work in C++.

"C++ is the right choice for a language that will open more doors in your career than any other."

Identify a Solid Development Strategy

The third tip is identify a solid development strategy and find a company that adheres to such a strategy for creating software. The development strategy is one of the primary criteria you can use to predict the potential success of software projects, and consequently how your career at that company will add to or detract from your future job outlook. You can usually get a feel for a company's strategy in the interview process.

Programmer's Perspective

"If there aren't lots of grown-ups in a development organization, that can be an indicator that the development strategy and methodology aren't in place. Young programmers tend to be excited about working on products, and they're not as concerned with QA, scheduling, consistency, and other boring things like these. Companies that don't have boring grown-ups around in a pretty good ratio to the programmers tend to collapse and often just fail to deliver products, or they deliver products that are too buggy or late."

Jeffrey Tarter
Editor, *Softletter*

Pick the Right Product

Steve Singh, the general manager of Symantec's Contact Management Division, recommends that during the interview you should try to calibrate the software experience of the company management. Steve suggests finding out "how realistic the company is about product ship dates. Management should have an understanding of the customer that they're creating products for and of that customer's needs. They should also have a pragmatic approach to software development."

Sometimes the most important factor to consider in deciding whether to work at a particular company is the product you would be working on. Steve Singh gave me his viewpoint on selecting the right company:

"The thing I'd concentrate on is the product you're going to work on because your success is often tied to the product more than the company you work for. When evaluating companies and products, you often need to stand back and take a look at the product from a different perspective than the programmer's perspective. For instance, you need to think about the possible market for the product and whether it's large and growing or not. You need to ask if customers will be willing to pay to use your product on a regular basis. Indeed, you should try to figure out if you yourself would use it on a regular basis, and if you wouldn't use it, then you have to question whether the product will be a strong one."

Steve goes on to say that "all software programs are products, even if they're not sold outside of the company. There are always customers, and in an MIS organization you also have to ask yourself who are the customers. They may be internal to the company, but they're still customers. I'd ask what organization in the company is going to use this? Do they have a lot of pull? Can they cut through the bureaucracy and help get the project funded and done? I'd want to have these pieces defined."

Have a Career Plan

The fifth tip is to keep in mind your own career plan. As mentioned earlier, it's important to figure out what your goals are, how you plan to achieve them, and what milestones you need to meet along the way as you progress toward your ultimate goal.

It's easy to see how the choice of which company to work for fits into an overall career plan. You may want to move from a small company to a larger one. If that's the case, then keep this goal in mind as you conduct your job search. Sometimes one company will be right for you when you start out but won't provide the opportunities you need later on. You may want to take your career down the path of management, or you may wish to stay in pure programming and advance along that road. The path you want to follow is a very important consideration in selecting a company to work for. You need to know what opportunities the company offers in both the technical and management tracks. If you don't determine what opportunities will be available later in your career at a particular company, you won't be able to adequately determine whether your career plan will fit into the future of the company.

Choose an Organization You Like

The sixth tip is to join a company you like. Since you are going to be spending so much time working, make sure you find a company with the kind of people and culture you can fit into. How do you tell from an interview what the company culture and the opportunities within a company are going to be like?

Scott Adams, creator of the wonderful *Dilbert* comic strip, contributed some great insights into how to figure out what kind of company you may be getting into from just a casual visit:

"The Dilbert Index helps. You walk through the cubicles of the company and note how many Dilbert cartoons are hung up. If there are just a few Dilbert cartoons hung up, then that probably means the company can tolerate different opinions, but there aren't so many problems in the company that the place is just littered with them. The two worst things that can happen are that there aren't any Dilbert cartoons, which means that the company may have problems but is not willing to talk about them, or that there are a lot of Dilbert cartoons, which means that the company has a lot of problems, though they are willing to talk about them."

Scott told me that his greatest love other than cartooning is creating software. He has written some games, as well as a communication program. One had a great user interface. Instead of menus, a zipper appeared on the screen. When the user clicked it, the zipper opened, and the menu items came out to the side. He has also created a great Dilbert screen saver, which is available for Windows and the Macintosh from Symantec. Scott says, "It's the funniest thing you'll ever see in your life but be careful if you leave it in the mode where it cycles through all the modules with the sound on, as the intermittent screaming can frighten your co-workers."

Scott goes on to say, "You can usually tell the level of creativity at a company by looking at the physical surroundings, the business cards, and what people are wearing. I have a theory that you can't do anything to create creativity. It's an uncontrollable force. The employees are either going to use it on the job or they're going to use it personally by writing clever e-mail messages that are a parody of the management style. My theory is you can't really control creativity. You can only get out of the way and hope that some of the natural creativity gets used for the company's benefit. If a company requires business suits without a customer reason behind it, that's a sure sign that the company may not be the best for creativity. And companies that have gone to 'casual Fridays' may have achieved the ultimate in missing the point. Either it's appropriate to wear casual clothes or it's not, and things don't change at the end of the week. Also, if you go into a company and the boss makes a big deal about the employees' being empowered, then that means they're not by definition because in a company where the employees are empowered, the boss wouldn't know what 'empowerment' is and wouldn't use the term. If you have to say it, then it can't possibly exist."

Establish Balance in Your Life

The seventh and last tip that I want to give you is establish balance in your life. My father, Professor William Wang, always told me that to be a success in life you need to carefully cultivate three important areas: body, mind, and soul. All are equally important, and all of them require attention. Never neglect any of these three areas of your life and never give up on them. I've seen too many programming geniuses who were unsuccessful because they couldn't get along with the rest of their team. I've seen people fail because their bodies couldn't tolerate the stress of the final push to get the software out the door. To be productive, you need to be healthy and have a clear mind. Remember to take the time to invest in yourself. The extra time that it takes will make you happier and get you farther ahead in your career as well.

"My father, Professor William Wang, always told me that to be a success in life you need to carefully cultivate three important areas: body, mind, and soul. All are equally important, and all of them require attention."

The Top 100 Software Companies

What follows is Jeffrey Tarter's list of the top 100 software companies in the United States, based on calendar 1994 revenues. Use this as a valuable resource to start your job search and to focus your future job searches. These companies all make software products. There are corporations where you can just as easily find the start of a great career; and although one of those may be the right place for you, it never hurts to explore the software industry itself. These companies are more than likely to treat programmers with the proper respect and consideration since programmers provide the essence of their business. Symantec, as this book goes to press, has over 200 job openings for programmers, and new jobs are always opening up. Check out Symantec at **www.symantec.com** on the Internet and you'll see what I mean.

Programming offers the smart and motivated person a wealth of opportunities. Good luck, live long, and prosper.

1 Microsoft Corp. $5,266,000,000

1 Microsoft Way, Redmond, WA 98052
206-882-8080 Fax: 206-936-7329

Chairman:	William Gates		
CFO	Mike Brown		
Ownership:	Public (MSFT)		
Employees:	16,379	**Sales/Emp.:**	$321,509
Established:	1975	**International**:	50%
1994 Rank:	#1	**'93-'94 Growth:**	28%
1993:	$4,109,000,000	**1990:**	$1,477,000,000
1992:	$3,252,000,000	**1989:**	$952,800,000
1991:	$2,275,000,000		

BEST-SELLING TITLES: MS DOS (OEM pricing) Operating system **Microsoft Windows** (OEM pricing) Operating system **Microsoft Office** (price varies) General business (DOS, Macintosh) **Microsoft Excel** (price varies) General business (Windows, Macintosh)

2 Novell $2,003,024,000

1555 N. Technology Way, Orem, UT 84057
801-429-7000 Fax: 801-222-2676

Chairman:	Robert J. Frankenberg		
CFO	James Tolonen		
Ownership:	Public (NOVL)		
Employees:	7,914	**Sales/Emp.:**	$253,099
Established:	1983	**International:**	43%
1994 Rank:	#2	**'93-'94 Growth:**	6%
1993:	$1,881,621,000	**1990:**	$1,032,200,000
1992:	$1,567,717,000	**1989:**	$745,530,000
1991:	$1,332,412,000		

BEST-SELLING TITLES: NetWare 4 ($1,095) Communications/networking (DOS, Windows, Macintosh, OS/2, Unix) **Unix** ($1,695) Operating system **WordPerfect** ($395) General business (DOS, Windows, Macintosh, OS/2, Unix) **Perfect Office** ($659) General business (Windows)

3 Lotus Development Corp. $970,700,000

55 Cambridge Pkwy., Cambridge, MA 02142
617-577-8500 Fax: 617-693-1779

Chairman:	Jim Manzi		
CFO:	Edwin Gillis		
Ownership:	Public (LOTS)		
Employees:	5,545	**Sales/Emp.:**	$175,059
Established:	1982	**International:**	48%
1994 Rank:	#3	**'93-'94 Growth:**	–1%
1993:	$981,200,000	**1990:**	$692,242,000
1992:	$900,100,000	**1989:**	$556,000,000
1991:	$826,900,000		

BEST-SELLING TITLES: Lotus1-2-3 ($329) General business (DOS, Windows, Macintosh, OS/2, Unix) **SmartSuite** ($499) General business (Windows, OS/2) **Lotus Notes** (price varies) Communications/networking (Windows, Macintosh, OS/2, Unix) **cc:Mail** ($34) Communications/networking (DOS, Windows, Macintosh, OS/2, Unix)

4 Adobe Systems $597,722,000

1585 Charleston Rd., Mountain View, CA 94039
415-961-4400 Fax: 415-961-5707

Chairman:	John Warnock		
CFO:	M. Bruce Nakao		
Ownership:	Public (ADBE)		
Employees:	1,584	**Sales/Emp.:**	$377,350
Established:	1982	**International:**	20%
1994 Rank:	#7	**'93-'94 Growth:**	15%
1993:	$520,240,000	**1990:**	$303,710,000
1992:	$440,060,000	**1989:**	$219,974,000
1991:	$397,180,000		

BEST-SELLING TITLES: Adobe Photoshop ($895) General business (DOS, Windows, Macintosh, OS/2, Unix) **Adobe PageMaker** ($895) General business (DOS, Windows, Macintosh, OS/2, Unix) **Adobe Illustrator** ($495) General business (DOS, Windows, Macintosh, OS/2, Unix)

5 Autodesk $454,612,000

111 McInnis Pkwy., San Rafael, CA 94903
415-507-5000 Fax: 415-507-6129

CEO:	Carol Bartz		
CFO:	Eric Herr		
Ownership:	Public (ACAD)		
Employees:	1,788	**Sales/Emp.:**	$254,257
Established:	1982	**International:**	60%
1994 Rank:	#6	**'93-'94 Growth:**	12%
1993:	$405,596,000	**1990:**	$230,403,000
1992:	$353,154,000	**1989:**	$173,512,000
1991:	$273,974,000		

BEST-SELLING TITLES: AutoCAD R.13 ($3,995) Vertical/industry- or job-specific (DOS, Windows, Unix) **AutoCAD** ($3,995 Vertical/industry- or job-specific (DOS, Windows, Unix) **3D Studio** ($2,995) Vertical/industry- or job-specific (DOS) **AutoCAD LT** ($495) Vertical/industry- or job-specific (Windows)

6 Attachmate Corp. $390,000,000

3617 131st Ave. SE, Bellevue, WA 98006
206-644-4010 Fax: 206-649-6662

CEO:	Frank Pritt		
CFO:	Geoff Revelle		
Ownership:	Private		
Employees:	2,000	**Sales/Emp.:**	$195,000
Established:	1983	**International:**	34%
1994 Rank:	n/a	**'93-'94 Growth:**	169%
1993:	$145,116,000	**1990:**	$79,406,000
1992:	$121,663,000	**1989:**	$55,810,000
1991:	$103,228,000		

BEST-SELLING TITLES: Extra! ($425) Communications/networking (DOS, Windows, Macintosh, OS/2) **Irma** ($495) Communications/networking (DOS, Windows, Macintosh, OS/2) **Rally!** ($395) Communications/networking (Windows) **Crosstalk** ($99–$295) Communications/networking (DOS, Windows, Macintosh)

7 Symantec Corp. — $323,449,000

10201 Torre Ave., Cupertino, CA 95014
408-253-9600 Fax: 408-253-3968

President:	Gordon Eubanks, Jr.		
CFO:	Robert Dykes		
Ownership:	Public (SYMC)		
Employees:	1,404	**Sales/Emp.:**	$230,377
Established:	1982	**International:**	34%
1994 Rank:	#8	**'93-'94 Growth:**	–6%
1993:	$342,794,000	**1990:**	$213,364,000
1992:	$351,291,000	**1989:**	$143,498,000
1991:	$333,067,000		

BEST-SELLING TITLES: Norton Utilities ($179) Utility (DOS, Windows, Macintosh, OS/2) **ACT!** ($279) General business (DOS, Windows, Macintosh) **pcAnywhere** ($199) Communications/networking (DOS, Windows) **Norton Administration for Networks** ($329) Utility (DOS, Windows) **Symantec C++** Programming tool/language ($199; DOS, Windows), ($499; Macintosh)

8 Intuit — $290,000,000

155 Linfield Dr., Menlo Park, CA 94025
415-322-0573 Fax: 415-329-3689

President:	Bill Campbell		
CFO:	Bill Lane		
Ownership:	Public (INTU)		
Employees:	1,400	**Sales/Emp.:**	$207,143
Established:	1983	**International:**	5%
1994 Rank:	#9	**'93-'94 Growth:**	39%
1993:	$209,015,000	**1990:**	$36,622,000
1992:	$150,866,000	**1989:**	$24,285,000
1991:	$54,812,000		

BEST-SELLING TITLES: Quicken ($49.95) Accounting/finance/tax (DOS, Windows, Macintosh) **QuickBooks** ($99.95) Accounting/finance/tax (DOS, Windows, Macintosh) **TurboTax** ($69.95) Accounting/finance/tax (DOS, Windows, Macintosh) **MacInTax** ($69.95) Accounting/finance/tax (DOS, Windows, Macintosh)

9 Borland International — $249,609,000

100 Borland Way, Scotts Valley, CA 95066
408-431-1000 Fax: 408-431-4128

CEO:	n/a		
CFO:	Gary Wetsel		
Ownership:	Public (BORL)		
Employees:	1,713	**Sales/Emp.:**	$145,715
Established:	1983	**International:**	50%
1994 Rank:	#5	**'93-'94 Growth:**	–46%
1993:	$459,541,000	**1990:**	$421,328,000
1992:	$463,690,000	**1989:**	$369,481,000
1991:	$499,420,000		

BEST-SELLING TITLES: Borland C++ ($499) Programming tool/language (DOS, Windows, OS/2) **Paradox** ($495) Programming tool/language (DOS, Windows) **dBase** ($495) Programming tool/language (DOS, Windows)

10 Santa Cruz Operation $190,409,000

400 Encinal St., Santa Cruz, CA 95061
408-425-7222 Fax: 408-458-4227

CEO:	Lars Turndal		
CFO:	John Jarris		
Ownership:	Public (SCOC)		
Employees:	1,200	**Sales/Emp.:**	$158,674
Established:	1979	**International:**	50%
1994 Rank:	#11	**'93-'94 Growth:**	7%
1993:	$178,243,000	**1990:**	$118,900,000
1992:	$170,700,000	**1989:**	$82,800,000
1991:	$137,500,000		

BEST-SELLING TITLES: SCO Unix Operating System ($1,295) **SCO Open Server Enterprise** ($2,395) General business (Unix) **SCO Open Server Network** ($1,895) Operating system (Unix)

11 Brøderbund Software $132,068,000

500 Redwood Blvd., Novato, CA 94948
415-382-4400 Fax: 415-382-4665

Chairman:	Douglas Carlston		
CFO:	Michael Shannahan		
Ownership:	Public (BROD)		
Employees:	450	**Sales/Emp.:**	$293,484
Established:	1980	**International:**	10%
1994 Rank:	#14	**'93-'94 Growth:**	38%
1993:	$95,814,000	**1990:**	$51,348,000
1992:	$86,126,000	**1989:**	$38,874,000
1991:	$60,517,000		

BEST-SELLING TITLES: The Print Shop ($20–$100) Consumer/entertainment (DOS, Windows, Macintosh) **Where in the World is Carmen Sandiego?** ($30–$70) Consumer/entertainment (DOS, Windows, Macintosh, CD-ROM) **Playroom** ($20–$50) Consumer/entertainment (DOS, Windows, Macintosh) **Kid Pix** ($20–$50) Consumer/entertainment (DOS, Windows, Macintosh)

12 SoftKey International $121,287,000

201 Broadway, Cambridge, MA 02139
617-494-1200 Fax: 617-494-1219

Chairman:	Michael Perik		
CFO:	Scott Murray		
Ownership:	Public (SKEY)		
Employees:	450	**Sales/Emp.:**	$269,527
Established:	1982	**International:**	26%
1994 Rank:	#13	**'93-'94 Growth:**	11%
1993:	$109,704,000	**1990:**	
1992:	$119,518,000	**1989:**	
1991:	$76,026,000		

BEST-SELLING TITLES: Calendar Creator ($49.95) Consumer/entertainment (Windows) **American Heritage Talking Dictionary** ($39.95) Consumer/entertainment (Windows) **BodyWorks** ($49.95) Consumer/entertainment (Windows) **Time Almanac** ($29.95) Consumer/entertainment (Windows)

13 Cheyenne Software — $104,761,000

3 Expressway Plaza, Roslyn Heights, NY 11577
516-484-5110 Fax: 516-484-3446

President:	ReiJane Huai		
CFO:	Elliot Levine		
Ownership:	Public (CYE)		
Employees:	495	**Sales/Emp.:**	$211,638
Established:	1983	**International:**	52%
1994 Rank:	#18	**'93-'94 Growth:**	33%
1993:	$78,684,000	**1990:**	$3,800,000
1992:	$31,015,000	**1989:**	
1991:	$10,239,000		

BEST-SELLING TITLES: ArcServe ($295) Communications/networking (Windows, OS/2, Unix) **FaxServe** ($395) Communications/networking (DOS) **Inoculan** ($395) Communications/networking (DOS, Windows) **Monitrix** ($495) Communications/networking (DOS)

14 Wall Data — $101,240,000

11332 NE 122nd Way, Kirkland, WA 98034
206-883-4777 Fax: 206-885-9250

President:	James Simpson		
CFO:	Angelo Grestoni		
Ownership:	Public (WALL)		
Employees:	654	**Sales/Emp.:**	$154,801
Established:	1982	**International:**	23%
1994 Rank:	#20	**'93-'94 Growth:**	57%
1993:	$64,641,000	**1990:**	$4,400,000
1992:	$31,800,000	**1989:**	$2,400,000
1991:	$14,600,000		

BEST-SELLING TITLES: Rumba Office ($500) Communications/networking (OS/2) **Rumba for Mainframe** ($400) Communications/networking (Windows) **Rumba for AS/400** ($400) Commications/networking (Windows)

15 FTP Software — $93,245,000

100 Brickstone Sq., Andover, MA 01810
508-685-4000 Fax: 508-794-4488

President:	David H. Zirkle		
CFO:	Robert W. Goodnow		
Ownership:	Public (FTPS)		
Employees:	491	**Sales/Emp.:**	$189,908
Established:	1986	**International:**	43%
1994 Rank:	n/a	**'93-'94 Growth:**	59%
1993:	$58,726,000	**1990:**	
1992:	$33,132,000	**1989:**	
1991:	$21,419,000		

BEST-SELLING TITLES: PC/TCP ($450) Communications/networking (DOS, Windows, OS/2) **PC/TCP Network** ($350) Communications/networking (Windows, OS/2, DOS)

16 Walker Richer & Quinn — $89,280,000

1500 Dexter Ave. North, Seattle, WA 98109
206-217-7500 Fax: 206-217-0293

President:	Doug Walker		
CFO:	Gerry Smith		
Ownership:	Private		
Employees:	392	**Sales/Emp.:**	$227,755
Established:	1981	**International:**	33%
1994 Rank:	#19	**'93-'94 Growth:**	35%
1993:	$66,003,000	**1990:**	$25,783,000
1992:	$47,023,000	**1989:**	$19,544,000
1991:	$33,039,000		

BEST-SELLING TITLES: Reflection Series ($249) Communications/networking (DOS, Windows, Macintosh)

17 Spectrum Holobyte — $87,970,000

2490 Mariner Sq.Loop, Alameda, CA 94501
510-522-3584 Fax: 510-522-9305

CEO:	Patrick S. Feely		
CFO:	Richard A. Gelhaus		
Ownership:	Public (SBYT)		
Employees:	430	**Sales/Emp.:**	$204,581
Established:	1986	**International:**	26%
1994 Rank:	n/a	**'93-'94 Growth:**	n/a
1993:	n/a	**1990:**	$7,295,000
1992:	n/a	**1989:**	$5,850,000
1991:	$8,100,000		

BEST-SELLING TITLES: Colonization (price varies) Consumer/entertainment (DOS, Window) **Falcon Gold** (price varies) Consumer/entertainment (DOS, Windows) **Master of Magic** (price varies) Education/consumer/entertainment (DOS, Windows) **Xcom:UFO Defense** (price varies) Consumer/entertainment (Windows, DOS)

18 Davidson & Associates — $87,914,000

19840 Pioneer Ave., Torrance, CA 90503
310-793-0600 Fax: 310-793-0601

Chairman:	Bob Davidson		
CFO:	Jack Allenwaert		
Ownership:	Public (DAVD)		
Employees:	531	**Sales/Emp.:**	$165,563
Established:	1982	**International:**	5%
1994 Rank:	#22	**'93-'94 Growth:**	50%
1993:	$58,569,000	**1990:**	$9,883,000
1992:	$39,608,000	**1989:**	$7,422,000
1991:	$16,559,000		

BEST-SELLING TITLES: Math Blaster ($40) Education (DOS, Windows, Macintosh) **Reading Blaster** ($40) Education (Windows) **Kid Works 2** ($40) Education (DOS, Windows, Macintosh)

19 Phoenix Technologies — $77,177,000

770 De La Cruz Blvd., Santa Clara, CA 95050
408-654-9000 Fax: 408-452-1985

President:	Ronald D. Fisher		
CFO:	Robert J. Kiopel		
Ownership:	Public (PTEC)		
Employees:	331	**Sales/Emp.:**	$233,163
Established:	1979	**International:**	50%
1994 Rank:	#17	**'93-'94 Growth:**	14%
1993:	$67,589,000	**1990:**	$33,687,000
1992:	$62,331,000	**1989:**	$40,000,000
1991:	$53,081,000		

BEST-SELLING TITLES: Phoenix BIOS 4.0 (OEM pricing) **Phoenix Note BIOS 4.0** (OEM pricing) **Phoenix Pico** (OEM pricing) **Phoenix Home Office Environment** (OEM pricing) Consumer/entertainment (Windows)

20 Sierra On-Line — $76,500,000

3380 146th Place SE, Bellevue, WA 98027
206-649-9800 Fax: 206-649-0340

Chairman:	Kenneth Williams		
CFO:	Michael Brochu		
Ownership:	Public (SIER)		
Employees:	650	**Sales/Emp.:**	$117,692
Established:	1979	**International:**	10%
1994 Rank:	#21	**'93-'94 Growth:**	21%
1993:	$63,354,000	**1990:**	$26,962,000
1992:	$43,269,000	**1989:**	$19,898,000
1991:	$32,075,000		

BEST-SELLING TITLES: King's Quest VII ($65.95) Consumer/entertainment (Windows, Macintosh) **Leisure Suit Larry** ($59.95) Consumer/entertainment (Windows, Macintosh) **Red Baron** ($49.95) Consumer/entertainment (DOS, Macintosh) **Out Post** ($55.95) Consumer/entertainment (Windows)

21 Caere Corp. — $59,130,000

100 Cooper Ct., Los Gatos, CA 95030
408-395-7000 Fax: 408-395-5263

CEO:	Robert Teresi		
CFO:	Blanche Sutter		
Ownership:	Public (CAER)		
Employees:	250	**Sales/Emp.:**	$236,520
Established:	1976	**International:**	31%
1994 Rank:	#28	**'93-'94 Growth:**	23%
1993:	$48,264,000	**1990:**	$44,248,000
1992:	$57,093,000	**1989:**	
1991:	$51,529,000		

BEST-SELLING TITLES: OmniPage Professional ($695) General business (DOS, Windows, Macintosh, OS/2) **OmniPage Direct** ($99) General business (DOS, Windows, Macintosh, OS/2) **WordScan Plus** ($595) General business (DOS, Windows, Macintosh, OS/2) **PageKeeper** ($195) General business (DOS, Windows, Macintosh, OS/2)

22 Micrografx $58,238,000

1303 Arapaho Rd., Richardson, TX 75081
214-234-1769 Fax: 214-944-6026

Chairman:	J. Paul Grayson		
CFO:	Gregory A. Peters		
Ownership:	Public (MGXI)		
Employees:	234	**Sales/Emp.:**	$248,880
Established:	1982	**International:**	59%
1994 Rank:	#23	**'93-'94 Growth:**	0%
1993:	$58,228,000	**1990:**	$26,685,000
1992:	$62,927,000	**1989:**	$16,201,000
1991:	$43,240,000		

BEST-SELLING TITLES: Designer ($695) General business (Windows) **ABC FlowCharter** ($349.95) General business (Windows) **Picture Publisher** ($299.95) General business (Windows) **Crayola Art Studio** ($59.95) Consumer/entertainment (Windows)

23 Interplay Productions $56,999,000

17922 Fitch Ave., Irvine, CA 92714
714-553-6655 Fax: 714-252-2820

President:	Brian Fargo		
CFO:	Chuck Camps		
Ownership:	Private		
Employees:	200	**Sales/Emp.:**	$284,995
Established:	1983	**International:**	15%
1994 Rank:	#24	**'93-'94 Growth:**	28%
1993:	$44,704,000	**1990:**	$3,179,000
1992:	$19,268,000	**1989:**	$1,517,000
1991:	$4,715,000		

BEST-SELLING TITLES: Cyberia ($59.95) Consumer/entertainment (DOS) **Mario Teaches Typing** ($39.95) Consumer/entertainment (DOS, Macintosh) **Battle Chess** ($29.95) Consumer/entertainment (DOS, Macintosh) **Star Trek: Judgement Rights** ($59.95) Consumer/entertainment (DOS)

24 Platinum $53,400,000

195 Technology Dr., Irvine, CA 92718
714-453-4000 Fax: 714-453-4091

CEO:	Dr. Carmelo Santoro		
CFO:	Michael Simmons		
Ownership:	Public (RSQL)		
Employees:	500	**Sales/Emp.:**	$106,800
Established:	1984	**International:**	28%
1994 Rank:	n/a	**'93-'94 Growth:**	90%
1993:	$28,100,000	**1990:**	$8,900,000
1992:	$15,000,000	**1989:**	$5,900,000
1991:	$11,100,000		

BEST-SELLING TITLES: Platinum Series ($595) Accounting/finance/tax (DOS, Windows) **SQL NT** ($10,000) Accounting/finance/tax (Windows) **SQL Enterprise** ($45,000) Accounting/finance/tax (OS/2, Unix)

25 SPSS — $51,757,000

444 N. Michigan Ave., Chicago, IL 60611
312-329-2400 Fax: 312-329-3668

President:	Jack Noonan		
CFO:	Ed Hamburg		
Ownership:	Public (SPSS)		
Employees:	408	**Sales/Emp.:**	$126,855
Established:	1968	**International:**	50%
1994 Rank:	n/a	**'93-'94 Growth:**	21%
1993:	$42,724,000	**1990:**	$33,791,000
1992:	$37,863,000	**1989:**	$30,116,000
1991:	$34,592,000		

BEST-SELLING TITLES: SPSS ($695) General business (DOS, Windows, Macintosh, Unix) **QI Analyst** ($495) General business (DOS, Windows, Macintosh) **SYSTAT** ($895) General business (DOS, Windows, Macintosh)

26 Software Publishing Corp. — $51,300,000

3165 Kifer Rd., Santa Clara, CA 95056
408-986-8000 Fax: 408-450-7915

President:	Ifran Salim		
CFO:	Miriam Frazer		
Ownership:	Public (SPCO)		
Employees:	225	**Sales/Emp.:**	$228,508
Established:	1980	**International:**	34%
1994 Rank:	#15	**'93-'94 Growth:**	–43%
1993:	$90,490,000	**1990:**	$153,496,000
1992:	$151,897,000	**1989:**	$110,401,000
1991:	$141,258,000		

BEST-SELLING TITLES: Harvard Graphics for Windows ($395) General business (DOS, Windows)

27 Learning Company — $44,761,000

6493 Kaiser Dr., Fremont, CA 94555
510-792-2101 Fax: 510-792-9628

President:	William Dinsmore		
CFO:	Jack Parsons		
Ownership:	Public (LRNG)		
Employees:	206	**Sales/Emp.:**	$217,286
Established:	1980	**International:**	5%
1994 Rank:	#29	**'93-'94 Growth:**	36%
1993:	$32,873,000	**1990:**	$12,395,000
1992:	$23,852,000	**1989:**	
1991:	$16,085,000		

BEST-SELLING TITLES: Reader Rabbit I ($69.95) Education (DOS, Windows, Macintosh) **Reader Rabbit 2** ($69.95) Education (DOS, Windows, Macintosh) **Interactive Reading Journey** ($139.95) Education (Windows, Macintosh) **Treasure Mathstorm** ($59.95) Education (DOS, Windows, Macintosh)

28 Macromedia $43,386,000

600 Townsend St., San Francisco, CA 94103
415-252-2000 Fax: 415-626-0554

President:	John C. Colligan		
CFO:	Richard B. Wood		
Ownership:	Public (MACR)		
Employees:	275	**Sales/Emp.:**	$157,767
Established:	1992	**International:**	35%
1994 Rank:	#35	**'93-'94 Growth:**	22%
1993:	$35,705,000	**1990:**	
1992:		**1989:**	
1991:			

BEST-SELLING TITLES: Macromedia Director ($1,195) Programming tool/language (Windows, Macintosh) **Authorware** ($4,995) Programming tool/language (Windows, Macintosh) **FreeHand** ($595) Programming tool/language (Windows, Macintosh) **Macro Model** ($895) Programming tool/language (Windows, Macintosh)

29 Datastorm Technologies $43,000,000

2401 Lemone Blvd., Columbia, MO 65205
314-443-3282 Fax: 314-875-0595

President:	Bruce Barkelew		
CFO:	Chris Force		
Ownership:	Private		
Employees:	244	**Sales/Emp.:**	$176,230
Established:	1985	**International:**	5%
1994 Rank:	#34	**'93-'94 Growth:**	61%
1993:	$26,769,000	**1990:**	$9,944,000
1992:	$24,983,000	**1989:**	$7,749,000
1991:	$17,744,000		

BEST-SELLING TITLES: ProComm Plus for Windows ($179) Communications/networking **ProComm Plus for DOS** ($129) Communications/networking **ProComm Plus Network** ($645) Communications/networking (DOS)

30 Insignia Solutions $39,361,000

1300 Charleston Rd., Mountain View, CA 94043
415-335-7100 Fax: 415-335-7105

President:	Robert Lee		
CFO:	Roger Friedberger		
Ownership:	Private		
Employees:	205	**Sales/Emp.:**	$192,005
Established:	1986	**International:**	14%
1994 Rank:	#44	**'93-'94 Growth:**	113%
1993:	$18,500,000	**1990:**	$7,857,000
1992:	$18,675,000	**1989:**	$6,045,000
1991:	$14,457,000		

BEST-SELLING TITLES: SoftWindows ($499) Communications/networking (Macintosh, Unix)

31 Activision — $38,132,000

11601 Wilshire Blvd., Los Angeles, CA 90025
310-473-9200 Fax: 310-479-4005

CEO:	Robert Kotick		
CFO:	Brian Kelly		
Ownership:	Public (ATVI)		
Employees:	92	**Sales/Emp.:**	$414,478
Established:	1979	**International:**	30%
1994 Rank:	#36	**'93-'94 Growth:**	44%
1993:	$26,525,000	**1990:**	$41,043,000
1992:	$18,875,000	**1989:**	$64,071,000
1991:	$7,996,000		

BEST-SELLING TITLES: Pitfall: The Mayan Adventure ($48) Consumer/entertainment (Video game) **Return to Zork** (price varies) Consumer/entertainment (DOS, Macintosh) **Radical Rex** ($42) Consumer/entertainment (Video game)

32 Maxis — $37,357,000

2 Theatre Sq., Orinda, CA 94563
510-254-9700 Fax: 510-253-3736

President:	Sam Poole		
CFO:	Fred Gerson		
Ownership:	Private		
Employees:	136	**Sales/Emp.:**	$274,684
Established:	1987	**International:**	15%
1994 Rank:	#43	**'93-'94 Growth:**	102%
1993:	$18,521,000	**1990:**	$5,329,000
1992:	$15,209,000	**1989:**	$2,901,000
1991:	$10,376,000		

BEST-SELLING TITLES: Sim City Classic ($29.95) Consumer/entertainment (DOS, Windows, Macintosh, Amiga, Unix) **Sim City 2000** ($59.95) Consumer/entertainment (DOS, Windows, Macintosh) **Sim Earth** ($29.95) Consumer/entertainment (DOS, Windows, Macintosh, Amiga) **Sim Ant** ($29.95) Consumer/entertainment (DOS, Windows, Macintosh, Amiga)

33 State of the Art — $37,300,000

56 Technology Dr., Irvine, CA 92677
714-753-1222 Fax: 714-453-8849

Chairman:	David W. Hanna		
CFO:	Joe R. Armstrong		
Ownership:	Public (SOTA)		
Employees:	300	**Sales/Emp.:**	$124,333
Established:	1981	**International:**	1%
1994 Rank:	#33	**'93-'94 Growth:**	0%
1993:	$37,300,000	**1990:**	$21,200,000
1992:	$33,100,000	**1989:**	$17,700,000
1991:	$24,900,000		

BEST-SELLING TITLES: M-A-S 90 Evolution/2 ($799/module) Accounting/finance/tax (DOS, Windows, Unix) **Business Works** ($399) Accounting/finance/tax (Macintosh) **MAC P&L** (price varies) Accounting/finance/tax (Macintosh) **Flexware** (price varies) Accounting/finance/tax (Macintosh)

34 Stac Electronics $35,973,000

12626 High Bluff Dr., San Diego, CA 92130
619-794-4300 Fax: 619-794-4570

President:	Gary W. Clow		
CFO:	John W. Witzel		
Ownership:	Public (STAC)		
Employees:	209	**Sales/Emp.:**	$172,120
Established:	1983	**International:**	17%
1994 Rank:	#30	**'93-'94 Growth:**	17%
1993:	$30,783,000	**1990:**	
1992:	$40,265,000	**1989:**	
1991:	$13,284,000		

BEST-SELLING TITLES: Stacker ($149) Utility (DOS, Windows, Macintosh, OS/2) **Reach Out Remote Control** ($199) Communications/networking (DOS, Windows)

35 Best Programs $33,334,000

11413 Isaac Newton Sq., Reston, VA 22090
703-709-5200 Fax: 703-709-9359

President:	James Petersen		
CFO:	Melody Ranelli		
Ownership:	Private		
Employees:	278	**Sales/Emp.:**	$119,906
Established:	1982	**International:**	5%
1994 Rank:	#27	**'93-'94 Growth:**	36%
1993:	$24,528,000	**1990:**	$7,320,000
1992:	$14,548,000	**1989:**	$5,661,000
1991:	$10,614,000		

BEST-SELLING TITLES: FAS For Windows ($1,595) Accounting/finance/tax **FAS 2000** ($1,795) Accounting/finance/tax (DOS) **Abra 2000** ($695–$1,895) Accounting/finance/tax (DOS) **Envoy HR** ($695–$3,995) Accounting/finance/tax (Windows)

36 McAfee Associates $32,900,000

2710 Walsh Ave., Santa Clara, CA 95051
408-988-3832 Fax: 408-970-9727

President:	Bill Larson		
CFO:	n/a		
Ownership:	Public (MCAF)		
Employees:	128	**Sales/Emp.:**	$257,031
Established:	1989	**International:**	24%
1994 Rank:	#46	**'93-'94 Growth:**	84%
1993:	$17,911,000	**1990:**	
1992:	$13,683,000	**1989:**	
1991:			

BEST-SELLING TITLES: Viruscan (price varies) Utility (DOS, Windows, OS/2) **NetShield** (price varies) Utility (DOS, Windows, OS/2) **Sitemeter** (price varies) Utility (DOS, Windows, OS/2) **Brightworks** (price varies) Utility (DOS, Windows, OS/2)

37 MapInfo $32,765,000

1 Global View, Troy, NY 12180
518-285-6000 Fax: 518-285-6060

CEO:	Brian Owen		
CFO:	D. Joseph Gersuk		
Ownership:	Public (MAPS)		
Employees:	228	**Sales/Emp.:**	$143,706
Established:	1986	**International:**	27%
1994 Rank:	#40	**'93-'94 Growth:**	56%
1993:	$21,000,000	**1990:**	$5,600,000
1992:	$12,000,000	**1989:**	$4,100,000
1991:	$8,200,000		

BEST-SELLING TITLES: MapInfo Desktop Mapping Software ($1,295–$2,495) General business (Windows, Macintosh, Unix) **MapBasic Development Environment** ($795–$1,595)) Programming tool/language (Windows, Macintosh, Unix)

38 Quarterdeck Office Systems $28,273,000

150 Pico Blvd., Santa Monica, CA 90405
310-392-9851 Fax: 310-314-3219

President:	Gaston Bastiaens		
CFO:	Ron Hammond		
Ownership:	Public (QDEK)		
Employees:	206	**Sales/Emp.:**	$137,248
Established:	1982	**International:**	22%
1994 Rank:	#25	**'93-'94 Growth:**	–33%
1993:	$41,988,000	**1990:**	$36,255,000
1992:	$51,845,000	**1989:**	$10,357,000
1991:	$49,924,000		

BEST-SELLING TITLES: QEMM ($99.95) Utility (DOS, Windows) **DESQview** ($99.95) Utility (DOS) **DESQview/X** ($275) Utility (DOS)

39 XcelleNet $26,900,000

5 Concourse Pkwy., Atlanta, GA 30328
404-804-8100 Fax: 404-804-8102

CEO:	Dennis Crumpler		
CFO:	Sidney Sack		
Ownership:	Public (XNET)		
Employees:	180	**Sales/Emp.:**	$149,444
Established:	1986	**International:**	8%
1994 Rank:	#47	**'93-'94 Growth:**	55%
1993:	$17,400,000	**1990:**	$3,800,000
1992:	$10,350,000	**1989:**	$900,000
1991:	$5,500,000		

BEST-SELLING TITLES: RemoteWare Communications Management Systems (price varies) Communications/networking (DOS, Windows, Macintosh, OS/2, Unix) **RemoteWare Applications Management Systems** (price varies) General business (Windows, OS/2) **Remote Mail System** (price varies) Communications/networking (DOS, Windows, OS/2)

40 ON Technology $25,000,000

320 Washington St., Brookline, MA 02146
617-374-1400 Fax: 617-374-1433

CEO:	Christopher Risley		
CFO:	John Bogdan		
Ownership:	Private		
Employees:	182	**Sales/Emp.:**	$137,363
Established:	1987	**International:**	15%
1994 Rank:	#64	**'93-'94 Growth:**	166%
1993:	$9,400,000	**1990:**	$800,000
1992:	$3,500,000	**1989:**	
1991:	$1,500,000		

BEST-SELLING TITLES: Notework E-Mail ($59/user) Communications/networking (DOS, Windows) **DaVinci E-Mail** ($79/user) Communications/networking (DOS, Windows, Macintosh) **Softrack** ($895) Utility (DOS, Windows, Macintosh, OS/2) **Meeting Maker** ($79/user) Communications/networking (DOS, Windows, Macintosh)

41 MECC $24,633,783

6160 Summit Dr. N., Minneapolis, MN 55430
612-569-1500 Fax: 612-569-1551

President:	Dale LaFrenz		
CFO:	Don Anderson		
Ownership:	Public (MECC)		
Employees:	190	**Sales/Emp.:**	$129,651
Established:	1973	**International:**	2%
1994 Rank:	#41	**'93-'94 Growth:**	18%
1993:	$20,795,000	**1990:**	
1992:	$17,960,000	**1989:**	
1991:	$16,210,000		

BEST-SELLING TITLES: Oregon Trail II ($89.95) Education (Windows, Macintosh) **Yukon Trail** ($69.95) Education (Windows, Macintosh) **Amazon Trail** ($69.95) Education (Windows, Macintosh)

42 Primavera Systems $24,584,000

2 Bala Plaza, Bala Cynwyd, PA 19004
610-667-8600 Fax: 610-660-5857

President:	Joel Koppelman		
CFO:	Michael Moran		
Ownership:	Private		
Employees:	177	**Sales/Emp.:**	$138,893
Established:	1983	**International:**	30%
1994 Rank:	#38	**'93-'94 Growth:**	11%
1993:	$22,208,000	**1990:**	$16,269,000
1992:	$20,841,000	**1989:**	$11,500,000
1991:	$19,161,000		

BEST-SELLING TITLES: Primavera Project Planner ($4,000) Vertical/industry- or job-specific (DOS, Windows) **Expedition** ($2,500) Vertical/industry- or job-specific (DOS) **SureTrak Project Manager** ($695) General business (Windows)

43 SoftDesk $24,021,000

7 Liberty Hill Rd., Henniker, NH 03242
603-428-3199 Fax: 603-428-7901

President:	David Arnold		
CFO:	James A. Harsch		
Ownership:	Public (SDSK)		
Employees:	183	**Sales/Emp.:**	$131,262
Established:	1985	**International:**	21%
1994 Rank:	n/a	**'93-'94 Growth:**	26%
1993:	$19,002,000	**1990:**	$8,938,000
1992:	$13,746,000	**1989:**	
1991:	$11,180,000		

BEST-SELLING TITLES: Auto-Architect ($1,000) Vertical/industry- or job-specific (DOS, Windows, Macintosh) **Advanced Design** ($2,500) Vertical/industry- or job-specific (DOS, Windows, Macintosh) **Design** ($399) Vertical/industry- or job-specific (DOS, Windows, Macintosh) **Survey** ($1,000) Vertical/industry- or job-specific (DOS, Windows, Macintosh)

44 InfoSoft International $23,463,000

222 Berkely St., Boston, MA 02116
617-351-3000 Fax: 617-351-1115

President:	Steven R. Vona-Paxhia		
CFO:	Betty J. Savage		
Ownership:	Public (INSO)		
Employees:	118	**Sales/Emp.:**	$198,839
Established:	1982	**International:**	18%
1994 Rank:	n/a	**'93-'94 Growth:**	71%
1993:	$13,757,000	**1990:**	$6,040,000
1992:	$9,487,000	**1989:**	$4,133,000
1991:	$7,733,000		

BEST-SELLING TITLES: CorrecText Grammar Correction Systems (OEM pricing) General business (Unix, Windows) **International CorrectSpell** (OEM pricing) General business (DOS, Windows, Macintosh) **American Heritage Electronic** (OEM pricing) General business (DOS, Windows, Macintosh)

45 Mathsoft $22,938,000

101 Main St., Cambridge, MA 02142
617-577-1017 Fax: 617-577-8829

President:	Charles J. Digate		
CFO:	Robert Orlando		
Ownership:	Public (MATH)		
Employees:	130	**Sales/Emp.:**	$176,446
Established:	1984	**International:**	34%
1994 Rank:	#32	**'93-'94 Growth:**	–20%
1993:	$28,619,000	**1990:**	$6,093,000
1992:	$17,668,000	**1989:**	$5,048,000
1991:	$7,928,000		

BEST-SELLING TITLES: MathCad Plus ($299.95) Vertical/industry- or job-specific (Windows) **MathCad 5.0** ($99.95) Vertical/industry- or job-specific (Windows) **S+** ($1,450–$3,400) Vertical/industry- or job-specific (Windows, Macintosh, Unix) **Electronic Books** ($99) Vertical/industry- or job-specific (DOS, Windows, Unix)

46 Shapeware — $22,588,000

520 Pike St., Seattle, WA 98101
206-521-4500 Fax: 206-521-4501

President:	Jeremy Jaech		
CFO:	Marty Chilberg		
Ownership:	Private		
Employees:	135	**Sales/Emp.:**	$167,319
Established:	1990	**International:**	19%
1994 Rank:	#54	**'93-'94 Growth:**	87%
1993:	$12,090,000	**1990:**	
1992:	$448,000	**1989:**	
1991:			

BEST-SELLING TITLES: Visio ($199) General business (Windows) **Visio Express** ($99) General business (Windows) **Visio Home** ($79) Consumer/entertainment (Windows)

47 IMSI — $21,966,000

1938 Fourth St., San Rafael, CA 94901
415-454-7101 Fax: 415-454-8901

President:	Martin Sacks		
CFO:	Mark H. Cosmez II		
Ownership:	Public (IMSI)		
Employees:	102	**Sales/Emp.:**	$215,353
Established:	1982	**International:**	29%
1994 Rank:	#42	**'93-'94 Growth:**	15%
1993:	$19,051,000	**1990:**	$4,700,000
1992:	$10,472,000	**1989:**	$5,400,000
1991:	$6,000,000		

BEST-SELLING TITLES: TurboCAD ($149.95) Vertical/industry- or job-specific (DOS, Windows, Macintosh) **FormTool Gold** ($99.95) General business (DOS, Windows) **WinDelete** ($49.95) Utility (Windows) **MasterClips** ($59.95) General business (DOS, Windows)

48 Traveling Software — $21,812,000

18702 North Creek Pkwy., Bothell, WA 98011
206-483-8088 Fax: 206-487-1284

President:	Jonathan Scott		
CFO:	David Payne		
Ownership:	Private		
Employees:	106	**Sales/Emp.:**	$205,774
Established:	1983	**International:**	23%
1994 Rank:	#39	**'93-'94 Growth:**	0%
1993:	$21,781,000	**1990:**	$12,704,000
1992:	$19,310,000	**1989:**	$13,589,000
1991:	$14,091,000		

BEST-SELLING TITLES: LapLink V ($169.95) Communications/networking (DOS) **LapLink for Windows** ($199.95) Communications/networking **Casio PC-Link** (price varies) Communications/networking (Casio) **CommWorks** ($199.95) Communications/networking (Windows)

49 Timberline Software Corp. $21,641,000

9600 SW Nimbus, Beaverton, OR 97005
503-626-6775 Fax: 503-526-8040

President:	John Gorman		
CFO:	Thomas Cox		
Ownership:	Public (TMBS)		
Employees:	245	**Sales/Emp.:**	$88,331
Established:	1972	**International:**	3%
1994 Rank:	#45	**'93-'94 Growth:**	19%
1993:	$18,205,000	**1990:**	$12,684,000
1992:	$14,902,000	**1989:**	$10,741,000
1991:	$12,697,000		

BEST-SELLING TITLES: Construction Gold (price varies) Vertical/industry- or job-specific (Windows, OS/2) **Precision Estimating** (price varies) Vertical/industry- or job-specific (DOS) **Property Management Gold** (price varies) Vertical/industry- or job-specific (OS/2) **AEasy Plus** (price varies) Vertical/industry- or job-specific (DOS)

50 DataEase International $21,000,000

7 Cambridge Dr., Trumbull, CT 06611
203-374-8000 Fax: 203-365-2317

President:	Stephen Page		
CFO:	Todd Ryder		
Ownership:	Private		
Employees:	190	**Sales/Emp.:**	$110,526
Established:	1982	**International:**	62%
1994 Rank:	#31	**'93-'94 Growth:**	–31%
1993:	$30,500,000	**1990:**	$28,000,000
1992:	$33,000,000	**1989:**	
1991:	$31,000,000		

BEST-SELLING TITLES: DataEase ($695) General business (DOS, OS/2) **DataEase Express** ($395) General business (Windows)

51 IQ Software Corp. $20,097,000

3295 River Exchange Dr., Norcross, GA 30092
404-446-8880 Fax: 404-448-4088

President:	Charles R. Chitty		
CFO:	Michael J. Casey		
Ownership:	Public (IQSW)		
Employees:	160	**Sales/Emp.:**	$125,606
Established:	1984	**International:**	31%
1994 Rank:	n/a	**'93-'94 Growth:**	5%
1993:	$19,119,000	**1990:**	$7,194,000
1992:	$15,211,000	**1989:**	$4,892,000
1991:	$10,359,000		

BEST-SELLING TITLES: Intelligent Query ($500–$42,000) General business (DOS, Windows, Unix) **IQ Access** ($500–$42,000) General business (DOS, Windows, Unix)

52 Expert Software $19,727,000

800 Douglas Rd., Coral Gables, FL 33134
305-567-9990 Fax: 305-443-0786

CEO:	Ken Currier		
CFO:	Bob Muccini		
Ownership:	Private		
Employees:	75	**Sales/Emp.:**	$263,027
Established:	1992	**International:**	5%
1994 Rank:	n/a	**'93-'94 Growth:**	57%
1993:	$12,555,000	**1990:**	
1992:	$8,673,000	**1989:**	
1991:			

BEST-SELLING TITLES: Expert Home Design 3-D ($14.95) Consumer/entertainment (Windows, Macintosh) **Travel Planner** ($14.95) Consumer entertainment (Windows) **Power Publisher** ($14.95) Consumer/entertainment (Windows) **Expert Maps** ($14.95) Consumer/entertainment (Windows)

53 Systems Plus $17,600,000

500 Clyde Ave., Mountain View, CA 94043
415-969-7047 Fax: 415-969-0118

President:	Richard Mehrlich		
CFO:	Eve Christensen		
Ownership:	Private		
Employees:	65	**Sales/Emp.:**	$270,769
Established:	1980	International:	0%
1994 Rank:	#50	**'93-'94 Growth:**	22%
1993:	$14,400,000	**1990:**	$11,100,000
1992:	$14,200,000	**1989:**	$8,500,000
1991:	$12,100,000		

BEST-SELLING TITLES: The Medical Manager (price varies) Vertical/industry- or job-specific (DOS, Windows, OS/2, Unix)

54 Globalink $17,300,000

9302 Lee Hwy., Fairfax, VA 22031
703-273-5600 Fax: 703-273-3866

President:	Michael Tacelosky		
CFO:	Jorge Forgues		
Ownership:	Public (GLNK)		
Employees:	100	**Sales/Emp.:**	$173,000
Established:	1989	**International:**	35%
1994 Rank:	#80	**'93-'94 Growth:**	49%
1993:	$11,600,000	**1990:**	$2,200,000
1992:	$5,700,000	**1989:**	$700,000
1991:	$3,500,000		

BEST-SELLING TITLES: Language Assistant ($59) Consumer/entertainment (DOS, Windows, Macintosh) **Power Translator** ($149) Consumer/entertainment (DOS, Windows, Macintosh) **Power Translator Professional** ($595) Consumer/entertainment (DOS, Windows, Macintosh)

55 MicroHelp — $17,232,000

4359 Shallowford Industrial Pkwy., Marietta, GA 30066
404-516-0899 Fax: 404-516-1099

President:	Tim O'Pry		
CFO:	Janet Van Pelt		
Ownership:	Private		
Employees:	36	**Sales/Emp.:**	$478,667
Established:	1985	**International:**	8%
1994 Rank:	#97	**'93-'94 Growth:**	299%
1993:	$4,315,000	**1990:**	$675,000
1992:	$1,384,000	**1989:**	$738,000
1991:	$748,000		

BEST-SELLING TITLES: UnInstaller 2 ($69.95) Utility (Windows) **VBTools 4** ($129) Programming tool/language (Windows)

56 Edmark — $16,807,000

6727 185th Ave. N.E., Redmond, WA 98073
206-556-8400 Fax: 206-556-8998

CEO:	Sally Narodick		
CFO:	Paul Bialek		
Ownership:	Public (EDMK)		
Employees:	115	**Sales/Emp.:**	$146,148
Established:	1970	**International:**	10%
1994 Rank:	#60	**'93-'94 Growth:**	66%
1993:	$10,118,000	**1990:**	$3,654,000
1992:	$7,268,000	**1989:**	$2,981,000
1991:	$5,087,000		

BEST-SELLING TITLES: Bailey's Book House ($30–$35) Education (DOS, Windows, Macintosh) **Millie's Math House** ($30–$35) Education (DOS, Windows, Macintosh) **Sammy's Science House** ($30–$35) Education (DOS, Windows, Macintosh) **Thinkin' Things Collection I** ($35–$40) Education (DOS, Windows, Macintosh)

57 Blyth Holdings — $16,252,000

989 E. Hillsdale Blvd., Foster City, CA 94404
415-571-0222 Fax: 415-571-1322

President:	Michael J. Minor		
CFO:	Jeffrey W. Beaumont		
Ownership:	Public (BLYH)		
Employees:	195	**Sales/Emp.:**	$83,344
Established:	1987	**International:**	26%
1994 Rank:	#51	**'93-'94 Growth:**	13%
1993:	$14,352,000	**1990:**	$3,926,000
1992:	$11,297,000	**1989:**	$2,996,000
1991:	$5,120,000		

BEST-SELLING TITLES: Omnis ($5,000) Programming tool/language (Windows, Macintosh)

58 Persoft — $16,100,000

465 Science Dr., Madison, WI 53711
608-273-6000 Fax: 608-273-8227

President:	Thomas Wolfe		
CFO:	Martin Chiaro		
Ownership:	Private		
Employees:	105	**Sales/Emp.:**	$153,333
Established:	1982	**International:**	28%
1994 Rank:	#56	**'93-'94 Growth:**	44%
1993:	$11,200,000	**1990:**	$6,796,000
1992:	$8,770,000	**1989:**	$6,546,000
1991:	$7,350,000		

BEST-SELLING TITLES: SmarTerm 420 ($295) Communications/networking (DOS, Windows) **SmarTerm 340** ($375–$395) Communications/networking (Windows) **SmarTerm 470** ($395) Communications/networking (DOS, Windows) **SmarTerm 320** ($225) Communications/networking (DOS)

59 SBT Accounting Systems — $14,000,000

1401 Los Gamos Dr., San Rafael, CA 94903
415-444-9900 Fax: 415-444-9901

President:	Robert Davies		
CFO:	Bill Meyer		
Ownership:	Private		
Employees:	120	**Sales/Emp.:**	$116,667
Established:	1980	**International:**	3%
1994 Rank:	#57	**'93-'94 Growth:**	26%
1993:	$11,100,000	**1990:**	$10,500,000
1992:	$11,000,000	**1989:**	$10,500,000
1991:	$11,000,000		

BEST-SELLING TITLES: Professional Series ($895/module) Accounting/finance/tax (DOS, Windows, Unix) **VisionPoint** ($395/module) Accounting/finance/tax (DOS, Unix) **Small Business Accountant** ($395/user) Accounting/finance/tax (DOS, Unix)

60 American Small Business Computer — $13,830,000

327 South Mill, Pryor, OK 74361
918-825-7555 Fax: 918-825-6359

President:	Bruce Taylor		
CFO:	Robert Webster		
Ownership:	Private		
Employees:	35	**Sales/Emp.:**	$395,143
Established:	1981	**International:**	12%
1994 Rank:	#52	**'93-'94 Growth:**	1%
1993:	$13,685,000	**1990:**	$8,381,000
1992:	$13,485,000	**1989:**	$7,200,000
1991:	$13,057,000		

BEST-SELLING TITLES: DesignCAD 2D ($349) Vertical/industry- or job-specific (DOS, Windows) **Design CAD 3D** ($499) Vertical/industry- or job-specific (DOS, Windows) **DesignCAD Macintosh** ($299) Vertical/industry- or job-specific (Macintosh) **Instant Architect/Instant Engineer** ($79.00) Vertical/industry- or job-specific (DOS)

61 CE Software $12,541,000

1801 Industrial Cir., W. Des Moines, IA 50265
515-221-1801 Fax: 515-221-1806

President:	Ford Goodman		
CFO:	Curtis Lack		
Ownership:	Public (CESH)		
Employees:	134	**Sales/Emp.:**	$93,940
Established:	1981	**International:**	21%
1994 Rank:	#63	**'93-'94 Growth:**	32%
1993:	$9,534,390	**1990:**	$6,720,574
1992:	$10,197,314	**1989:**	$3,486,900
1991:	$9,165,620		

BEST-SELLING TITLES: QuickMail ($649/10 users) Communications/networking (DOS, Windows, Macintosh) **QuicKeys** ($119) Utility (Macintosh) **Time Vision Network Scheduler** ($59.95) General business (Windows)

62 Eagle Point Corp. $11,660,000

4131 Westmark Dr., Dubuque, IA 52002
319-556-8392 Fax: 319-556-5321

President:	Rod Blum		
CFO:	Dennis George		
Ownership:	Private		
Employees:	160	**Sales/Emp.:**	$72,875
Established:	1983	**International:**	7%
1994 Rank:	#59	**'93-'94 Growth:**	10%
1993:	$10,554,000	**1990:**	$1,434,000
1992:	$6,954,000	**1989:**	$763,000
1991:	$3,917,000		

BEST-SELLING TITLES: RoadCalc ($2,495) Vertical/industry- or job-specific (DOS, Windows, Unix) **Surface Modeling** ($1,095) Vertical/industry- or job- specific (DOS, Windows, Unix) **Site Design** ($1,495) Vertical/industry- or job-specific (DOS, Windows, Unix) **Advanced Architecture** ($1,195) Vertical/industry- or job-specific (DOS, Windows, Unix)

63 RealWorld $11,300,000

282 Loudon Rd., Concord, NH 03302
603-224-2200 Fax: 603-224-1955

President:	Murray P. Fish		
CFO:	n/a		
Ownership:	Private		
Employees:	110	**Sales/Emp.:**	$102,727
Established:	1980	**International:**	3%
1994 Rank:	n/a	**'93-'94 Growth:**	–13%
1993:	$13,002,000	**1990:**	$15,620,000
1992:	$16,010,000	**1989:**	$15,540,000
1991:	$16,800,000		

BEST-SELLING TITLES: RealWorld General Ledger ($795) Accounting/finance/tax (Windows, Unix) **RealWorld Payroll** ($795) Accounting/finance/tax (Windows, Unix) **RealWorld Order Entry** ($795) Accounting/finance/tax (Windows, Unix)

64 Banner Blue Software — $10,930,000

39500 Stevenson Pl., Fremont, CA 94539
510-794-6850 Fax: 510-794-9152

President:	Kenneth Hess		
CFO:	Bonnie Anderson		
Ownership:	Private		
Employees:	55	**Sales/Emp.:**	$198,727
Established:	1984	**International:**	4%
1994 Rank:	#77	**'93-'94 Growth:**	55%
1993:	$7,062,000	**1990:**	$3,412,000
1992:	$5,637,000	**1989:**	$2,784,000
1991:	$4,624,000		

BEST-SELLING TITLES: Family Tree Maker ($55–$70) Consumer/entertainment (DOS, Windows) **Org Plus** ($75–$150) General business (DOS, Windows, Macintosh)

65 Now Software — $10,181,000

921 SW Washington St., Portland, OR 97205
503-274-2800 Fax: 503-274-0670

President:	Duane Schulz		
CFO:	Tim Marcotte		
Ownership:	Private		
Employees:	51	**Sales/Emp.:**	$199,627
Established:	1990	**International:**	24%
1994 Rank:	#68	**'93-'94 Growth:**	18%
1993:	$8,663,000	**1990:**	$888,000
1992:	$5,547,000	**1989:**	
1991:	$1,830,000		

BEST-SELLING TITLES: Now Utilities ($129) (Macintosh) **Now Up to Date** ($99) General business (Macintosh) **Now Contact** ($99) General business (Macintosh)

66 Citrix Systems — $10,140,000

210 University Dr., Coral Springs, FL 33071
305-755-0559 Fax: 305-341-6880

Chairman:	Edward Iacobucci		
CFO:	Jim Felcyn		
Ownership:	Private		
Employees:	72	**Sales/Emp.:**	$140,833
Established:	1989	**International:**	20%
1994 Rank:	#91	**'93-'94 Growth:**	101%
1993:	$5,043,000	**1990:**	
1992:	$1,850,000	**1989:**	
1991:	$350,000		

BEST-SELLING TITLES: WinView for Networks ($2,995) Operating system (DOS, Windows, OS/2) **Citrix Multiuser** ($995) Operating system (DOS, Windows, OS/2)

67 Formgen $10,015,000

7641 E. Gray Rd., Scottsdale, AZ 85260
602-443-4109 Fax: 602-951-6810

President:	Randy MacLean		
CFO:	Peter Gibson		
Ownership:	Private		
Employees:	31	**Sales/Emp.:**	$323,065
Established:	1987	**International:**	10%
1994 Rank:	#70	**'93-'94 Growth:**	23%
1993:	$8,151,000	**1990:**	$3,050,000
1992:	$6,390,000	**1989:**	$2,350,000
1991:	$4,108,000		

BEST-SELLING TITLES: Doom ($7.95) Consumer/entertainment (DOS) **Gold Medallion Gamepack** ($19.95) Consumer/entertainment (DOS) **Spear of Destiny** ($59.95) Consumer/entertainment (DOS) **Raptor** ($7.95) Consumer/entertainment (DOS)

68 Software Shop Systems $10,000,000

1340 Campus Pkwy., Wall, NJ 07719
908-938-3200 Fax: 908-938-5631

President:	Harvey Kimmel		
CFO:	James Vena		
Ownership:	Private		
Employees:	68	**Sales/Emp.:**	$147,059
Established:	1978	**International:**	1%
1994 Rank:	#61	**'93-'94 Growth:**	0%
1993:	$10,000,000	**1990:**	$10,000,000
1992:	$10,000,000	**1989:**	$9,200,000
1991:	$10,000,000		

BEST-SELLING TITLES: The Construction Manager ($4,595) Vertical/industry- or job-specific (DOS, Windows) **ACE-CSI Estimating** ($4,495) Vertical/industry- or job-specific (DOS) **ESTMAT 2000 Estimating** ($4,495) Vertical/industry- or job-specific (DOS) **Pulsar** ($2,625) Vertical/industry- or job-specific (DOS, Windows, Unix)

69 Healthcare Communications $9,900,000

300 S. 68th St., Lincoln, NE 68510
402-489-0391 Fax: 402-489-6411

Chairman:	Michael Edwards		
CFO:	David Rice		
Ownership:	Private		
Employees:	100	**Sales/Emp.:**	$99,000
Established:	1983	**International:**	0%
1994 Rank:	#65	**'93-'94 Growth:**	6%
1993:	$9,300,000	**1990:**	$6,048,000
1992:	$7,648,000	**1989:**	$4,713,000
1991:	$6,994,000		

BEST-SELLING TITLES: MediMac ($4,295) Vertical/industry- or job-specific (Macintosh) **DentalMac** ($3,995) Vertical/industry- or job-specific (Macintosh) **ChiroMac** ($2,995) Vertical/industry- or job-specific (Macintosh)

70 Nova Logic $9,542,000

26010 Mureau Rd., Calabasas, CA 91302
818-880-1997 Fax: 818-880-1998

President:	John Garcia		
CFO:	Lee Milligan		
Ownership:	Private		
Employees:	27	**Sales/Emp.:**	$353,407
Established:	1985	**International:**	25%
1994 Rank:	#95	**'93-'94 Growth:**	93%
1993:	$4,941,000	**1990:**	
1992:	$2,216,000	**1989:**	
1991:			

BEST-SELLING TITLES: Armored Fist ($69.95) Consumer/entertainment (DOS) **Comanche** ($49.95) Consumer/entertainment (DOS) **Wolfpack** ($39.95) Consumer/entertainment (DOS, Macintosh)

71 MicroBiz Corp. $8,800,000

300 Corporate Dr., Mahwah, NJ 07430
201-512-0900 Fax: 201-512-1919

President:	Craig Aberle		
CFO:	William Huntington		
Ownership:	Private		
Employees:	55	**Sales/Emp.:**	$160,000
Established:	1986	**International:**	10%
1994 Rank:	#69	**'93-'94 Growth:**	2%
1993:	$8,660,000	**1990:**	$1,231,000
1992:	$6,637,000	**1989:**	$491,000
1991:	$3,525,000		

BEST-SELLING TITLES: Business Controller Plus ($1,595/user) General business (DOS) **Hair/Nail Salon Controller** ($1,195) Vertical/industry- or job-specific (DOS) **Auto Repair Shop Controller** ($2,495) Vertical/industry- or job-specific (DOS) **Liquor Store Controller** ($2,495) Vertical/industry- or job-specific (DOS)

72 Dantz Development Corp. $8,493,000

4 Orinda Way, Orinda, CA 94563
510-253-3000 Fax: 510-253-9099

President:	Lawrence Zulch		
CFO:	Doug Paul		
Ownership:	Private		
Employees:	52	**Sales/Emp.:**	$163,327
Established:	1984	**International:**	38%
1994 Rank:	#66	**'93-'94 Growth:**	–3%
1993:	$8,765,000	**1990:**	$2,050,000
1992:	$5,292,000	**1989:**	$629,721
1991:	$4,781,000		

BEST-SELLING TITLES: Retrospect ($249) Utility (Macintosh) **Retrospect Remote** ($449) Utility (Macintosh) **Remote 10-Pack** ($249) Utility (Macintosh) **DiskFit Pro** ($125) Utility (Macintosh)

73 FutureSoft — $8,456,000

12012 Wickchester, Houston, TX 77079
713-496-9400 Fax: 713-496-1090

Chairman:	J.T. Farrell		
CFO:	Warren White		
Ownership:	Private		
Employees:	80	**Sales/Emp.:**	$105,700
Established:	1982	**International:**	20%
1994 Rank:	#76	**'93-'94 Growth:**	15%
1993:	$7,359,000	**1990:**	$1,932,000
1992:	$5,538,000	**1989:**	$1,089,000
1991:	$3,325,000		

BEST-SELLING TITLES: DynaComm ($249) Communications/networking (Windows)
DynaComm/Elite ($395) Communications/networking (Windows)
DynaComm/OpenConnect TN32 ($395) Communications/networking (Windows)
DynaComm Open Connect 5250 ($395) Communications/networking (Windows)

74 Data Access Corp. — $8,400,000

14000 SW 119 Ave., Miami, FL 33186
305-238-0012 Fax: 305-238-0017

President:	Charles Casanave III		
CFO:	Charles Casanave Sr.		
Ownership:	Private		
Employees:	75	**Sales/Emp.:**	$112,000
Established:	1976	**International:**	61%
1994 Rank:	#71	**'93-'94 Growth:**	5%
1993:	$8,000,000	**1990:**	$6,500,000
1992:	$7,200,000	**1989:**	$6,266,000
1991:	$7,100,000		

BEST-SELLING TITLES: DataFlex ($995) Programming tool/language (DOS, Windows, OS/2, Unix) **FlexQL** ($295) Programming tool/language (DOS, Unix) **WinQL** ($250) Programming tool/language (Windows)

75 Campbell Services — $8,360,000

21700 Northwestern Hwy., Southfield, MI 48075
810-559-5955 Fax: 810-559-1034

President:	Donald Campbell		
CFO:	Jennifer Konitsney		
Ownership:	Private		
Employees:	92	**Sales/Emp.:**	$90,870
Established:	971	**International:**	4%
1994 Rank:	#79	**'93-'94 Growth:**	20%
1993:	$6,958,000	**1990:**	$917,000
1992:	$5,218,000	**1989:**	$346,000
1991:	$1,963,000		

BEST-SELLING TITLES: OnTime for Networks ($534/5 users) General business (DOS, Windows) **OnTime Enterprise/Banyan Vines** ($641/5 users) General business (DOS, Windows) **OnTime Enterprise/Novell Netware** ($641/5 users) General business (DOS, Windows)

76 Cosmi Corp. $8,169,000

2600 Homestead Pl., Rancho Dominguez, CA 90220
310-833-2000 Fax: 310-886-3500

President:	George Johnson		
CFO:	William DeMucci		
Ownership:	Private		
Employees:	45	**Sales/Emp.:**	$181,533
Established:	1982	**International:**	3%
1994 Rank:	#81	**'93-'94 Growth:**	34%
1993:	$6,106,000	**1990:**	$4,089,000
1992:	$5,252,000	**1989:**	$3,400,000
1991:	$4,539,000		

BEST-SELLING TITLES: Label Publisher ($14.95) General business (DOS, Windows, Macintosh) **PC Attorney** ($14.95) General business (DOS, Windows) **Desktop Publisher** ($14.95) Consumer/entertainment (DOS, Windows) **SwiftDraw** ($19.95) Consumer/entertainment (Windows)

77 Jandel Scientific $8,094,000

2591 Kerner Blvd., San Rafael, CA 94901
415-453-6700 Fax: 415-453-7769

President:	Joseph Osborn		
CFO:	Ross Garofalo		
Ownership:	Private		
Employees:	67	**Sales/Emp.:**	$120,806
Established:	1983	**International:**	36%
1994 Rank:	#75	**'93-'94 Growth:**	7%
1993:	$7,583,000	**1990:**	$5,100,000
1992:	$6,600,000	**1989:**	$3,338,000
1991:	$5,600,000		

BEST-SELLING TITLES: SigmaPlot ($495) Vertical/industry- or job-specific (DOS, Windows, Macintosh) **SigmaStat** ($495) Vertical/industry- or job-specific (DOS, Windows) **TableCurve** ($495) Vertical/industry- or job-specific (DOS, Windows)

78 ConnectSoft $7,900,000

11130 NE 33rd Pl. #250, Bellevue, WA 98004
206-827-6467 Fax: 206-822-9095

CEO:	Mitchell B. London		
CFO:	Paul McBride		
Ownership:	Private		
Employees:	91	**Sales/Emp.:**	$86,813
Established:	1988	**International:**	0%
1994 Rank:	n/a	**'93-'94 Growth:**	243%
1993:	$2,300,000	**1990:**	$200,000
1992:	$2,500,000	**1989:**	$40,000
1991:	$640,000		

BEST-SELLING TITLES: E-Mail Connection ($99.95) Communications/networking (Windows) **Kidmail Connection** ($34.95) Communications/networking (Windows)

79 SWFTE International $7,897,000

724 Yorklyn Rd., Hockessin, DE 19707
302-234-1740 Fax: 302-234-1760

President:	David Goodman		
CFO:	n/a		
Ownership:	Private		
Employees:	36	**Sales/Emp.:**	$219,361
Established:	1983	**International:**	0%
1994 Rank:	#78	**'93-'94 Growth:**	12%
1993:	$7,025,000	**1990:**	$2,002,000
1992:	$6,663,000	**1989:**	$1,382,000
1991:	$2,205,000		

BEST-SELLING TITLES: Bicycle Limited Edition ($69.95) Consumer/entertainment (DOS, Windows) **Brain Quest** ($29.95) Education (DOS, Windows) **Bicycle Solitaire** ($19.95) Consumer entertainment (DOS, Windows) **Gettysburg** ($69.95) Education(Windows)

80 Algor $7,798,000

150 Beta Dr., Pittsburgh, PA 15238
412-967-2700 Fax: 412-967-2781

President:	Michael Bussler		
CFO:	Virginia Goebel		
Ownership:	Private		
Employees:	60	**Sales/Emp.:**	$129,967
Established:	1977	**International:**	23%
1994 Rank:	#73	**'93-'94 Growth:**	3%
1993:	$7,589,000	**1990:**	$4,400,000
1992:	$7,000,000	**1989:**	$3,000,000
1991:	$5,800,000		

BEST-SELLING TITLES: The Professional Mech/E ($2,900–$4,350) Vertical/industry- or job-specific (DOS, Windows, Unix) **The Industrial Mech/E** ($3,900–$5,850) Vertical/industry- or job-specific (DOS, Windows, Unix) **Nonlinear Analysis Extender** ($2,750–$4,125) Vertical/industry- or job-specific (DOS, Windows, Unix) **The Graduate Mech/E** ($1,495–$2,245) Vertical/industry- or job-specific (DOS, Windows, Unix)

81 Touchstone $7,207,000

2130 Main St., Huntington Beach, CA 92648
714-969-7746 Fax: 714-960-1886

President:	C. Shannon Jenkins		
CFO:	Ronald Maas		
Ownership:	Public (TSSW)		
Employees:	35	**Sales/Emp.:**	$205,914
Established:	1982	**International:**	12%
1994 Rank:	#96	**'93-'94 Growth:**	47%
1993:	$4,900,000	**1990:**	$3,526,000
1992:	$3,495,000	**1989:**	$1,708,000
1991:	$3,680,000		

BEST-SELLING TITLES: WinCheck It ($79.95) Utility (Windows) **Setup Advisor** ($29.95) Utility (Windows) **CheckIt Pro** ($149.95) Utility (DOS)

82 Pinnacle Publishing — $6,500,000

18000 72nd Ave. S., Kent, WA 98032
206-251-1900 Fax: 206-251-5057

CEO:	Janice Machala		
CFO:	D. Robert Colliton		
Ownership:	Private		
Employees:	40	**Sales/Emp.:**	$162,500
Established:	1986	**International:**	10%
1994 Rank:	#83	**'93-'94 Growth:**	8%
1993:	$5,995,000	**1990:**	$2,947,000
1992:	$5,559,000	**1989:**	$2,021,000
1991:	$4,354,000		

BEST-SELLING TITLES: Graphics Server ($299) Programming tool/language (Windows) **NetLib** ($299) Programming tool/language (DOS, Windows) **CommTools** ($299) Programming tool/language (DOS, Windows) **ToolThings** ($179) Programming tool/language (Windows)

83 Mastersoft — $6,150,000

8737 E. Via De Commercio, Scottsdale, AZ 85258
602-948-4888 Fax: 602-948-8261

CEO:	Kent C. Mueller		
CFO:	Sally Lauden		
Ownership:	Private		
Employees:	32	**Sales/Emp.:**	$192,188
Established:	1986	**International:**	27%
1994 Rank:	n/a	**'93-'94 Growth:**	66%
1993:	$3,703,000	**1990:**	$1,480,000
1992:	$2,812,000	**1989:**	$650,000
1991:	$2,054,000		

BEST-SELLING TITLES: Word For Word ($149) Utility (DOS, Windows, Macintosh, Unix) **DocuComp** ($189) Utility (DOS, Windows, Macintosh)

84 Queue — $6,101,000

338 Commerce Dr., Fairfield, CT 06430
203-333-7268 Fax: 203-336-2481

CEO:	Jonathan Kantrowitz		
CFO:	Peter Uhrynowski		
Ownership:	Private		
Employees:	58	**Sales/Emp.:**	$105,190
Established:	1980	**International:**	5%
1994 Rank:	#84	**'93-'94 Growth:**	5%
1993:	$5,965,000	**1990:**	$5,890,000
1992:	$5,900,000	**1989:**	$5,400,000
1991:	$6,126,000		

BEST-SELLING TITLES: Black American History ($295) Education (DOS, Macintosh)

85 Micro Star Software — $6,000,000

2245 Camino Vida Roble, Carlsbad, CA 92009
619-931-4949 Fax: 619-931-4950

President:	Stephen H. Benedict		
CFO:	Chris Burnett		
Ownership:	Private		
Employees:	70	**Sales/Emp.:**	$85,714
Established:	1986	**International:**	18%
1994 Rank:	#99	**'93-'94 Growth:**	88%
1993:	$3,200,000	**1990:**	$1,300,000
1992:	$2,900,000	**1989:**	$1,800,000
1991:	$1,500,000		

BEST-SELLING TITLES: 200 Great Games ($29.95) Consumer/entertainment (Windows) **35 Great Games** ($19.95) Consumer/entertainment (Windows) **Doom-Shareware** ($7.99) Consumer/entertainment (DOS) **7000 Clip Art** ($29.95) General business (DOS, Windows)

86 Ray Dream — $5,343,000

1804 North Shoreline Blvd., Mountain View, CA 94043
415-960-0768 Fax: 415-960-1198

CEO:	Eric Hautemont		
CFO:	Joseph C. Consul		
Ownership:	Private		
Employees:	32	**Sales/Emp.:**	$166,969
Established:	1989	**International:**	24%
1994 Rank:	n/a	**'93-'94 Growth:**	81%
1993:	$2,960,000	**1990:**	$33,000
1992:	$1,147,000	**1989:**	
1991:	$673,000		

BEST-SELLING TITLES: Ray Dream Designer ($349) Vertical/industry- or job-specific (Windows, Macintosh) **Add Depth** ($149) Vertical/industry- or job- specific (Windows, Macintosh) **Jag II** ($129) Vertical/industry- or job-specific (Windows, Macintosh)

87 DeltaPoint — $5,185,000

2 Harris Ct., Monterey, CA 93940
408-648-4000 Fax: 408-648-4020

President:	Ray Kingman		
CFO:	n/a		
Ownership:	Private		
Employees:	34	**Sales/Emp.:**	$152,500
Established:	1989	**International:**	39%
1994 Rank:	#86	**'93-'94 Growth:**	–11%
1993:	$5,833,000	**1990:**	$2,658,000
1992:	$6,739,000	**1989:**	$1,100,000
1991:	$4,241,000		

BEST-SELLING TITLES: DeltaGraph Pro ($195) General business (Windows, Macintosh) **Graphics Tools** ($169) General business (Windows, Macintosh)

88 Individual Software — $5,150,000

5870 Stoneridge Dr., Pleasanton, CA 94588
510-734-6767 Fax: 510-734-8337

President:	Jo-L Hendrickson		
CFO:	n/a		
Ownership:	Private		
Employees:	35	**Sales/Emp.:**	$147,143
Established:	1981	**International:**	10%
1994 Rank:	#85	**'93-'94 Growth:**	–13%
1993:	$5,953,000	**1990:**	$4,800,000
1992:	$7,000,000	**1989:**	$4,400,000
1991:	$6,400,000		

BEST-SELLING TITLES: Professor Windows ($39.95) Education (Windows) **AnyTime** ($39.95) General business (DOS, Windows) **MultiMedia Typing Instructor** ($39.95) Education (Windows) **Resume Maker** ($29.95) Consumer/entertainment (DOS, Windows)

89 Graphsoft — $4,866,000

10270 Old Columbia Rd., Columbia, MD 21046
410-290-5114 Fax: 410-290-8050

President:	Richard Diehl		
CFO:	Joseph Schmelzle		
Ownership:	Public (DIEG)		
Employees:	30	**Sales/Emp.:**	$162,200
Established:	1985	**International:**	38%
1994 Rank:	n/a	**'93-'94 Growth:**	40%
1993:	$3,470,000	**1990:**	$1,205,000
1992:	$2,274,000	**1989:**	$896,000
1991:	$1,521,000		

BEST-SELLING TITLES: Minicad ($795) Vertical/industry- or job-specific (Macintosh) **Blueprint** ($295) Vertical/industry- or job-specific (Macintosh) **Azimuth** ($395) Vertical/industry- or job-specific (Macintosh)

90 Softdisk Publishing — $4,219,000

606 Common St., Shreveport, LA 71101
318-221-8718 Fax: 318-221-8870

CEO:	W.A. Vekovius		
CFO:	Stephen Vekovius		
Ownership:	Private		
Employees:	52	**Sales/Emp.:**	$81,135
Established:	1981	**International:**	10%
1994 Rank:	#88	**'93-'94 Growth:**	–23%
1993:	$5,509,000	**1990:**	$7,127,000
1992:	$4,938,000	**1989:**	$6,105,000
1991:	$4,749,000		

BEST-SELLING TITLES: Softdisk PC VGA ($69.95) Consumer/entertainment (DOS) **Softdisk PC for Windows** ($69.95) Consumer/entertainment **Load Star** ($69.95) Consumer/entertainment (C64/128, Apple II)

91 Sound Source Unlimited — $4,200,000

2985 E. Hillcrest Dr., Westlake Village, CA 91362
805-494-9996 Fax: 805-495-0016

CEO:	Vincent Bitetti		
CFO:	n/a		
Ownership:	Private		
Employees:	25	**Sales/Emp.:**	$168,000
Established:	1988	**International:**	5%
1994 Rank:	n/a	**'93-'94 Growth:**	91%
1993:	$2,200,000	**1990:**	$1,000,000
1992:	$2,200,000	**1989:**	$490,000
1991:	$1,200,000		

BEST-SELLING TITLES: Star Trek AudioClips ($20) Consumer/entertainment (DOS, Macintosh) **T2: Screen Saver** ($30) Consumer/entertainment (Windows) **Star Wars AudioClips** ($20) Consumer/entertainment (DOS, Macintosh) **The Secret Garden** ($30) Consumer/entertainment (Windows)

92 7th Level — $4,174,000

1771 International Pkwy., Richardson, TX 75081
214-498-8100 Fax: 214-437-2717

President:	George D. Grayson		
CFO:	David R. Henkel		
Ownership:	Public (SEVL)		
Employees:	75	**Sales/Emp.:**	$55,653
Established:	1993	**International:**	15%
1994 Rank:	n/a	**'93-'94 Growth:**	398%
1993:	$838,000	**1990:**	
1992:		**1989:**	
1991:			

BEST-SELLING TITLES: Monty Python's Complete Waste of Time ($49.95) Consumer/entertainment (Windows) **TuneLand** ($39.95) Consumer/entertainment (Windows) **Take Your Best Shot** ($19.95) Consumer/entertainment (Windows)

93 Silton-Bookman Systems — $4,082,000

20230 Stevens Creek Blvd., Cupertino, CA 95014
408-446-1170 Fax: 408-446-5705

President:	Richard Silton		
CFO:	Sarah Padfield		
Ownership:	Private		
Employees:	43	**Sales/Emp.:**	$94,930
Established:	1984	**International:**	5%
1994 Rank:	#98	**'93-'94 Growth:**	–5%
1993:	$4,287,000	**1990:**	$2,424,000
1992:	$3,644,000	**1989:**	$1,739,000
1991:	$3,066,000		

BEST-SELLING TITLES: Registrar ($1,995–$2,995) Vertical/industry- or job-specific (DOS, Windows)

94 CYMA Systems $4,000,000

2330 West University, Tempe, AZ 85281
602-303-2962 Fax: 602-303-2969

President:	Michael Glaser		
CFO:	James Norton		
Ownership:	Private		
Employees:	40	**Sales/Emp.:**	$100,000
Established:	1980	**International:**	2%
1994 Rank:	#100	**'93-'94 Growth:**	0%
1993:	$4,000,000	**1990:**	
1992:	$4,800,000	**1989:**	
1991:	$4,000,000		

BEST-SELLING TITLES: Professional Accounting Series ($675/module) Accounting/finance/tax (DOS)

95 KnowledgePoint $3,900,000

1129 Industrial Ave., Petaluma, CA 94952
707-762-0333 Fax: 707-762-0802

President:	Michael Troy		
CFO:	Jerri Brown		
Ownership:	Private		
Employees:	33	**Sales/Emp.:**	$118,182
Established:	1987	**International:**	0%
1994 Rank:	n/a	**'93-'94 Growth:**	50%
1993:	$2,600,000	**1990:**	$1,100,000
1992:	$1,900,000	**1989:**	$800,000
1991:	$1,200,000		

BEST-SELLING TITLES: Performance Now! ($129) General business (Windows) **Descriptions Now!** ($49.95) General business (DOS, Windows) **Policies Now!** ($69.99) General business (DOS)

96 Cambridge Scientific Computing $3,863,000

875 Massachusetts Ave., Cambridge, MA 02139
617-491-2200 Fax: 617-491-8208

President:	Stewart D. Rubenstein		
CFO:	Michael G. Tomasic		
Ownership:	Private		
Employees:	24	**Sales/Emp.:**	$160,958
Established:	1986	**International:**	30%
1994 Rank:	n/a	**'93-'94 Growth:**	7%
1993:	$3,621,000	**1990:**	$1,635,000
1992:	$2,364,000	**1989:**	$1,362,000
1991:	$1,862,000		

BEST-SELLING TITLES: CS ChemOffice ($1,295) Vertical/industry- or job-specific (Windows, Macintosh) **CS ChemDraw** ($495) Vertical/industry- or job-specific (Windows, Macintosh, Unix) **CS Chem3D** ($795) Vertical/industry- or job-specific (Windows, Macintosh) **CS ChemFinder** ($795) Vertical/industry- or job-specific/Education (Macintosh)

97 GeoWorks $3,700,000

960 Atlantic Ave., Alameda, CA 94501
510-814-1660 Fax: 510-814-4250

President:	Gordon Mayer		
CFO:	n/a		
Ownership:	Public (GWRX)		
Employees:	120	**Sales/Emp.:**	$30,833
Established:	1983	**International:**	50%
1994 Rank:	n/a	**'93-'94 Growth:**	–26%
1993:	$5,000,000	**1990:**	$4,000,000
1992:	$5,000,000	**1989:**	$3,000,000
1991:	$9,000,000		

BEST-SELLING TITLES: GEOS (OEM pricing) Operating system

98 AMSI $3,639,000

9801 Westheimer, Houston, TX 77042
713-785-0265 Fax: 713-785-2674

President:	Dean Schmidt		
CFO:	Gene Burgen		
Ownership:	Private		
Employees:	30	**Sales/Emp.:**	$121,300
Established:	1980	**International:**	0%
1994 Rank:	n/a	**'93-'94 Growth:**	29%
1993:	$2,827,000	**1990:**	$1,904,000
1992:	$2,431,000	**1989:**	$1,920,000
1991:	$2,124,000		

BEST-SELLING TITLES: Power Site ($2,000) Vertical/industry- or job-specific (DOS, Windows) **Budget Control Ledger** ($700) Vertical/industry- or job-specific (DOS, Windows) **Power Suite** ($3,500) Vertical/industry- or job-specific (DOS, Windows) **Power Books Accountant** ($2,500) Vertical/industry- or job-specific (DOS, Windows)

99 Campbell Software $3,500,000

1603 Orrington Ave., Evanston, IL 60201
708-328-3200 Fax: 708-328-3459

President:	Michael H. Campbell		
CFO:	David B. Menzel		
Ownership:	Private		
Employees:	44	**Sales/Emp.:**	$79,545
Established:	1989	**International:**	14%
1994 Rank:	n/a	**'93-'94 Growth:**	169%
1993:	$1,300,000	**1990:**	
1992:	$900,000	**1989:**	
1991:	$500,000		

BEST-SELLING TITLES: StaffWorks ($4,000) Vertical/industry- or job-specific (DOS, Windows, OS/2, Unix) **Campbell Time and Attendance** ($1,500) Vertical/industry- or job-specific (DOS, Windows, OS/2, Unix) **POS Gateway** ($395) Vertical/industry- or job-specific (DOS, Windows, OS/2, Unix) **Campbell File Exchange** ($395) Vertical/industry- or job-specific (DOS, Windows, OS/2, Unix)

100 Software Products International **$3,261,000**

6620 Flanders Dr., San Diego, CA 92121
619-450-1526 Fax: 619-450-1921

President:	John C. Bowne		
CFO:	Carl Hempel		
Ownership:	Private		
Employees:	18	**Sales/Emp.:**	$181,167
Established:	1979	**International:**	33%
1994 Rank:	#72	**'93-'94 Growth:**	–58%
1993:	$7,727,000	**1990:**	$20,504,000
1992:	$13,240,000	**1989:**	$14,302,000
1991:	$17,255,000		

BEST-SELLING TITLES: Open Access IV ($595) General business (DOS)
WindowBase ($199) General business (Windows)

Notes on Methodology

The Softletter 100, published annually since 1984, is defined formally as a ranking of the top 100 personal computer software companies in the U.S., based on calendar year revenues. That definition (which continues to evolve with the industry itself) helps explain why some companies appear on our list and why others are excluded.

Our basic eligibility rules are simple: To be ranked, a company must be an independent, U.S.–based company (subsidiaries do not qualify) that generates at least 50 percent of its revenues from personal computer software development or publishing. For the great majority of the companies we review, eligibility is a straightforward issue. But every year we are challenged by several dozen or more difficult cases that we try—not always to everyone's satisfaction—to treat logically and consistently.

Perhaps the biggest problem is creating a workable definition of personal computing. Traditionally, personal computer software was any product that ran on a microcomputer-based machine. That definition has become increasingly obsolete, now that microcomputer architectures and operating systems have taken over large portions of the server, workstation, and minicomputer markets. Hardware platforms and operating systems simply do not tell us much any more about the nature of the software they support.

So what defines personal computer software? In determining eligibility, we now look at several issues: patterns of use (does the user perform personal tasks or function as part of a workgroup or enterprise-wide system?), pricing (is the price level appropriate for an individual purchase?), distribution channels (in particular, is the product marketed to individual end users or to MIS departments?), and the local computing environment (does the product function in an open, multiproduct world or only as part of a closed and centralized system?).

Even with these guidelines, we're always left with borderline cases, especially in the area of development tools for client-server and workgroup applications. We continue to watch market trends closely in these areas, because we recognize that the client-server model will become increasingly important for the software industry.

On another front, we currently don't include companies that create software for dedicated or single-purpose hardware platforms. This rule applies primarily to the video game segment, where the basic platforms as yet don't support general-purpose applications.

Finally, it's important to note that our rankings only include companies that supply data on the record. To ensure accountability, we don't accept estimates from analysts or other outside sources; thus, several privately held companies do not appear in our rankings because they declined to provide us with revenue data.

Internet Job Search Fundamentals

The Internet is not only one of the most exciting developments in hot new technologies today but is also one of the best places to look for programming jobs. Every day more companies are using the Internet to describe their operations, products, and services and to post job openings. An Internet Web page or server is now expected of major software companies, systems integrators, and VARs, and practically all of them list their current job openings. In addition, the Internet offers career placement services, headhunters, and job marts in abundance, with more being added all the time.

For programmers, who are often the most avid net surfers, an Internet job hunt is a natural. After all, it's easy, it's quick, and with just a touch of aptitude for technology (which you undoubtedly have), it's fun. Chances are you've already had at least a little experience with local online bulletin boards and some of the commercial online services such as CompuServe or America Online (AOL). I know many programmers who surf the net for pleasure each evening, chatting with friends they've made electronically yet never physically met, checking out new public-domain and shareware programs that can be easily downloaded, or catching up on the latest news. Indeed, electronic communications is so fascinating that it sometimes displaces television or going to the movies as a programmer's main form of entertainment, sometimes to the dismay of other family members.

If you've been caught up in these activities, it's just a short hop to accessing the Internet and using it as a tool for finding the job you really want. Even if you're new to this medium, it's not hard to get connected and start browsing for hot job opportunities. This appendix gives you the basics of how to get connected, explore the Internet, and apply for jobs electronically—all from your own computer screen.

Getting Connected

If you have a relatively late model computer, a modem, a communications program of some sort, and a telephone outlet, you have all the basic hardware you need to get started.

A fast computer of the 486-variety or later will make net surfing more fun because you'll be able to display graphics more quickly, but most computers made in the last 10 years will do. More important is a fast modem. Be sure to get one that can receive and transmit at no less than 14.4 kilobits per second. Even better is a modem with a transmission speed of at least 28.8 kilobits per second. Using a modem slower than 14.4 kilobits per second can be tedious because of the time required to transmit information, and you'll never be able to access the graphical World Wide Web with such a modem unless you have extreme patience and a very long attention span.

Communications programs, usually simply called comm programs, are available almost everywhere as shareware, as public-domain programs, or as commercial software. Some are usually shipped along with a modem or preinstalled on a new computer. Web browsers such as Mosaic or Netscape are also available quite reasonably and are a good investment. In any case, finding a good comm program shouldn't be a problem.

When you have your equipment in place, it's time to consider your Internet connection. You can connect to the Internet in three different ways: through a dedicated T1 or T3 line, a commercial service, or a point-to-point protocol (PPP) or serial line Internet protocol (SLIP) line.

Connecting via a Dedicated T1 or T3 Line

The fastest and most elegant way to connect is also often the hardest to arrange. A dedicated T1 or T3 line will put you into instant contact with World Wide Web sites all over the world. You can download graphics with amazing speed and truly surf the graphical World Wide Web sites in amazing style. However, T1 lines, which transmit data at a rate of 1.54 million bits per second, or T3 lines, which transmit data at 44.7 million bits per second, can cost thousands of dollars per month to maintain and are usually so expensive to install that they aren't a viable home alternative. The only way you can expect to use T1 or T3 lines is if you are already working for a large company that has one and you conduct your job search after hours using your company's connection, or if you have access to a connection through a university or other organization.

Unfortunately, although the World Wide Web is a fantastic new tool for graphically transmitting bitmapped images and even information in multimedia format, using its graphical features really isn't feasible at this time without a T1 or T3 connection. Using anything else is just too slow. But don't despair. All the other forms of connection to the Web can provide access to most sites, so long as you donn't expect to get the fancy graphics. What you really want is the basic information anyway.

The nice thing about the Internet is that it can often give you a much better feel for the culture of a company (in addition to the information about a company). For instance, I recently was looking through the pages of the Netscape home site, shown in Figure A-1, and found not only job listings at that company but also pictures of some of the key people working at Netscape along with some personal information they'd posted on their own pages and great graphics of their products. It did give me a feel for the type of company culture that Netscape has, and that was very interesting. Of course, Netscape isn't a typical company, and if I'd been looking for a job, that personal information wouldn't have been important at all. All you really need are the job listings and the Internet address of where to send your résumé.

Connecting via a Commercial Service

Another way to connect to the Internet is through a commercial online service such as CompuServe, AOL, Prodigy, or Genie. In contrast to T1 and T3 lines, these services cost very little, and they provide many extra services such as special-interest group bulletin boards, news services, and entertainment services. These services also provide a lot a software, usually available for downloading at no cost.

Typically, you connect to a commercial service through a packet-switched network such as SprintNet or Xstream (formerly called Tymnet), and the phone cost is minimal since almost all towns of any size have a local number to call to access the packet-switched network. The major expense is for the time you

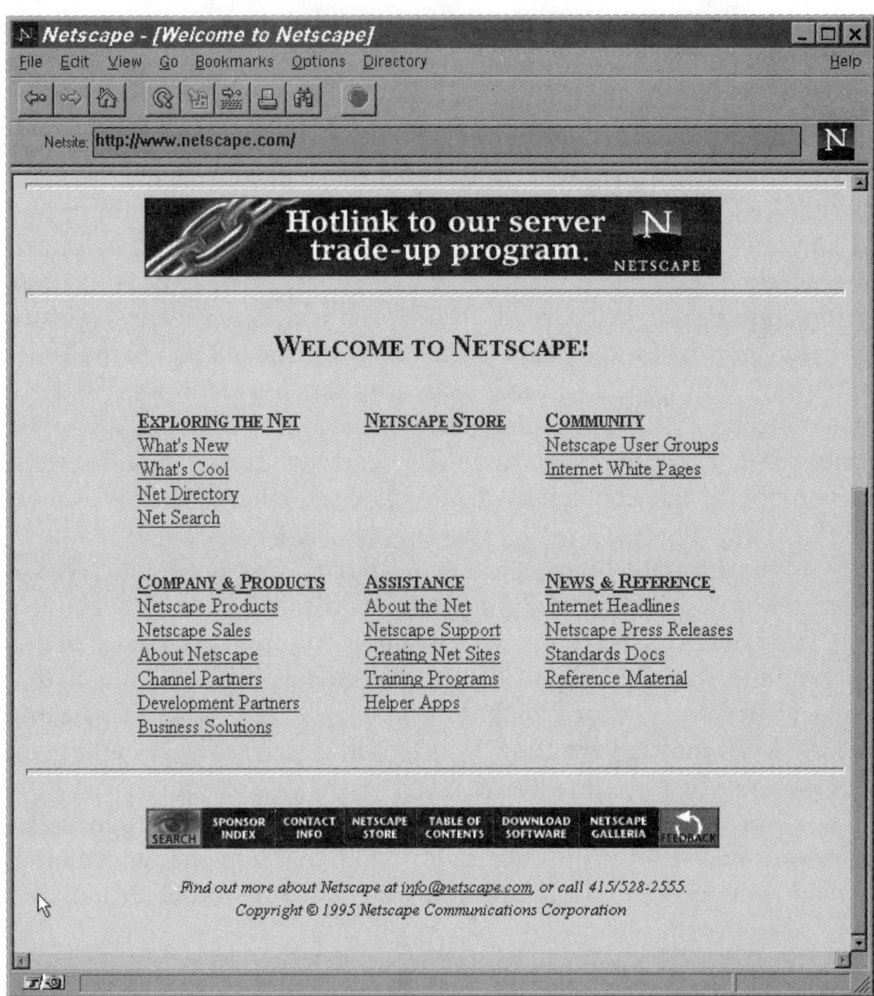

Figure A-1 *Netscape provides very detailed information on the company and its personnel through its World Wide Web site.*

actually spend connected, and even that is not very great; you could easily conduct a good job search for under $20 a month, providing you don't get sidetracked into one of the many other services offered. If you're watching your pennies, be sure *not* to get involved in playing online games, as these not only divert you from your original goal of job hunting but can also greatly increase your online time—and your expenses.

The main drawbacks to using a commercial online service are that Internet connections are a bit more cumbersome, you'll have to use an address that betrays your method of connection by listing the service provider and sometimes a long series of numbers as your address, and most services don't provide all Internet features.

Connecting via a PPP or SLIP Line

Another way of connecting is through a point-to-point protocol (PPP) or serial line Internet protocol (SLIP) line. These weren't so easy to find just a few years ago, but today there are many providers in almost every area. Chances are there's a company in your town selling Internet access through one of these methods. A PPP or SLIP line is bit more expensive than a commercial dial-up service, but not much, and this type of connection is a lot faster and provides all Internet services. You can usually hook up to a PPP or SLIP line for about $20 per month, plus some minor charges, and you'll have an access speed of up to 28.8 kilobits per second. In addition, you can specify your own address, without the fuss connected with commercial online services.

A good tool for finding a PPP or SLIP service is *Providers of Commercial Internet Access*, published by Celestin. This is a directory of such services throughout the country.

Since the Internet is evolving at a phenomenal rate, with new services and sites being added every day, a PPP or SLIP line seems like the best way to go for home access. Also, if you're planning on doing any contract work, or if you'd just like to project a more professional image, having your own domain address is a big plus.

Exploring the Internet

Once you understand the makeup of an Internet address, you can easily use the Internet to go to company sites, job sites, and newsgroups. Gophers and Yahoo are some of the tools that can aid your search.

Internet Addresses

The Internet began as a government project. Universities then hooked in, and recently all sorts of commercial companies have clambered onboard. The addresses that all sites use show this heritage and also reveal quite a bit about the organization at a particular site.

Internet addresses are divided into two parts, separated by an at (@) sign. The part of an address to the left of the @ sign indicates an individual or group of individuals at a particular site. The part of the address to the right of the @ sign, called the domain, indicates the actual site and also tells you something about the organization. Bits of information in the domain are separated by periods, referred to as dots. Thus, the address

Gwang@symantec.com

would be pronounced "G. Wong at Symantec dot com" and would indicate a person named G. Wang who receives Internet mail at the Symantec Internet site. The .com part of the address shows that this is a commercial site, and Symantec, of course, shows which commercial site it is.

The most commonly used abbreviations for the last part of domain names show what type of site is being accessed and tell something about the organization. These are as follows:

.com	A commercial site, or a private company
.edu	An educational site, usually a university
.org	A nonprofit organization or sometimes a local service
.gov	A government organization
.int	An international organization, such as the United Nations

These abbreviations are pretty easy to remember and tell you a lot about who you're calling before you even dial.

Objects on the Internet are often described with uniform resource locators (URLs). An object can be anything: a company Internet server, a menu, a newsgroup, anything. Everything on the Internet can have a URL.

The letters "http" in an Internet address stand for Hypertext transport protocol and indicate a World Wide Web site. Two forward slashes after http indicate the server name.

An interesting side benefit of all this interest in the Internet for programmers looking for jobs is the current demand for Hypertext markup language (HTML) programming. HTML is used to create Web pages for Internet server sites. HTML is a very simple language and is easy to learn and use, and since Web sites are in such heavy demand today, proficiency in HTML could be a good starting point for any beginning programmer.

Company Sites

Using the preceding information, it's not a large leap to figure out that you can connect to the Internet sites of most companies without ever looking up their addresses, if you know a company's name. Browsing company sites is a great way to start your job search, since you can explore for jobs quickly and easily. For instance, if you want to see if there's any job openings at Microsoft, you can simply type **http://www.microsoft.com** and you will be sent to the main Microsoft Internet server, as shown in Figure A-2. From there, it's just a matter of following menus to get to the posted job openings. The same is true for almost all large software companies, as well as for quite a few systems integrators and even corporate sites.

Job Sites

Several online career service providers, such as the Online Career Center, provide information about jobs at many different companies. Jobs are often listed by geographical location or job category, as Figure A-3 shows. Online career centers provide an excellent place to start your search.

You can find an equally rich source of jobs simply by browsing the sites of companies for which you may want to work. Although some companies post only one-line descriptions of the jobs, other post comprehensive job descriptions. You should use these, of course, to customize the résumé you send. Figure A-4 shows the listing at the Novell job site.

Note: *To help you get started on your search, a list of hardware computer companies and how they can be reached on the Internet appears at the end of this appendix.*

Newsgroups

Contrary to their name, newsgroups are really akin to bulletin boards on which users can post questions, observations, and other information for other users to respond to. Each newsgroup is dedicated to a particular topic, and so newsgroups can be used to find people with related interests. This, of course, can be valuable in job hunting, as it can put you in contact with people at companies you might like to work for or who might know of current openings. Newsgroups can be lots of fun if you get involved in the discussions (called *threads* in Internet parlance), and you never know who you might chat with electronically.

One caveat when connecting to newsgroups is that since you literally don't know who will be reading the threads, it's not wise to post your résumé in a

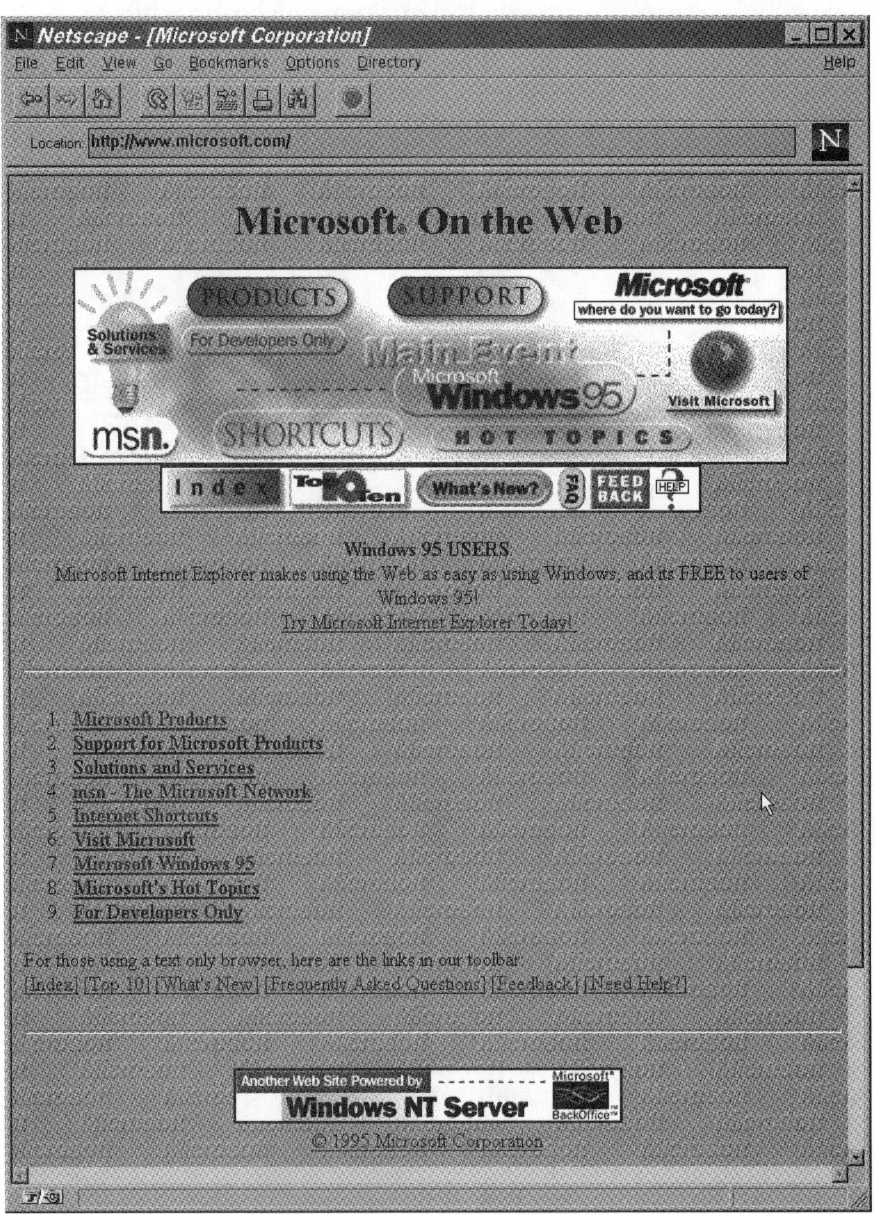

Figure A-2 *Microsoft's home page*

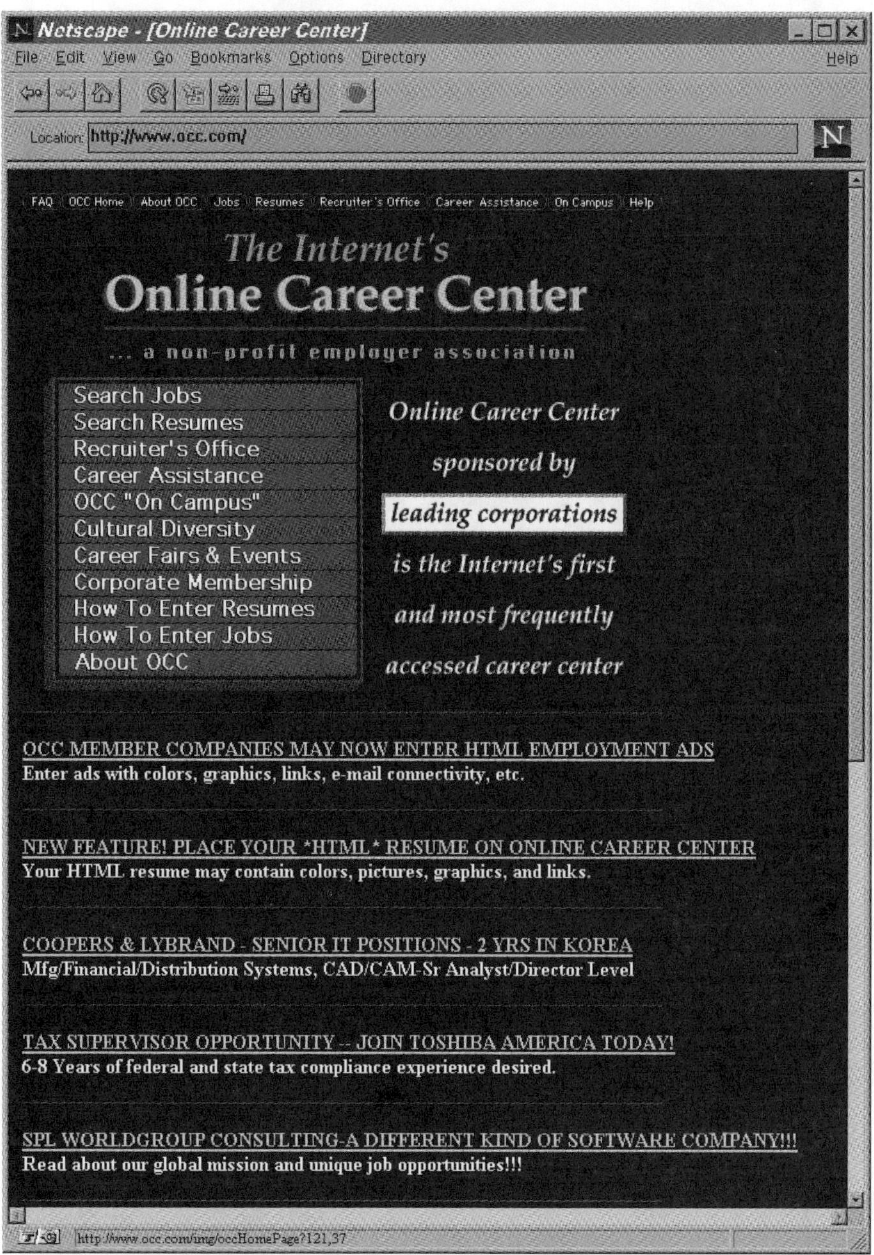

Figure A-3 *Online Career Center's home page*

newsgroup. After all, if you're currently employed, it could be your boss who sees it. It's better to use newsgroups to gather information and make contacts.

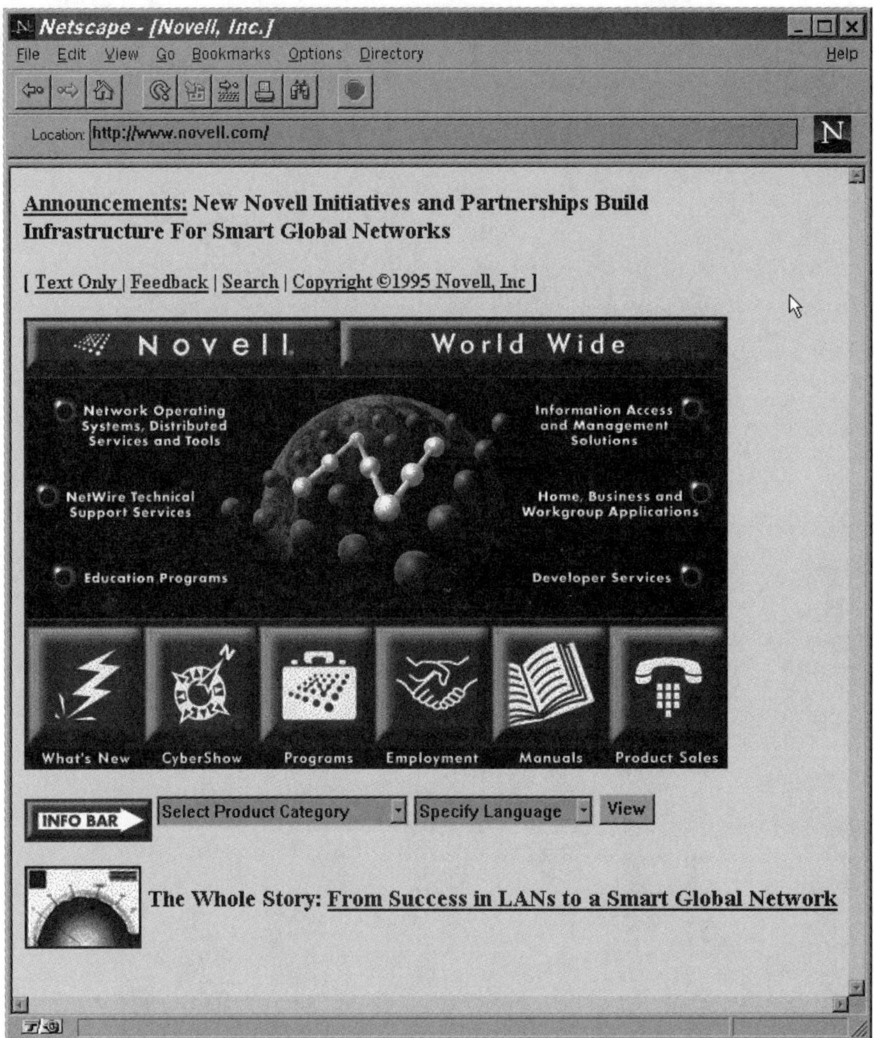

Figure A-4 *Novell's home page*

Gophers

Gophers are one of the most useful devices on the Internet. They can help you locate almost anything. A gopher is a menu system set up by an administrator at a particular Internet site and so is unique to the site. When you find a gopher menu, it will not only tell you what's available at a site but will actually go and get whatever information you request.

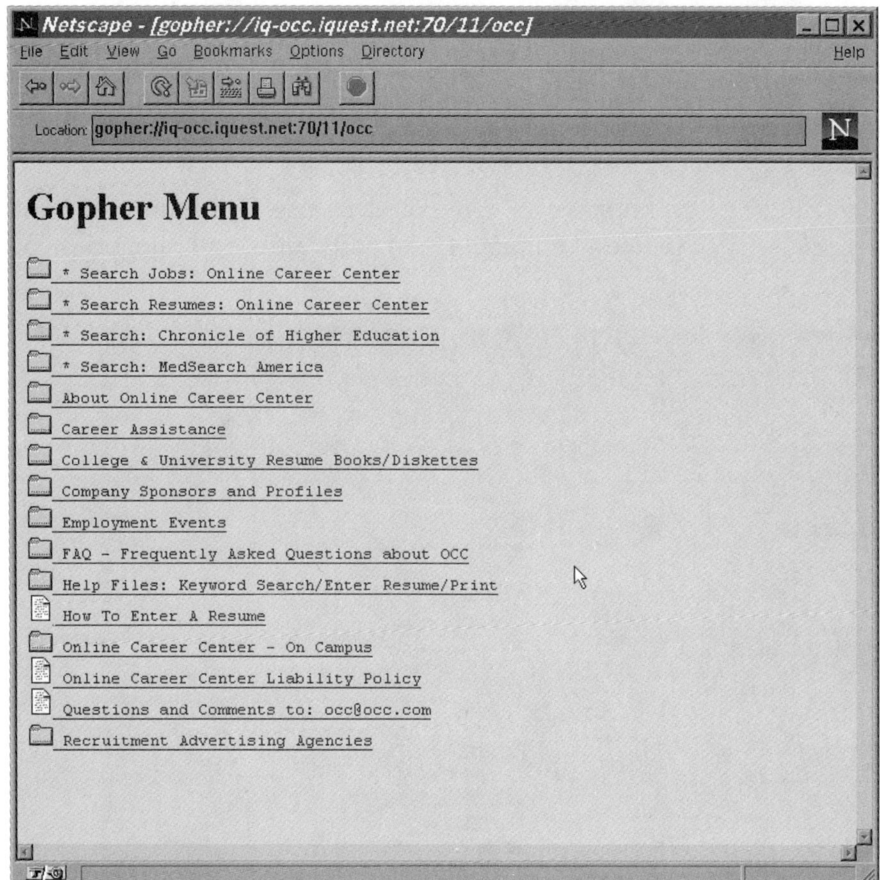

Figure A-5 *Online Career Center's gopher*

You can find a gopher by typing the word **gopher** and then a colon (**:**) and a double slash (**//**) to get to a server, and then typing the name of the server you wish to access. For example, if you type **gopher://occ.com**, you'll go immediately to the gopher at the Online Career Center. If you're displaying graphics when you do this, a menu like the one in Figure A-5 will appear. You can usually access information from a gopher menu simply by selecting it and either clicking it or pressing ENTER

Yahoo

Yahoo is a terrific Internet directory you can use in your job search to find companies posting programmer jobs and newsgroups on the particular programming category or language you're interested in and a host of other subjects. Yahoo spans many companies, and is not a gopher. To get to Yahoo, simply enter **yahoo.com**. You'll see a screen listing various subject headings. Select the heading "Computers and Internet" to go to a screen similar to the one in Figure A-6.

As you can see, several subjects here could be useful in your job hunt. Computer Science, Companies, Languages, and Software are all categories you

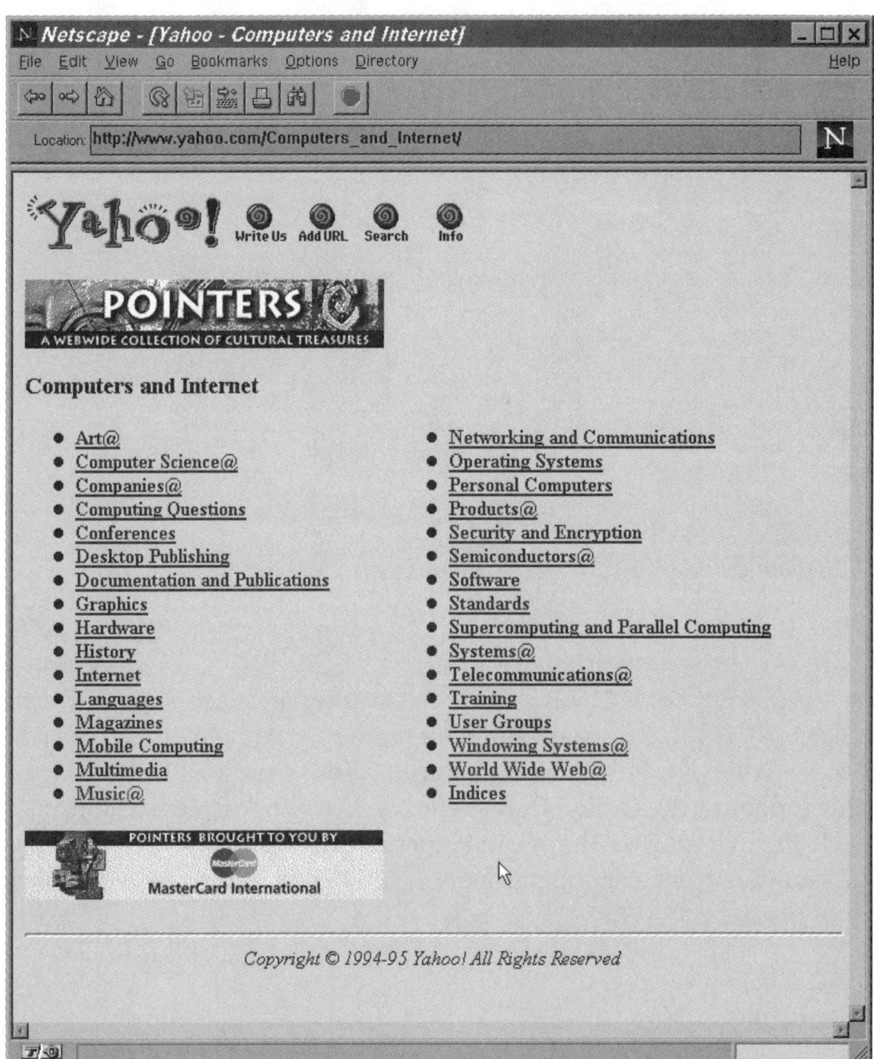

Figure A-6 *A Yahoo directory*

may want to explore. If you select the heading "Languages," a listing like the one in Figure A-7 appears.

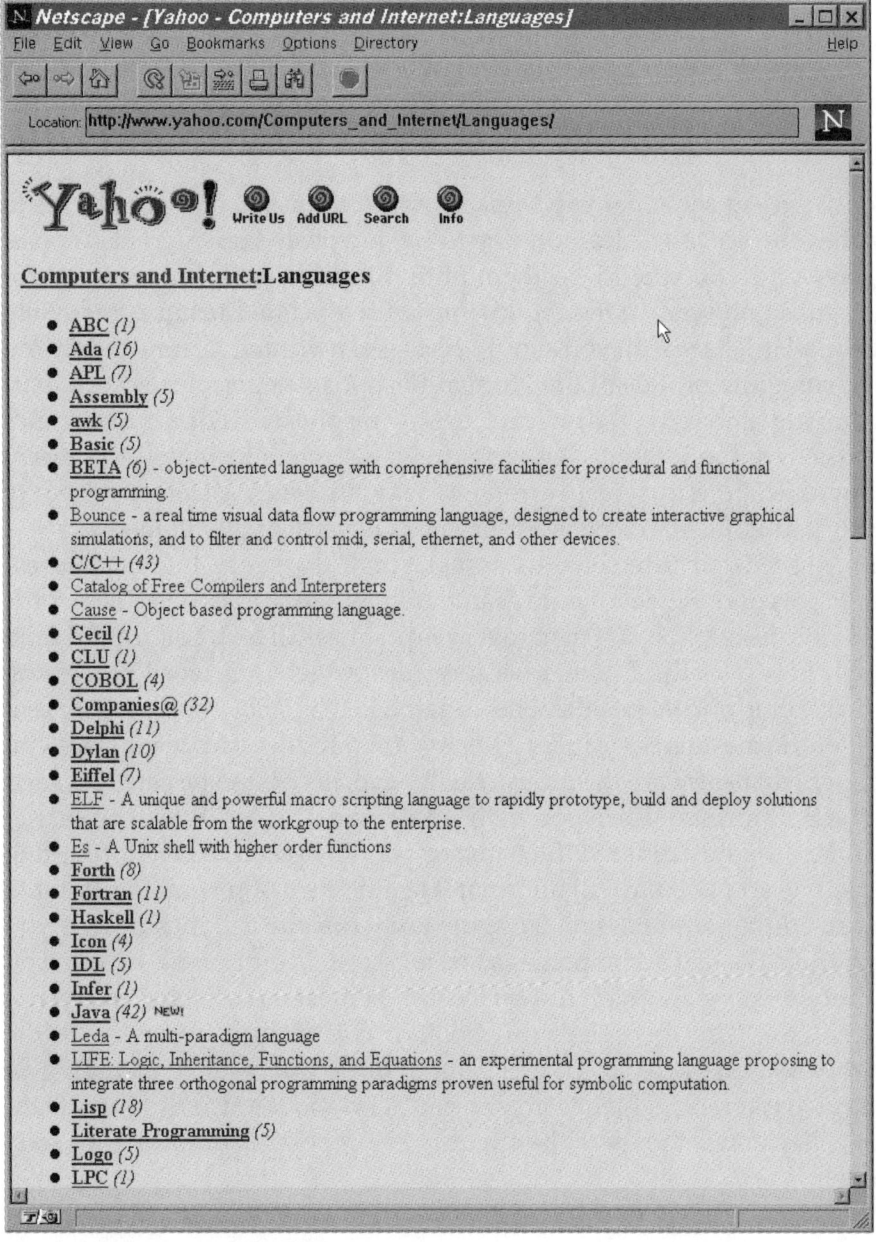

Figure A-7 *A Yahoo directory of language subjects*

From here you can select the language you're proficient in and then follow the tree further to find more specific information. Notice the little search icon at the top of the screen (if you're using graphics). This feature lets you search for information based on keywords in URLs, titles, and even comments. Yahoo is a great tool for navigating the Internet.

Responding to an Internet Job Listing

Once you've found a job that you think looks right for you and you decide to respond, how do you do it? Responding to any job posted on Internet involves two actions--and you should do them both. First, prepare your résumé for Internet e-mail and send it; then follow up with a printed résumé and cover letter and mail it. The reason you should also send a printed résumé is that you cannot be sure how proficient the Human Resources department at any particular company is in using the Internet, or how responsive they are to résumés they receive over the Internet. Also, a printed résumé allows you to present your job qualifications in a nicely formatted way and gives you an opportunity to exhibit thoroughness, which is a trait that is usually highly valued.

When you see a job listed on the Internet, you'll also see an Internet address to which to respond. Review your résumé to make sure it lists any keywords used in the job description and then save it as plain ASCII text. You should send only ASCII files over the Internet because files saved with word processing formats may come out on the other end as garbage files. I have successfully sent and received via the Internet standard Microsoft Word files. However, since you can't be sure what software the receiver will have, it's best to be safe and send the file in ASCII format. When you save your résumé as ASCII text, be sure to save it under a slightly different filename or you'll wipe out all the formatting in your résumé and will have to reformat it again when you want to print it.

You can add the résumé directly in the body of your text message, or you can attach it as a file that accompanies a text message. In either case, be sure you add an introductory paragraph or two to the text message, which is in essence your cover letter. Use the tips in this book to create some interest with the introductory text, so the recipient will want to read your résumé. Including an introductory paragraph is plain common courtesy, and it's also to your advantage. After all, you want to spark the interest of your potential employer as soon as possible.

Getting the Job Electronically

What could be more natural? After all, you're a programmer, and as a programmer you naturally have an inclination toward all forms of electronic media. The Internet is blossoming all around us and is a constant source of new ways to exchange information and to interact with people all over the globe. It's entirely possible to find a job in India while sitting at your PC in Ohio. It's possible to find several jobs per day that you might be suited for in all categories of programming over the Internet. In fact, it's hard to pin down anything that is *not* possible over the Internet. It is a great new medium, and it promises to change the way we work and conduct business transactions and even the way we live. You are in the best possible position to take advantage of this new tool—so do it. Use the resources listed in the remainder of this chapter to help you get underway.

Using the Internet to Find Jobs in Computer Hardware

The following pages provide the Internet addresses of many leading makers of computer hardware and summarize the main operations of each company and what you can expect to find at each site. This list of resources was taken from *The World Wide Web Complete Reference,* written by Rick Stout (Berkeley, CA: Osborne/McGraw-Hill, 1995).

You'll find that many programming jobs are available at software as well as hardware companies. In addition to the sites listed here, be sure to visit the Web sites of the software companies listed in Chapter 9.

Adaptec

Adaptec is a leading manufacturer of SCSI interface cards, network devices, and other I/O products. Adaptec's page includes information on hot topics, a summary of the company's complete product line, access to drivers, and technical information on Adaptec products.

Address: **http://www.adaptec.com**

Advanced Logic Research

ALR is a leading PC manufacturer. ALR's Web server provides information on the company's product lines and awards the products have won, as well as employment opportunities.

Address: **http://www.alr.com**

Advanced Micro Devices

AMD is one of the largest merchant-suppliers of integrated circuits in the United States. AMD's pages offer information on their microprocessors, embedded processors, memory products, logic devices, and other products.

Address: **http://www.amd.com**

APC

APC is a manufacturer of products that protect computers from power surges and brownouts. Through its Web site, APC offers product information, customer service, and technical support.

Address: **http://www.apcc.com**

Apple Computer

Apple offers information on its line of Macintosh computers and software as well as technical support, information on research and technology, and developer services.

Address: **http://www.apple.com**

BusLogic

BusLogic manufactures SCSI and RAID products, including SCSI host adapters and controllers for ISA, EISA, Microchannel, VLB, and PCI buses.

Address: **http://www.buslogic.com**

Compaq

On its pages, this leading PC manufacturer offers information on new products, service and support, how to upgrade Compaq products to Windows 95, and much more.

Address: **http://www.compaq.com**

Data Exchange

Data Exchange specializes in repairing computer peripherals, contract manufacturing, and end-of-life product support. Data Exchange currently repairs more than 750 products.

Address: **http://www.dex.com**

Data General

Data General creates advanced computer systems that employ the newest technologies and offers a complete set of information management services.

Address: **http://www.dg.com**

Dell

Dell is a major manufacturer of PCs and peripheral equipment. The company offers technical support through its Web site, as well as corporate information and a list of employment opportunities.

Address: **http://www.dell.com**

Design Acceleration

Design Acceleration provides hardware design engineers with simulation analysis tools to reduce design time.

Address: **http://www.designacc.com**

Digital Equipment Corporation

DEC offers access to a wealth of information about the company and its products and services.

Address: **http://www.digital.com**

Digital Products

DP manufactures a complete line of network print-server products. Product descriptions are available online, as is technical support for the company's growing customer base.

Address: **http://www.digprod.com**

Direct Data Storage

DDS sells SCSI controllers and SCSI disk and tape drives online. DDS says it will try to beat anybody else's prices on identical products and offers a 30-day money-back guarantee.

Address: **http://www.harddisk.com**

Encore Computer

Encore is a supplier of open, massively parallel, scalable computer and storage systems for mission-critical applications.

Address: **http://www.encore.com**

Gilltro-Electronics

Gilltro-Electronics developed the Giltronix line of products, including local connectivity products, peripheral sharing devices, low-cost workgroup connectivity, and high-performance local- and remote-access systems.

Address: **http://www.giltronix.com**

Heurikon

Heurikon manufactures single-board computers that typically are embedded in larger systems, such as video-on-demand systems, simulation systems, and printer controls.

Address: **http://www.heurikon.com**

Hewlett Packard

As a major manufacturer of computers and peripheral devices such as printers, HP offers volumes of company and product information on a substantial group of Web pages. HP also offers news and tips for people upgrading to Windows 95.

Address: **http://www.hp.com**

IBM

This company needs no introduction. IBM's Web site offers volumes of information on the company and its operations, technology, research, and products.

Address: **http://www.ibm.com**

IBM Personal Computers

This is the home page for IBM's Personal Computer division. It offers product information, file libraries, support, and news about the PC industry.

Address: **http://www.pc.ibm.com**

Intel

Check out Intel's Web site for detailed information on their latest CPUs, PCs, and components. Intel also offers developer support, information on embedded design products, and communications and networking products.

Address: **http://www.intel.com**

National Instruments

National Instruments develops software and hardware products for PCs and workstations to help scientists and engineers in their research. National's pages offer information on developer programs and a news update option.

Address: **http://www.natinst.com**

NEC

NEC makes computers and peripherals ranging from monitors to CD-ROM drives. Besides the basics, NEC's pages offer product overviews, support, service, information on events and trade shows, information on R&D, and even information on how to buy used equipment directly from NEC.

Address: **http://www.nec.com**

NECX Direct

This online computer store sells hardware, software, and networking and accessory products. This secure site features more than 20,000 products, daily specials, and good prices.

Address: **http://www.necx.com**

Network Wizards

Network Wizards makes temperature sensors and system console managers.

Address: **http://www.dicon.com**

Online Computer Market

OCM is an online center for computer products and information ranging from software, hardware, and research companies to resellers and consultants. OCM offers information on trade shows and upcoming computer events, as well as a list of clients and a directory of computer links on the Web.

Address: **http://www.ocm.com**

Overland Data

Overland Data supplies everything you need for desktop applications—half-inch tape drives, software, connecting cables, and expert service.

Address: **http://www.cts.com/browse/odisales**

PC Market

PC Market is a computer store doing business on the Web. Its products are categorized into hardware, software, and communications, and it also offers technical support through its Web site.

Address: **http://www.pcmarket.com/browse/nms**

Play, Inc.

Play, Inc., manufactures a video-frame grabber called the Snappy Video Snapshot, which attaches to a PC parallel port and captures still images from a camcorder, VCR, or TV tuner.

Address: **http://www.play.com**

Power Computing

Power Computing is a manufacturer of Macintosh clones. The company claims its systems are 100 percent Macintosh compatible but exceed the Mac in features, expandability, service, and support.

Address: **http://www.powercc.com**

RICOH California Research Center

RICOH manufactures computers, printers, copy machines, fax machines, and other technology products.

Address: **http://www.crc.ricoh.com**

Road Warrior International

Road Warrior Outpost offers products, services, and information for portable computers. One option lets customers shop for used computers or advertise their own. The page provides information on new products, monthly specials, and past issues of the company's newsletter.

Address: **http://www.warrior.com**

Seagate

Seagate is a leading manufacturer of data storage products (such as hard disk drives). In addition to product and company information, Seagate offers technical support and human resource information through its Web site.

Address: **http://www.seagate.com**

Silicon Graphics

Silicon Graphics manufactures high-end UNIX workstations. Its pages offer extensive information on the company's computer services and products, including the Indy, Indigo2, and Onyx systems.

Address: **http://www.sgi.com**

Sparco Communications

Sparco supplies computer hardware and software products. In addition to product and services information, they provide a list of manufacturers, special offers, and frequently asked questions.

Address: **http://www.sparco.com**

Standard Microsystems

SMC is a leading manufacturer of networking products for PCs, including Ethernet network interface cards, switches, LSI chips, and Fast Ethernet products. SMC's Web pages offer product overviews, drivers, and technical information.

Address: **http://www.smc.com**

Sun Microsystems

Sun is the largest manufacturer of turnkey UNIX computers. Sun's pages describe the company's hardware and software products and offer links for sales and service, technology and developers, and back issues of Sun's magazine-style Web pages. You can't order products online, but you can leave your name and address for more information.

Address: **http://www.sun.com**

Supra

Supra is a leading manufacturer of modems for PCs and Macintosh computers. Supra's pages include product and support information, and a file library that includes drivers and flash ROM upgrades. You can also enter a contest to receive a free SupraFAXModem 288.

Address: **http://www.supra.com**

Texas Instruments

Texas Instruments is a high-profile supplier of technological products, including defense electronics, notebook computers, software development tools, calculators, and other technology products.

Address: **http://www.ti.com**

Toshiba America

Toshiba America is the American branch of the Japanese electronics giant. Toshiba's page offers information on the company's divisions and products.

Address: **http://www.toshiba.com**

TouchWindow

TouchWindow, a product of SCT, Inc., is a touch screen for the ultimate in user-friendly interfaces. TouchWindow works on any computer that has a graphical user interface and a mouse.

Address: **http://www.touchwindow.com**

U.S. Robotics

No, USR doesn't make robots—it makes digital and analog communications equipment, including modems, remote-access servers, fax servers, and communications hubs. Check out RoboWeb and find out more about the company's products and services.

Address: **http://www.usr.com**

WebFactory

WebFactory sells top-quality computers and Internet products, both hardware and software. Products include workstations from Silicon Graphics; routers from Cisco, Livingston, and Ascend; and bridges from Combinet.

Address: **http://www.webfac.com**

Well-Connected Mac

The Well-Connected Mac is the online information source for everything regarding the Macintosh computer. This page lists related Mac sites on the Web, current and back issues of *MacWeek*, and extensive information on Mac products and services.

Address: **http://www.macfaq.com**

Wiltec

Wiltec manufactures IBM-compatible nine-track and cartridge tape systems. The company guarantees its products and provides free expert advice and support to customers.

Address: **http://www.wiltec.com/wiltec**

Xerox

Xerox's page provides links and information on the company's divisions, operations, and products.

Address: **http://www.xerox.com**

More Great Sources of Information for Your Programming Career

B

Baran, Nicholas. *Inside the Information Superhighway.* Coriolis Group, Inc., 1995.

Beizer, Boris. *Software Testing Techniques.* New York: Van Nostrand Reinhold Computer Books, 1990.

Bentley, Michael Brian. *The Viewport Technician: A Guide to Portable Software Design.* Glenview, Ill.: Scott Foresman and Company, 1987.

Booch, Grady. *Object-Oriented Analysis and Design with Applications.* Redwood City, Calif.: Benjamin/Cummings Publishing Company, 1993.

Brockschmidt, Kraig. *Inside OLE 2: The Fast Track to Building Powerful Object-Oriented Applications.* Redmond, Wash.: Microsoft Press, 1993.

Carnegie, Dale. *How To Win Friends and Influence People.* New York: Simon & Schuster, 1981.

Carter, Daniel R. *Writing Localizable Software for the Macintosh.* Reading, Mass.: Addison-Wesley Publishing Company, 1991.

DeMarco, Tom. *Controlling Software Projects: Management, Measurement and Estimation.* Englewood Cliffs, N.J.: Yourdon, Inc., 1982.

Eckel, Bruce. *Thinking in C++.* Upper Saddle River, N.J.: Prentice-Hall Computer Books, 1995.

Glass, Robert L. *Building Quality Software.* Englewood Cliffs, N.J.: Prentice-Hall, 1992.

Holland, Kelley, and Amy Cortese. "The Future of Money." *Business Week,* June 12, 1995, 66–78.

Hutchins, W. John, and Harold Somers. *An Introduction to Machine Translation.* San Diego: Academic Press, 1992.

Kernighan, Brian W., and Dennis M. Ritchie. *The C Programming Language.* Englewood Cliffs, N.J.: Prentice-Hall, 1988.

Kernighan, Brian W. *The Elements of Programming Style.* New York: McGraw-Hill, 1978.

Krol, Natasha, and David Yockelson. Meta Group. *Component Software.* Sunnyvale, Calif.: Component Integration Labs, 1995.

Laurel, Brenda, ed. *The Art of Human-Computer Interface Design.* Reading, Mass.: Addison-Wesley Publishing Company, 1990.

Maddell, T., C. Parsons, and J. Abegg. *Developing and Localizing International Software.* Englewood Cliffs, N.J.: Prentice-Hall, 1994.

Maguire, Steve. *Writing Solid Code: Microsoft's Techniques for Developing Bug-Free C Programs.* Redmond, Wash.: Microsoft Press, 1993.

Martin, Justin. "How Does Your Pay Really Stack Up?" *Fortune,* June 26, 1995, 79–86.

McConnell, Steve. *Code Complete: A Practical Handbook of Software Construction.* Redmond, Wash.: Microsoft Press, 1993.

Metzger, Philip W. *Managing a Programming Project.* Englewood Cliffs, N.J.: Prentice-Hall, 1981.

Meyer, Bertrand. *Object-Oriented Software Construction.* Englewood Cliffs, N.J.: Prentice-Hall, 1994.

Mills, Harlan D. *Software Productivity.* New York: Dorset House, 1988.

Realizing the Information Future: The Internet and Beyond. Washington, D.C.: National Academy Press, 1994.

Negroponte, Nicholas. *Being Digital.* New York: Alfred Knopf, 1995.

Object Linking and Embedding Programmer's Reference. Redmond, Wash.: Microsoft Press, 1992.

Parker, Richard O. *Mastering the THINK Class Library: Using Symantec C++ and Visual Architect.* Reading, Mass.: Addison-Wesley Publishing Company, 1995.

Petzold, Charles. *Programming Windows 3.1.* Redmond, Wash.: Microsoft Press, 1992.

Petzold, Charles. *Programming Windows 95.* Redmond, Wash.: Microsoft Press, 1995.

Pooley, James H.A. *Trade Secrets: A Guide to Protecting Proprietary Business Information.* New York: Amacom, 1989.

Price Waterhouse. *Technology Forecast.* Menlo Park, Calif.: Price Waterhouse World Firm Technology Centre, 1994.

Schulmeyer, G. Gordon. *Zero Defect Software.* New York: McGraw-Hill, 1990.

Uren, E., R. Howard, and T. Perinotti. *Software Internationalization and Localization: An Introduction.* New York: Van Nostrand Reinhold, 1993.

Yourdon, Edward. *Classics in Software Engineering.* Englewood Cliffs, N.J.: Yourdon, Inc., 1979.

Zultner, Richard. "Quality Function Deployment (QFD) for Software: Satisfying Customers." Princeton, N.J.: Zultner & Company, 1992.

Index

A

B

J

K

L

P

Q

R

S

Revolutionary Information on the Information REVOLUTION

Alluring opportunities abound for the global investor. But avoiding investment land mines can be tricky business. The first release in the Business Week Library of Computing lets you master all the winning strategies. Everything is here—from analyzing and selecting the best companies, to tax planning, using investment software tools, and more. Disks include MetaStock, Windows On WallStreet, and Telescan, the leading investment analysis software.

The Business Week Guide to Global Investments Using Electronic Tools
by Robert Schwabach
Includes Three 3.5-Inch Disks
$39.95 U.S.A. ISBN: 0-07-882055-3

The Business Week Guide to Multimedia Presentations
Create dynamic presentations that inspire.
by Robert Lindstrom
Includes One CD-ROM
$39.95 U.S.A.
ISBN: 0-07-882057-X

The Internet Yellow Pages
Second Edition
by Harley Hahn and Rick Stout
$27.95 U.S.A.
ISBN: 0-07-882098-7

Fundamental Photoshop: A Complete Introduction Second Edition
by Adele Droblas Greenberg and Seth Greenberg
$27.95 U.S.A.
ISBN: 0-07-882093-6

Multimedia: Making It Work, Second Edition
by Tay Vaughan
Includes One CD-ROM
$34.95 U.S.A.
ISBN: 0-07-882035-9

BC640SL

ORDER BOOKS DIRECTLY FROM OSBORNE/McGRAW-HILL

For a complete catalog of Osborne's books, call 510-549-6600 or write to us at 2600 Tenth Street, Berkeley, CA 94710

Call Toll-Free: ***1-800-822-8158***
24 hours a day, 7 days a week in U.S. and Canada

Mail this order form to:
McGraw-Hill, Inc.
Customer Service Dept.
P.O. Box 547
Blacklick, OH 43004

Fax this order form to:
1-614-759-3644

EMAIL
7007.1531@COMPUSERVE.COM
COMPUSERVE GO MH

Ship to:

Name ____________________

Company ____________________

Address ____________________

City / State / Zip ____________________

Daytime Telephone: ____________________
(We'll contact you if there's a question about your order.)

ISBN #	BOOK TITLE	Quantity	Price	Total
0-07-88				
0-07-88				
0-07-88				
0-07-88				
0-07-88				
0-07088				
0-07-88				
0-07-88				
0-07-88				
0-07-88				
0-07-88				
0-07-88				
0-07-88				
0-07-88				
	Shipping & Handling Charge from Chart Below			
	Subtotal			
	Please Add Applicable State & Local Sales Tax			
	TOTAL			

Shipping & Handling Charges

Order Amount	U.S.	Outside U.S.
Less than $15	$3.50	$5.50
$15.00 - $24.99	$4.00	$6.00
$25.00 - $49.99	$5.00	$7.00
$50.00 - $74.99	$6.00	$8.00
$75.00 - and up	$7.00	$9.00

Occasionally we allow other selected companies to use our mailing list. If you would prefer that we not include you in these extra mailings, please check here: ❑

METHOD OF PAYMENT

❑ Check or money order enclosed (payable to Osborne/McGraw-Hill)

❑ AMERICAN EXPRESS ❑ DISCOVER ❑ MasterCard ❑ VISA

Account No. ____________________

Expiration Date ____________________

Signature ____________________

In a hurry? Call 1-800-822-8158 anytime, day or night, or visit your local bookstore.

Thank you for your order

Code BC640SL